Praise for

The

9.9 PERCENT

"Brilliant. . . . Stewart is both cartographer and critic, serving as a kind of appalled anthropologist. . . . What gives the book its relentlessly sharp edge is his exposure of so much conventional wisdom as ultimately self-serving and deluded."
— Nick Romeo, The *Washington Post*

"In *The 9.9 Percent*, Matthew Stewart studies . . . the social class just below the new millennial robber barons—the overcompensated, self-regarding, yet terminally anxious cohort of the merely extravagantly privileged. . . . [a] clear-eyed and incisive study."
— Chris Lehmann, The *New Republic*

"*The 9.9 Percent* is a bracing and necessary read. Matthew Stewart does not pull his punches, making clear that the inequality and social stagnation plaguing the United States cannot be blamed on the billionaires. The ideology of meritocracy has been perverted to support a growing aristocracy, even as many of us passionately profess our commitment to universal equal opportunity. Highly recommended."
— Anne-Marie Slaughter, CEO, New America

"Matthew Stewart's new book is a captivating account of how America got into our current plight of extreme inequality and why that should concern all of us—especially those of us in the top 9.9 percent. It closes with some suggestions about what we might do about it."
— Robert D. Putnam, author of *Bowling Alone* and *Our Kids*

"In contemporary America, the lives of the wealthy bear increasingly little resemblance to those of working-class people, much less to those who are poor. Stewart is surely right to view this as a problem and to question why it has generated so much less outrage and concern than the obscene fortunes of the superrich."

—Eyal Press, *The New York Times*

"A charged study of the second-tier wealthy in America, the principal engine of inequality. . . . A sharp-tongued, altogether readable, and welcome assault on unrestrained wealth."

—*Kirkus Reviews* (starred review)

"[A] withering assessment of the overweighted, nearly intractable socio-economic power of that 9.9 percent—all conveyed with an acid humor that recalls the late social critics Henry Fairlie and Paul Fussell. . . . Holding out a sliver of hope for positive change, Stewart's study has the power to transform minds not yet closed to the possibility."

—*Booklist* (starred review)

"A rip-roaring argument against oblivious privilege. Stewart is an agile, witty writer with philosophical gifts. He can make you laugh while you make better sense of America."

—Alissa Quart, author of *Squeezed: Why Our Families Can't Afford America* and executive director, Economic Hardship Reporting Project

"Like the ancient curse of Midas, today's extreme inequality poisons even those it privileges, as Matthew Stewart reveals in this urgent and convincing book. It's not just the plutocrats who are ruining lives; it's all of us who enable the toxic myth that our society is a meritocracy."

—Nancy MacLean, author of *Democracy in Chains: The Deep History of the Radical Right's Stealth Plan for America*

"At a time when there is much focus on billionaires—the top 0.1 percent of American households—Matthew Stewart's book *The 9.9 Percent* provides us with a welcome, in-depth look at another vitally important group. . . . This important, often gripping book gives us a much-needed analysis of a powerful group, the 9.9 percent, that is too often overlooked as it plays a pivotal role in shaping—and mis-shaping—twenty-first century America."

—Steven Greenhouse, author of *Beaten Down, Worked Up: The Past, Present, and Future of American Labor*

The

9.9 PERCENT

The New Aristocracy

That Is Entrenching Inequality

and Warping Our Culture

MATTHEW STEWART

SIMON & SCHUSTER PAPERBACKS

New York   London   Toronto   Sydney   New Delhi

Simon & Schuster Paperbacks
An Imprint of Simon & Schuster, Inc.
1230 Avenue of the Americas
New York, NY 10020

First Simon & Schuster trade paperback edition October 2022

SIMON & SCHUSTER PAPERBACKS and colophon are registered trademarks of Simon & Schuster, Inc.

For information about special discounts for bulk purchases, please contact Simon & Schuster Special Sales at 1-866-506-1949 or business@simonandschuster.com.

The Simon & Schuster Speakers Bureau can bring authors to your live event. For more information or to book an event, contact the Simon & Schuster Speakers Bureau at 1-866-248-3049 or visit our website at www.simonspeakers.com.

Interior design by Kyle Kabel

Manufactured in the United States of America

1   3   5   7   9   10   8   6   4   2

Library of Congress Cataloging-in-Publication Data

Names: Stewart, Matthew
Title: The 9.9 percent : the new aristocracy that is entrenching inequality and warping our culture / Matthew Stewart. Description: New York : Simon & Schuster, [2021] | Includes bibliographical references and index. | Summary: "A trenchant analysis of how the wealthiest 9.9 percent of Americans—those just below the tip of the wealth pyramid—have exacerbated the growing inequality in our country and distorted our social values"— Provided by publisher.
Identifiers: LCCN 2021002076 | ISBN 9781982114183 (hardcover) | ISBN 9781982114190 (trade paperback) | ISBN 9781982114206 (ebook)
Subjects: LCSH: Upper class—United States. | Rich people—United States. | Wealth—Moral and ethical aspects—United States. | Social stratification—United States. | Equality—United States.
Classification: LCC HT653.U6 S74 2021 | DDC 305.5/20973—dc23
LC record available at https://lccn.loc.gov/2021002076

ISBN 978-1-9821-1418-3
ISBN 978-1-9821-1419-0 (pbk)
ISBN 978-1-9821-1420-6 (ebook)

For K, S, and A

Contents

— 1 —

Who We Are

When you are young, the past seems very far away, and maybe a little comical. That's the way my grandparents looked to me when I was a child. With his slicked-back hair, tortoiseshell glasses, and bright red trousers pulled way up high, Grandfather would greet us like he had stepped out of the first color movie ever made. Grandmother usually showed up in oversized jewelry that she invested with many superstitious meanings, drawling like a slightly campy southern belle. They lived in country clubs, as far as I could tell, mostly on the island of Palm Beach, and those clubs seemed like antique amusement parks to me. There was endless French toast, card games that lasted all day, and lots of funny rules, most of them involving what to wear and when not to speak.

Once or twice a year, usually around Christmas or the Fourth of July, the family would gather around tables piled high with chilled shrimp and cheesecake, and, in between puffs on his cigar, Grandfather would unwind long stories with enough loose ends to fill a bowl of spaghetti. At around the age of eleven or twelve, I learned that we owed our holiday bounty to Great-Grandfather, Colonel Robert W. Stewart, a onetime Rough Rider with Teddy Roosevelt who made a great big pile of money in the oil business.[1] I gathered that we were very lucky to come from such a distinguished family. Our roots—and my own middle name!— went all the way back to William Stewart, a lieutenant in the Continental Army who was seated at the right hand of George Washington.

As I entered my teenage years, the comedy of our holidays in grandparent-land slowly ripened into farce. The pomp of our clubroom luncheons began to feel tedious and even ridiculous, like an interminable birthday party for people whose main accomplishment was just showing up in life. One day, at the age of thirteen, I was rushed to an unctuous tailor to be fitted in time for the dedication of a gold-plated bicentennial eagle on which Grandfather had lavished some of his evaporating inheritance. I remember getting the distinct impression that I had become a prop in a ludicrous costume drama. I inspected that cartoonish bird of prey closely and imagined that it must have been stuffed with papier-mâché on the inside. It struck me that my grandparents wouldn't know papier-mâché if it showed up across from them at the dinner table. They had no clue what life was like off the island.

My actual home was the militantly middle-class world of United States Marine Corps bases and suburban public high schools. I saw myself as a proud member of the Space Age. The present was a rocket ship to the future, and we weren't going to get there by inhaling the last fumes of some bygone way of life. I didn't believe in inheriting your money (a good thing, given the grandparents' spending habits), or in dedicating your life to joining clubs that excluded the greatest number of people, or in hiding from the world on some fantasy island. I believed in grades, test scores, new gadgets, working for what you have, and playing to win in pickup basketball. I was an eager representative of a generation that put its faith in all those things that we now call "merit." I was more or less committed to a form of life that I will call, for reasons I explain in this chapter, "the 9.9 percent."

SOME YEARS AGO, however, I began to feel that the past was catching up with the present, like a familiar face approaching unexpectedly over the shoulder. Maybe it started when I found myself in the fray of parents scrambling for spots at city preschools that, on second thought, seemed more exclusive than any of the old country clubs and no less self-satisfied. Maybe it was the way that buying a bag of mixed greens at the grocery store had come to seem like an act of class warfare, or the vague awareness that there was a category of vacation resort so special that I didn't even know about its existence. Or maybe it was just the odd sense that snuck up on me during pleasant conversations in my favorite coastal enclaves, chatting about fitness options and real estate opportunities as if the rest of the world simply did not exist, that an old and insular form of life had come back, except that now it was sipping vegetable smoothies and wearing brightly colored, sweat-wicking spandex. It felt as if I had stepped out of that rocket ship to the future and found myself a few blocks down the road, stumbling around some alternate version of the past. We've been here before, I thought—only this time, I am part of the problem.

This uncanny feeling of déjà vu, I think, will be familiar to many people who have very different family stories, not at all like my own. Really, it can happen to anyone who has tried to relax in recent years with a good history book. Time was when the chronicles of ancient Rome, China, or Mesopotamia would offer escape from the present. No more. The holiday from history is over. These days, you'll get to the end of a learned tome on the rise of fascism and realize that several chapters remain to be written. You'll read about the "lost cause" of the Confederacy and wonder when they will finally give up. You'll consult George Orwell's 1984, not to speculate about the future, but to analyze the latest pronouncements from on high. Or you'll thumb through an old novel about the fading American dream, like *The Great Gatsby*, and wonder which one of the characters is you. The so-called arc of the moral universe seems to have acquired a dark sense of humor.

It's usually best to imagine that we create our own circumstances in life. But it is often more accurate to say that our circumstances create us. In retrospect, the small dramas of my family story look like a spotty commentary on forces that remain mostly out of view. The same is true for the form of life that I aspired to join, or so I tend to think. The closest thing to a defining attribute of the way of thinking that now dominates American life is our lack of awareness of the causes that brought us to the present state and of the ancient patterns we thoughtlessly retrace in our lives. To an unexpected degree, we are living in the past. We just don't know it.

In this book, I argue that those forces which have set us rowing backward into the past can be explained mostly in terms of a single fact: the rapid rise in economic inequality over the past half century. At the same time, I contend that language in which we talk about this fact has come to obscure the reality. In particular, we systematically overlook the way in which inequality reaches into our own thoughts and desires and so involves us all. In this chapter—spoiler alert—I lay out all of the main lines of the argument in the book. The evidence in support of that argument will have to wait for subsequent chapters. My aim here is to supply some of the intuitions out of which the argument evolved. The family memories are idiosyncratic, I grant, but the experiences they represent are now close to universal, or so I believe.

WHEN YOU ARE NOT RICH, you are quite sure you know what it would feel like to be rich. Once you become rich, you are not so sure. You come to see that there are many people much richer than you, and you can't help but wonder what it would be like to be them. This was one of the thoughts I picked up from Grandfather, rather indirectly, when he complained, as he often did, of the monstrous injustice of the estate tax.

The government, I learned early, taxed away three quarters of the Colonel's fortune upon his death. The remaining quarter was divided among four siblings. Thus, the Colonel at death must have been worth an impressive sixteen times more than Grandfather at his peak, or so I calculated with my sixth-grade math skills. I thought this might explain some of the deference—or was it fear?—that crept around the edges of Grandfather's voice when the subject turned to the Colonel. I wondered if it also explained the occasional outbursts of hostility that Grandfather directed at the Rockefellers. They must have been worth sixteen times more than the Colonel, or maybe much more.

I never quite got all the numbers down, but then again, I realized that the perceptions of wealth that organized my grandparents' lives were not all that reliable either. On the one hand, they lived in a world that was transparently ordered by money, with all of the poor people out on the mainland, all of the rich people on the island, and the richest people in the biggest houses on the island. On the other hand, the exact relationship between house size and wealth was always measured in imprecise terms. And, having spent some time across the water in West Palm Beach on the way in, I got the sense that it was not actually a pestilent wasteland.

What stayed with me, in any event, was this Russian-doll experience of not quite knowing when you will finally arrive at the innermost sanctum of wealth. An unequal world, according to the usual way of thinking, is one that is angrily divided between the rich and the poor. But in reality, it may also be one that is united in the universal awareness that there is always someone richer than you—a lot richer. And sometimes it isn't the actual wealth but the impressions of wealth that determine where you will end up. These simple intuitions seem worth bearing in mind as we turn to the extraordinary increase in economic inequality in the United States over the past half century.

THE STORY OF RISING ECONOMIC INEQUALITY is by now so familiar that it fits easily onto a T-shirt. But the way the story is told is often imprecise enough to leave out much of the plot. "We are the 99 percent" sounds righteous enough, but it's a slogan, not an analysis. It suggests that the whole issue is about "them," a tiny group of crazy rich people, who are nothing at all like "us." But that's not how inequality has ever worked. You can glimpse the outlines of the problem if you take a closer look at the math of inequality.

Supposing we stick for the moment with the questionable suggestion that "we" are merely a collection of percentiles in the wealth distribution tables—and I will question that suggestion in a moment—the first thing to note is that "99 percent" is not the right number. Contrary to popular wisdom, it is not the "top 1 percent" but the top 0.1 percent of households that have captured essentially all of the increase in the relative concentration of wealth over the past fifty years.[2]

Between 1963 and 2016, this top one-thousandth of the population have tripled their share of the pie and now own almost one quarter of everything of economic value in the country. The top 0.01 percent have done even better, and the 0.001 percent better still. In 1982, the price of entry into the *Forbes* list of the 400 wealthiest Americans ("the 0.00025 percent") was $75 million and the prize at the top was $2 billion and change. As of 2019, $2 billion doesn't even get you onto the list, and you'll need a couple of extra digits to break into the top two spots.[3] Even adjusting for inflation and economic growth, the rich today are an order of magnitude richer than they were just forty years ago. The last time the rich were this rich, in relative terms, was in 1928, or right around the time that my great-grandfather's fortunes peaked.

And yet not all of the percentiles below the fabulous 0.1 percent lost ground over the past half century. Only the bottom 90 percent did. In the years between 1963 and 2016, every percentile below the 90th saw its relative share of the wealth decline. Collectively, the bottom 90 percent is down about one third in its piece of the pie, even while the top 0.1 percent is up by the corresponding amount. All of the 401(k)s, checking accounts, mattress money, and college savings plans of the bottom 90 percent now add up to a mere 10 percent of the nation's financial wealth. Throw in the houses, cars, old pianos, and the other things that people generally can't afford to sell, and the aggregate wealth of the bottom 90 percent totals up to about the same as the wealth of the top 0.1 percent. If our society had $2 to share between the richest 0.1 percent and the bottom 90 percent, it would give $1 to the guy in the private jet and the other $1 to the other 900, or about enough people to fill 20 city buses. Back in the 1960s, by contrast, the people on the buses shared $4 for every $1 among the sky people.

In between the 0.1 percent and the 90 percent, there is a collection of percentiles that has held on to its share of the growing economy. It has pulled away from the 90 percent, even as it has fallen far behind the 0.1 percent. Taken on the whole, the 9.9 percent is the richest segment of the distribution and controls more than half of the personal wealth in the nation. In fact, if the super-rich in the 0.1 percent and the masses in the 90 percent have $1 apiece, this group has about $2.50 to share among its members. As of 2016—the numbers will almost certainly be higher by the time you read this—$1.2 million in net assets will get

you into this stretch of the wealth spectrum, and about $20 million will
push you up to the 0.1 percent. This is the 9.9 percent.[4]

THE POPULATION THAT HAPPENS TO RESIDE in the 9.9 percent at
any one moment is diverse, and no generalization about the group is
accurate in more than a loose, statistical sense. Nonetheless, it is safe
to say that this isn't the place to look for superstar performers and the
great disruptors of free market lore, and it isn't a den for villains and
plotters either. For the most part, it is home for people who follow the
rules and do as they are told: professionals of all sorts, but especially
in medicine and law; platoons of midlevel bankers; managers of processes you've never heard of; small business owners; and older couples
who planned sensibly for retirement. One thing most of them have in
common is the conviction that the system works and that their own
success is the proof. The merit myth—the vague and sunny belief that
everything works out for those who try—is the first tenet of the Creed
of the 9.9 percent.

Another thing they have in common is that they are mostly—but not
entirely—white. The median Black household had wealth of $3,557 in
2016—down by almost half from 1983. Latinos had $6,591, up a couple
thousand dollars.[5] The median white family, on the other hand, had
$146,984, up over 80 percent in the same period. People of color are
not absent from the top 9.9 percent of the wealth distribution, to be
sure—a fact that is central to our collective self-image. It's just that white
people are eight times more likely to make it into those happy percentiles.

Another thing the 9.9 percent have in common is that they are lucky
to live in America. In this book I confine my focus on the United States;
but that is less of a limitation than it sounds. The United States represents
a little over 4 percent of the world's population and 24 percent of world
GDP, but its 9.9 percent would blow away the competition in any face-
off with the rest of the world's 9.9 percent. That's not because the United
States is wealthier; it's because the United States is that much more
unequal. In the thirty-seven industrialized countries that make up the
Organisation for Economic Co-operation and Development (OECD),

on average, the top decile has about as much wealth as the bottom nine deciles put together.[6] In the United States, the top decile has about four times as much wealth as the bottom nine. Between 1974 and 2014, while the ratio of income between the top decile and bottom decile rose from 3.5 to 7.3 in Sweden and from 5.3 to 7.8 in Holland, it rocketed from 9.1 to 18.9 in the United States.[7] In some respects, the U.S. socioeconomic hierarchy looks more like those of India and Brazil, say, than those of traditional peers in the industrialized world such as Germany and Japan.

Another marker of membership in the 9.9 percent in the wealth distribution, at least in numerical terms, is an individual's generational cohort. According to Census Bureau data, individuals who made the mistake of being born in the early 1980s, i.e., as one of the allegedly weak-willed and self-absorbed millennials, will have an average net worth 25 percent lower in 2016 in inflation-adjusted dollars than people born in the early 1950s had in the 1980s, when they were the same age. Meanwhile, those fat and happy baby boomers, now in their sixties and seventies, have seen their relative share of the wealth double.[8] But before we incite a generation war, consider this: the growing gaps in starting salaries and starter-home values indicate that the secession of the 9.9 percent from the rest of society is now happening earlier than ever in the American life cycle.

Homeownership is another feather in the cap of those who succeed in the 9.9 percent game. While the median homeowner has a net worth of $195,400, the median renter has $5,400.[9] That's not just because rich people buy homes; it's because buying (the right) home makes people rich. Some research suggests that homeownership has become such a central part of wealth formation that it may account for most of the increase in wealth inequality.[10]

A lesson for success among the 9.9 percent worth noting up front has to do with the importance of having good taste in parents. The Federal Reserve estimates that between 25 percent and 53 percent of all wealth in the United States is inherited[11]—the wide range has to do with assumptions about the rate of return on inherited wealth—and three quarters of inherited wealth ends up where approximately three quarters of all wealth starts off: in the pockets of the top decile. Setting aside the large financial fortunes at the top, a substantial part of that intergenerational wealth transfer passes through the family home.[12]

The spectacular rise of the 0.1 percent has received plenty of ink over the past decade, but the expanding chasm between the 90 percent and the 9.9 percent in some ways matters more to the real story of inequality in American life. In 1963, a household at the national median (that is, the 50th percentile) needed to increase its wealth by a factor of 10 to reach the median of the 9.9 percent. Now, the median household has to multiply its wealth by 24 times to achieve the same result. If you think of the American Dream as a mountain, that mountain is now more than twice as steep.

According to the same math, the Dream is now also at least twice as cruel. The traditional theory of the Dream says that the universal striving for material riches is a good thing because, win or lose, everybody gains in the end. A rising tide lifts all boats, or so the song goes. This was a credible view in the postwar decades, when economic growth generated matching increases in median wages. Over the past forty years, however, real wages have remained anchored to the sea floor, even as tuition, housing, and health care costs have raised the price of admission to the middle class.[13] Only the top decile have floated up with the tide. The new theory of the dream is: winning is everything, losers stay put.

From a statistical perspective, the 9.9 percent is more or less what you get when the middle class goes underwater. (Or, maybe more accurately, when the middle class turns on itself and shoves the other guys off the boat.) But there is no reason to get particularly fixated on the current number. By the time you read this, it may well be the 8.9 percent, or the 7.9 percent. The only certainty is that, as long as inequality is rising, the number will go down. Not all of the people on the boat have figured this out yet, but the nature of rising inequality is such that the circle of joy is always shrinking.

IN ALL OF THIS FAMILIAR STATISTICAL CHATTER about wealth distributions, it is vital not to lose sight of the fact that percentiles aren't people. Percentiles are just snapshots of where people happen to stand at any one moment on the economic hillside. Individuals move up and down the economic terrain all the time, as they advance in their careers, go into debt, have children, or slip on black ice. As the hillside gets steeper, however, they move more slowly, or so I will show in the chapters ahead. More than that, as the hillside gets steeper, people change. They start to think about themselves and about the nature of life itself in very different ways. They spend long hours looking up the hillside and, scary thought, looking down, and they often build their personalities around unspoken thoughts about what it would be like to live off the island, or in some other, unknown place.

Social class in general is misunderstood if we think of it merely as a label attached to one's toe at birth. It has much more to do with the way in which we imagine ourselves, and it usually comes with a certain amount of struggle, since it is not always easy to get the world to agree with the image we have of ourselves. Often, as on my grandparents' island, it is the misperceptions of wealth and station that matter most. It's better to think of the percentiles, then, not as a list of people but as a landscape of opportunities, imperfectly filtered through a variety of perceptions. It's like a grainy, composite photograph of what it means to live in the modern economy.

For most Americans most of the time, the salient feature of the economic landscape is not the shrouded peak occupied by the 0.1 percent. On the contrary, survey evidence consistently shows that most Americans have no clue how rich the rich really are. The average American thinks the average big-corporation CEO earns $1 million per year.[14] (The right answer: $17.2 million for the top 350 firms as of 2018.)[15] The average American doesn't get that when the top twenty hedge fund managers took home $500 million apiece in 2018, it was a *bad* year for them. (The $770 million they made in 2017—now *that* was good times.)[16] But most people do care a lot about the closer hillside occupied by the 9.9 percent. You can drive through their neighborhoods, you will come across them in all sorts of workplaces, and they are always on-screen. They are there to say that you can have it all, too, if you just put on your training shoes and lean in the right direction. The 9.9 percent is no exception to the rule that all consciousness is local.

The 9.9 percent, then, is more a state of mind than it is a group of people, even if it is embodied at this or that moment by some number of individuals. It is a way of being that is open to all those with the right attitude and the right assumptions. More than that, the 9.9 percent is the defining state of mind in America today. The ideas of the 9.9 percent are the ruling ideas of American society. In varying degrees, "we" are all the 9.9 percent—even if we are not yet or never will be precious-metal-card-carrying members of the group. In fact, much of the madness in America stems from the fact that most of us think we are in the 9.9 percent, even though only one in ten actually has the cash to show for it.

In this book, to repeat for emphasis, I use "the 9.9 percent" to describe a form of life rather than a set of people identified by their supposed net worth. It is a way of thinking and a system of values that characterizes many people who are not and have no realistic prospect of joining the top decile of the wealth distribution. Indeed, it matters most precisely insofar as it is shared by those who are not "paid-up" members of the 9.9 percent, as it were. This widespread culture of the 9.9 percent, I will argue in this book, is a fundamental consequence of rising inequality and it has transformed American life in profound, intimate, and often unacknowledged ways. It is in many senses the defining development in recent American history and the key to understanding the predicaments in which we find ourselves now.

Even so, I do not intend in this way to diminish concern with the extreme concentration of wealth at the very top of the economic spectrum. Quite to the contrary. The point rather is that oligarchs have never controlled anything with their own bare hands. Their power, like all human power, resides in the minds of other human beings. To understand how our ruling class came to be, and why it gets richer and more powerful with every passing crisis and act of universal impoverishment, it is necessary to know something about the illusions that accumulate down below as inequality rises. The pillars of the system ultimately rest on a ground of assumptions that guide the lives of people who look a lot like me and, probably, you.

MY GRANDPARENTS HAD ONE OF THOSE MARRIAGES that seem as inevitable as a matching sofa set. The effortless coordination of their minds, though hardly gender-neutral, made them a formidable presence in any country club luncheon or contract bridge tournament. Only after Grandmother was gone and Grandfather had lost some of the ability to control his narratives did I piece together the story of how destiny almost failed to organize the furniture of life in the appointed way.

In his first and only year at Yale, the nineteen-year-old version of Grandfather ran off to the speakeasies of New York and came back with a wife. Yale at the time did not permit marriage, and the Colonel and Mother did not permit marriage to the wrong sort of woman. This marriage, the elders resolved, was a case of "hot loins." The woman in question, however, was soon discovered to have "a nose for cold cash." She demanded $5,000 to go away (worth about $50,000 today). The Colonel forked over the money and saved most of his fury for his will, in which he specified that Grandfather's inheritance would take the form of a trust whose principal he would not be permitted to touch (until Grandfather learned how to game the trust). The twenty-three-year-old version of Grandfather went on to meet soon-to-be Grandmother, a debutante from Kentucky, who proved to be very much the right sort of woman, and the affair of the loins was consigned to that unlit basement where one places all of those unwelcome memories that somehow dictate the terms of a life.

This is a story I like to bear in mind when the conversation turns to economic inequality today. Most of our narratives about inequality tend to shape themselves around the economic data, and most of that data sits in some recently upgraded data sets on economic wealth and income distributions. The data are great to have (and I have already started to exploit the trove shamelessly here), but the love affair with spreadsheets gives the impression that understanding inequality is just a matter of comparing dollars and cents. Inequality, according to this line of thought, is what happens when Bill Gates walks into a bar. The average net worth goes through the roof—and everything else stays right where it is. The underlying assumption is that economic inequality answers to the laws of economics alone—laws that operate like a kingdom within the kingdom, entirely independent of the principles that govern the rest of human society.

But none of that is true. Money is never just about the money. Human beings always convert cold cash into good matches, elevated social status, higher education, better health, and political power—and then they turn around and exchange those other forms of advantage for money. Money is where the story of inequality begins and ends, but most of the plot happens in between. What looks like destiny is sometimes just the dead hand of an aging trust fund exercising its will. In many situations, too, the process works best when that handful of cash is curled up in a fist and hidden from view. I do not mean to pass judgment on this tendency among human beings to make markets out of all those things that money is not supposed to buy. It is what it is, and I tend to think that what is, if it really is, is good. The point is that the tendency necessarily increases in importance with rising inequality. You can't understand the rise and the role of the 9.9 percent in American life today without taking it into account, or so I will show in the pages that follow.

In Chapter 2, you will meet many amazing families: supermoms, cool dads, and their camera-ready offspring. Then we will consider the secret identity between the sociological data and the economic data. The rise of the 9.9 percent has turned parenting into an extreme sport. It has cheated the luckiest offspring of their childhood and robbed the unlucky ones of their future. The process starts with values that can only be good—what kind of people would not want to care for their children?—and then twists those values into weapons in a ruthless struggle that undermines families in order to better exploit individuals.

It would be strange to think that such changes in family patterns would leave gender relations untouched, and indeed they have not. In Chapter 3, I show that the rise of the 9.9 percent has turned marriage and a stable family life into a luxury good. Notwithstanding the enlightened ideals about gender equality that are cemented into the official Creed of the 9.9 percent, I further contend, the rise of the 9.9 percent has in reality reinvigorated misogyny as a political force and opened the door to new forms of old gender hierarchies.

In Chapter 4, we follow aspiring members of the 9.9 percent as they seek admission to the colleges that now serve as the gateways to status and success in America. Along the way I track the damage that uncontrolled inequality has wreaked on the system of higher education. The rise of the 9.9 percent has brought about what I will call the Great Reprivatization of America's university system. It has converted higher education from an engine of mobility into a machine for reproducing privilege. Above all, it has distorted the very idea of education in a way that strikes at the foundation of democracy.

In Chapter 5, we tour some of the nation's finest neighborhoods, where the rise of the 9.9 percent has hammered the idea of community into an excuse for exclusion and transformed the celebration of homeownership into a housing affordability crisis. Rising inequality, the history will reveal, has converted the indirect homeowner subsidies that once served as a welfare system for the white middle class into a device for transferring money upward from the 90 percent to the 9.9 percent and reinforcing racial divisions. Through their domination of local government, the paid-up members of the 9.9 percent have monopolized control over the economic geography and restored property in land to its ancestral role as a principal mechanism for dividing the desirable from the undesirable.

To be clear, I do not mean to suggest that there is something intrinsically wrong with the ideals of parenting, family, education, and community from which the 9.9 percent got its start in the world. I take for granted that people will do whatever possible to secure a happy future for themselves, and there would in any case be no point in shaming them for doing what only comes naturally. I doubt that anybody sets off in the morning with the malicious intent of breaking up other people's families, perverting the system of education, shortening average life expectancy, raising average commute times to toxic levels, or profiting from the race hatred of other people. The point is just that that is what happens in the twilight of the meritocracy. Rising inequality takes good values and quietly twists them into bad ones. The unconscious hoarding that has come to define the life of the 9.9 percent is a response to this underlying condition, not the cause, and it is a response born of weakness, not strength.

But none of that adds up to an excuse for not knowing how the system now works, which way it is headed, and the role we all play in its perpetuation. The distinguishing feature of the 9.9 percent is not that it has advantages and is willing to use them, but that it confuses its privileges with artifacts of nature. It sees its own virtues brightly in the mirror, and it has no trouble spotting the vices of other people. But it remains blind to the conditions on which both depend. That willful ignorance is the glue that holds the system together. It is our collective contribution to the triumph of the 0.1 percent and the fall of the 90 percent. Rising inequality makes accomplices of us all.

WHEN I FIRST HEARD THE STORIES about the Colonel, I pictured him in cowboy boots, tying his horse up next to an oil derrick, and making on-the-spot decisions about where to drill and when to sell. That, I imagined, is just what the chairman of the Standard Oil Company of Indiana does, especially if he happens to be a former Rough Rider and goes by the name of "the Colonel." Whenever I tried asking Grandfather exactly how the Colonel made his fortune, however, I usually got back an answer about the glories of capitalism and the evils of communism. Then he would remind me that the Rockefellers were our mortal enemies. This really confused me. Weren't the Rockefellers the capitalists?

I eventually figured out that the Colonel was a lawyer, not a petroleum-sniffing cowboy. He was the son of a poor farmer made good with a scholarship to Coe College in Iowa and then a degree from Yale Law School. He got his start defending the rights of John D. Rockefeller's Standard Oil Company to use its monopoly over the distribution of oil to crush its competitors and squeeze money out of the American public. From there he moved over to the executive side of the business. The high point and the low point of his career occurred around the same time, when he used his formidable legal skills to structure the offshore-shell-company scheme that supplied the raw money needed to bribe members of the Warren G. Harding administration to let Big Oil siphon off the vast reserves of publicly owned petroleum recently discovered under a rock in Wyoming shaped oddly like a teapot. (For those who slept through high school history: in the century preceding the Donald Trump administration, the Teapot Dome scandal was thought to have set the standard for corruption in American politics.)

The Colonel was never convicted of any crimes (though things did get dicey in the trial over his alleged contempt of Congress). But John D. Rockefeller Jr., who owned the largest block of shares in Standard of Indiana, knew a PR disaster when he saw one. The Colonel put up a fight—I knew for sure that was his style—but in the end the richer man won, and the Colonel was compelled to hang up his spurs. It all came as something of a surprise to me, when I read about the details in the textbooks. There was nothing in Grandfather's brunchtime stories about Canadian shell companies or teapots. And yet, in the end, it all made sense. The real mystery, I later thought, was how it was that I had let so many loose ends in Grandfather's tales escape my attention.

This is another one of those stories that come to my mind when the subject turns to inequality. The problem with inequality today—or at any rate, the part of the problem that should be of concern—is not that some people earn more or are worth more than others. It is that some people earn much more than they are worth and most people are worth much more than they earn. There isn't just one Standard Oil now; there are dozens of them slithering all over the economy. And Teapot Dome is starting to look like amateur hour. The basic form of a solution to the problem of inequality today is not to redistribute wealth from those who have allegedly earned it to those who have not, but to return wealth from those who expropriated it to those who actually created it. The only kind of inequality that matters is that which involves injustice.

All of this, I think can be easily known, though I will present the necessary evidence for the case throughout this book. The real question—or at least the one with which I will be primarily concerned—is why we consistently fail to see an injustice that is playing itself out before our eyes.

Conversations about inequality with successful members of the 9.9 percent today, I have noticed, often move swiftly toward the defenses. Do you understand how hard it is to get into Yale Law? I worked my tail off! You want to punish me for my success? Anyway, that's life, get over it! And so on. It's a funny thing to hear this sort of talk coming from a group whose statistically significant attributes, apart from their wealth, also include, among other things, the whiteness of their skin, the year of their birth, the nation in which they happen to reside, the nature of their housing arrangements, and the size of their parents' bank accounts. But we must take things as they are. The origin myth of the 9.9 percent is a certain idea of meritocracy.

Here it is important to distinguish meritocracy from certain false ideas about it, as I will explain further in Chapter 6. The problem with meritocracy is not the idea that merit should receive its just rewards, as many of its present critics seem to think. What could be wrong with rewarding people for their talent, effort, and accumulated skills? Much better to hear about the efficacy of face masks in a pandemic from an epidemiologist, I am inclined to think, than from the shouty guy at the other end of the bar. Indeed, rightly understood, meritocracy is simply one of many limited devices for holding power accountable to reason. It is a necessary component of a just democracy and a founding postulate of liberal democracy.

The real problem with meritocracy, or so I will argue, is the unstated, additional, and spurious assumption that the merit of isolated individuals is the principal human factor in the production of wealth and the moral foundation of our just rewards. It is not. This merit myth, as I will call it, becomes especially dangerous when it is used to explain and justify the growing imbalances in the distribution of economic and political power. It does not. The biggest problem of all is that, according to what I will call the Iron Law of Merit, the merit myth is itself a consequence of rising inequality. Indeed, it is the defining illusion of the 9.9 percent. Today we tend to blame inequality on the meritocracy, but the reality is that we should blame the problems with meritocracy on inequality.

In the medicine cabinet, right next the merit myth, you will find the other great opiate of the 9.9 percent. Call it the market myth. My grandfather ingested this one in very large quantities. It says that rising inequality is just the price we pay for a system that sets everyone free and leaves us all better off. It is the goose that lays our golden iPhones. And, blessed are we, it all comes down to timeless laws of economics written into the sky.

Bullshit, or so I argue in Chapter 7. Most of the supposed definitions of the existing economic system are merely statements of what its principal beneficiaries in the 9.9 percent and their bosses in the 0.1 percent would like it to be. What they really mean to say is: Wouldn't it be nice to have "free" enterprise in a "free" market where all "capital" is put to productive use in an endless cycle of "creative destruction"? The actual system we have is none of those things, or so I explain, and it generates inequality not as an accident or a by-product but as a necessary feature of its business model. In this system, moreover, the Creed of the 9.9 percent has a special role to play, and it is not an altogether happy one. By insisting that our struggles are the necessary consequence of a system that operates entirely according to the beneficent principles of free and fair competition, that Creed serves to keep the desperation flowing downward and the money flowing upward.

The market myth, I further contend in Chapter 7, has corroded certain ideals of economic justice that, paradoxically, were present at the creation of the 9.9 percent. Professionalism and managerialism are not intrinsically bad things. On the contrary, they were and remain to some degree buffers against the fanatical absurdities of the market myth. They are central to any system that wishes to benefit from the kind of competition and innovation to which markets may contribute and yet relies on the imperfect nature and circumscribed conditions of actual human beings and actual human societies. In the age of captured markets and escalating inequality, however, these ideals, like the rest of the worthy values that once guided the 9.9 percent, have been twisted into their opposites.

Practically speaking, as I will further explain, the options for aspiring members of 9.9 percent in the existing economic system come down to this. You can seek shelter from the pressures of living in a stacked market by hiding in a profession that has betrayed its principles and learned to protect itself. (That was more or less the Colonel's strategy when he came out of school as a lawyer.) Or you can join with the winners and organize the extraction of life-juices from your fellow human beings. (That was the horse that the Colonel rode when he took his pony up to the top of the legal oil field.) This is the why most of the paid-up members of the 9.9 percent wear white coats or white collars. Sadly, the white coats have not yet figured out that the white collars will soon eat them for lunch, before turning on themselves.

ONE OF THE THINGS that became clear when my grandparents passed away is that they had never been all that rich. Everything had gone into appearances. I don't mean that only in a financial sense (though there was that). In the end, the struggle to stay on the island came with some not insignificant personal costs, too. They lived in a home much smaller than they might have liked because living off-island was unthinkable. They ate and drank too much cheesecake and champagne in their efforts to keep up at the clubs. And they experienced quite a few cloudy days of disappointment and alienation, when family members blew in with unspoken regrets about their failure to achieve the status to which they were supposedly born. I don't doubt that my grandparents would have done it all again. But it was clear in retrospect that the land of endless French toast had never really been such a thing of splendor.

Quite possibly some of the paid-up members of the 9.9 percent will have experienced a similar moment of morning-after accounting. The overpriced homes, the overanxious offspring, the overpolished credentials, the over-policed and over-purified neighborhoods—they're usually better than the existing alternatives, but they aren't quite the unalloyed goods that they at first seem to be. The story on the surface of the 9.9 percent is about the class that gets everything it wants; the subtext is about a group that has simply played the game of self-subordination better than others.

The root of the trouble, I now tend to think, has to do with the ways with which we think about wealth and inequality. More precisely, it has to do with the ways in which inequality distorts our ideas about wealth, progress, and our own well-being. Inequality deforms consciousness, or so I contend; it makes us all unreasonable.

Now, we all know that human beings have always been unreasonable to some degree. They routinely draw conclusions about the way the world is from the way they wish it to be; they systematically overvalue evidence of recent experience and undervalue evidence that comes from far away; they are really bad at math, especially the math of risks and probabilities; they think their team is always in the right, and the other guys are always in the wrong; and so on. As inequality rises, however, all of these cognitive defects become catastrophically worse, or so I show. The human faculties of moral cognition are simply not built to work under conditions of extreme inequality. Even more important, inequality brings forth social forces with the means and the motive to amplify and exploit the growing vulnerabilities in the human cognitive apparatus. This self-combustion of reason, I think, is the real backstory behind the rise of the 9.9 percent.

In Chapter 8, I draw on parallels between ancient and modern civilization to illustrate how inequality inscribes itself on our own bodies and then distorts our ideas about the actual sources of our physical health and well-being. The rise of the 9.9 percent, I argue, accounts for the paradox of a nation where well-toned abs are an obsession even while pre-existing conditions multiply at pandemic levels, where billionaires look like fitness trainers while the average life expectancy declines. It is the fundamental reason why the nation with the most expensive health care system in the known universe is among the least able to protect its public health. Inequality disrupts progress by distorting our ideas about the only kind of well-being that actually matters, or about actual human prosperity.

In Chapter 9, I return to the role of inequality in enabling the growing political power of racism in twenty-first-century America. According to the theory favored by the 9.9 percent, racism is a legacy of the past, bound to fade as individuals slowly purify their souls of bad thoughts. The reality is that rising inequality today serves, as it has throughout history, to reproduce racism in new forms, and the 9.9 percent theory of racism is just a way of framing the problem that leaves its own contribution out of the picture. The race dividend, as I will call it, cultivates race hatred in society at large and converts it into higher real estate returns and higher income for those who live and work in mostly white spaces without regard to the purity of their souls or even necessarily their individual racial identities—and this dividend grows in times of rising inequality.

In Chapter 10, I argue that the triumph of unreason is the defining crisis of American politics and that this crisis is the principal manifestation of rising inequality. According to many of the usual narratives, by contrast, inequality is just one among many grim problems we face, and it has to stand in line alongside, and maybe behind, such worries as political polarization, hyperpartisanship, and corruption; climate change, runaway technology, and threats from foreign adversaries; racial injustice, gender injustice, religious bigotry, and the decay of moral and social institutions in general; the permanent crises in health care, education, and housing; and, well, the list could go on. Each of these issues does indeed deserve individual attention and tailored solutions. But compartmentalizing injustices is also one of the ways that injustice perpetuates itself. The real problem is the politics of unreason to which inequality necessarily gives rise, and the solution is to reestablish a politics of reason.

In this struggle to achieve a politics of reason, I further contend, the 9.9 percent have a peculiar and somewhat tragic role to play. The original charter of the meritocracy is to hold power accountable to reason. Its job is to make authority answer to scrutable laws, norms, and facts rather than the whims of rulers. Under the pressure of rising inequality, however, the intellectual vanguard of the 9.9 percent has abandoned its post. Some of its members have gone to work directly for the superwealthy in those ideological factories known as think-tanks. A larger number have preferred to hide behind the simulated justice of specious relativisms and the politics of posturing. Both have framed the crisis of our time in ways that leave their contribution out of the picture. Both have committed a kind of treason of the intellectuals.

GRANDFATHER'S BEST STORIES actually strayed far from the theme of the family tree. He chuckled to life when he talked about his years of service as a pilot in particular. In his early middle age, before the inheritance solved all problems, while he was still living under the shadow of the Colonel's wrath, he learned how to fly and went to work for Trans World Airlines. Grandmother, too, became a pilot, and joined the first generation of female pilots. For a time, they crossed the midwestern skies in a barnstorming plane, offering thrills to wide-eyed farming families for spare change. During World War II, Grandfather enlisted in the navy's air transport service and flew supply missions in the Pacific theater. The stories about Lieutenant William Stewart of Revolutionary War fame, I long knew, were so much baloney. (As best I can gather, William was an Irish peasant who moved out to western Pennsylvania and ended up on the wrong side of George Washington in the Whiskey Rebellion.) Grandfather's war service, on the other hand, was unglamorous but real. In an indirect way, it helped imbue me with an optimistic view of the American future.

In any discussion of the problem of inequality today, it is easy to fall into a doom loop. History supplies an abundance of evidence that inequality is a one-way street. It always ends badly. Even worse, you can see it all play out in real time. The self-regard and greedy paranoia of the super-rich, the nihilism of the resentful masses, the willful obliviousness of the those upper-middle operators of the machinery—it can sometimes seem like you're forced to sit through a bad movie with an all-too-predictable plot. That's why those unwelcome experiences of déjà vu today are so unnerving. It's easy to slip into the idea that the only option is to watch it all burn.

But I do not share this pessimism. I tend to think that mystical calls for a total revolution are just another one of the ways in which inequality perpetuates itself—mainly by representing the only alternative as impossible or dangerous. My optimism, such as it is, rests on a simple fact. Some degree of progress in human affairs has in fact happened. It has not been continuous or cumulative, and it is not irreversible, as its more naive champions today tediously insist. But it is real. And it has happened in America, too. The important thing is to understand its actual source, and to separate this from the self-congratulatory myths with which it is often traduced.

In the final chapter of this book, I frame the solutions to the problem represented by the rise of the 9.9 percent in the context of American history. We do not need to reject the promise of America in order to address the problem of inequality; we just need to recover it from the many false interpretations that have been imposed upon it, or so I contend. We aren't doomed to a politics of unreason, because there are reasonable steps we can take to advance reason itself. The same is true for the values that lie at the origin of the 9.9 percent. The belief in education, the commitment to scientific expertise, the principle of fair play and earning your privilege—these are all good things. We just need to clear away the baggage that rampant inequality has piled on top of them.

There is lots to do, and I will point to many solutions in the pages that follow. We need to change the way we understand and organize the care we provide for all children, not just our own. We need a new and democratic philosophy of education and a new way of funding and managing it. We need to accept that health has always been something we pursue collectively as well as individually. We should face the fact that there is no lasting hope for racial or gender justice without economic justice. We should take control of American geography back from those feudal overlords who have captured it through self-serving land use regulations and return it to productive use. We should obliterate the monopolies, reempower workers, and use the tax system to return wealth from those who have expropriated it to those who actually created it. We need to fix the disinformation system, return data to the people, and establish a genuinely open market in ideas. And while we're at it, let's get the money out of politics.

But I wouldn't put too much weight on the specifics of the to-do list offered here. The solutions are mostly obvious in their general form but complicated in the specifics. Tackling a problem like inequality requires attention to detail, smart tactics, and a lot of fight. It's far too much for a short book about everything that's wrong with the world. As a rule, I tend to think, books are not a great way to save the world. They're best when they stick to the job of trying to open a few eyes. The striking fact about inequality today is not that it exists but that we do nothing about it. We do nothing about it because we have figured out how not to see it. So now it is time to take a look.

Why We Have Such Amazing Children

It is a truth generally acknowledged that a working parent in possession of a fortune must be in want of a nanny. Menlo Mom, as I will call her, is one person who gets it. A technology executive and the single mother of twin ten-year-old boys, Menlo Mom lives in the Silicon Valley bedroom community of Menlo Park. Around the time of this writing, she posted a nanny-wanted ad, and in that ad she articulates with admirable precision the modern parent's vision of the ideal helpmeet.[1]

Nanny (or Manny: the text scrupulously avoids committing to gender) will have "high executive functioning" and a "university degree or equivalent knowledge." She (reality check: 97 percent of nannies are female) will have deep math and computer skills, too, as she will be asked to "correctly quantify how much fish to purchase for five people"; "compare and make recommendations using credit card points to booking vacations versus paying cash"; and ensure that her research is "populated into a simple Excel spreadsheet." She must also be highly literate, with a demonstrated ability to "read articles about eating beef and increases in breast cancer" and to summarize them succinctly: "i.e., beef is bad, fish and vegetables are good." She'll want to bone up on her master chef skills, so that she can prepare those fishy-veggie meals while managing the family's complex allergies (chicken eggs bad, duck eggs good). Ideally, Nanny will have already trained for a decathlon, as she will be called upon to lead the boys in regular "sit ups, lunges, squats, push-ups" and join them in body surfing, skiing, mountain hiking, and "river-swimming" (huh?). Even better, Nanny should bring MBA-caliber managerial talent to the position, as she will be charged with "building alliances" with the housekeeper, property manager, the gardener/handyman, and the au pair (Nanny's little helper!), not to mention the nannies of the boys' play date partners.

Most of all, Nanny must have "room in their heart to love the kids and the mom." But she had better not get any ideas. Nanny must respect "appropriate boundaries in relationships and interactions."

And one last thing. Nanny must come with an open mind, just as she will be greeted with a firmly open mind. "Our family is human civil rights oriented and does not discriminate against any candidate on the basis of age, race, sex, etc.," says Menlo Mom. You have to love that "etc." It says: I'm going to click on every damn one of these boxes, as long as I get my nanny. (Reality check: 54 percent of nannies are people of color; 35 percent are noncitizens; and, not coincidentally, 46 percent of child care workers are on some form of public assistance.)[2]

Menlo Mom really exists. A reporter from *Slate* tracked her down through her digital footprints, and she owned up to the post under condition of anonymity. Then, in a brilliant countermove, she justified her quest for the ideal nanny by pointing to Judy Syfers's 1971 feminist classic, "I Want a Wife."[3] Aside from supplying evidence that Women's Studies programs at elite universities have clearly left their mark on the business classes, Menlo Mom hit the nail of parenting in our times on the head. The service person once described as a "wife" is now the nanny. Change the title of Syfers's essay to "I Want a Nanny" and it could well be a manifesto for the supreme parents of the 9.9 percent today.

"If I were Scott McNealy, former CEO of Sun Microsystems, and I'd done this ad, nobody would think twice," Menlo Mom adds in her own defense. As far as spreading viral memes go, this is surely true. Much of the energy in the commentary on her post, as Menlo Mom herself notes, consists of women attacking women for not doing what women are supposed to do. "Women are sexist because they live in a sexist society," she argues. It's a good point—and no less interesting than the fact that Menlo Mom and her fellow supreme parents have outsourced what was formerly described as women's work to an exploitable pool of overwhelmingly female laborers. We'll get to all of that in the next chapter. But the fact of the matter is that the extraordinary assumptions about the task of parenting embedded in the message from Menlo are distinct from the question of who is on the hook to perform those tasks, and those assumptions now cut across all genders among the 9.9 percent.

The Menlo doctrine of parenting perfection through corporate management of a multidivisional household are not at all confined to Menlo Park. In my own Silicon-ish neighborhood in the Boston area, for example, a "busy professional couple" recently placed an ad that seems to be looking for the very same nanny, wherever she may be.[4] Nanny/Manny (the text has once again been cleansed of all incriminating pronouns) will be "a very good communicator, written and verbal," and will possess, it is hoped, a "college degree in early childhood education." But she had better stay in her lane. She "must know the proper etiquette in a professionally run household" and be prepared to "accommodate changing circumstances." This ad, too, is written in fluent management-speak, but the person it seeks is one that any decent nineteenth-century novelist would have instantly identified as a "governess"—assuming, that is, that governesses are willing to work part-time with no job security and zero health benefits.

Although nannies generally get paid very little, in relative terms, the freedom they deliver isn't free. The average base salary for nannies in the Boston area is now $37,000.[5] The times being what they are, there are economy, business, first-class, and off-label-titanium tiers of service, just like at the airport. A network for "professional women" called SWAAY recently ran a feature on five nannies making more than $100,000 per year.[6] Menlo Mom herself appears to be offering a package that, counting the free lodging in the pool house, generous hourly wage, and overtime, may come in close to that level. Some families in San Francisco "are paying over $220,000 a year," says Anita Rogers, the president of British American Household Staffing.[7] "There's a value in paying well for your employees, especially in your household," she intones. The relevant section of her firm's website, by the way, is titled

"Nannies & Governesses." At these exalted heights of the traffic in child care, the performative aspect of the arrangements is hard to overlook. Presumably one of the perks of having a "governess" is being able to say you have one.

In the time of Covid, the hunger for governesses combined with a thirst for in-home schooling took the competition for ultimate child care to still greater levels of achievement. An ad from a "fun and loving" Connecticut family, for example, seeks a "governess" to provide "structure, schedules, teach manners, and discipline." Your schedule will be ten hours per day, and "you must be open to traveling," as the family travels to "other homes." A Los Angeles family is looking for the same person, with the obligatory "background in early childhood education," only the schedule is eleven hours. And flexibility is a must—the family is not sure whether the position will last a few months or the whole year. A Boston family homes in on the educational qualifications: "Having some experience teaching at a private or charter school is a plus," reads their ad for a "top quality teacher/home educator." Public school teachers and others involved in educating the masses, presumably, need not apply. The winner of the Mary Poppins–coronavirus sweepstakes, however, will surely take up the offer from the family in the Hamptons. The position will be "a 7-day live-in due to covid," and you get meals provided by "the family's private chef." But you "must work well on a team," as you will be joined by two full-time nannies and a newborn care specialist. You are to be in charge only of "the educational space" for kids aged one, two, and five years.[8]

"All I really want to do is run my business and be the best mom ever," says Menlo Mom. "I love my children and I think about them 24 hours a day." And you know what? She probably does. She probably is going to ace the mom test. The charitable assumption is that the twins will survive the ordeal and turn out just fine. And it's not like she's going to save the world by skipping the nanny and leaving the kids at home alone with the au pair, the property manager, and the gardener. I, for one, would not place all of the burdens of world history on Menlo Mom's personal choices. I would, however, take a second look at the ideas about parenting that speak through her.

Looking on the bright side, one could say that Menlo Mom and her social-class-mates have solved the problem of child care in modern times. They may count as evidence that, contrary to the dire predictions of nay-saying reactionaries, the sexual revolution and the entry of women into the workforce not only need not undermine family values but may actually turbocharge them to insane levels of achievement. They show by example that that which was supposed to have destroyed the family appears to have saved it. They stand for the idea that you can indeed have it all. You can have the duck eggs, the river-swimming, the tech IPO, the gender-neutral human civil rights, and a house full of love where everyone knows their place! More precisely, they stand for the idea that you can have it all, as long as you start with it all in the first place. Or at least with most of the cash. And a supremely talented nanny. And maybe a housekeeper, a property manager, a gardener, and, why not, an au pair.

This revolution in parenting (or is it a counterrevolution?) comes to rest on a curious system of beliefs. The first article of the Menlo Doctrine, to give it a name, is just this: not only can you have it all, but *you must do it all*. You alone are the maker of your child. If your child fails, that's on you. Now, it is true that other people have children and that these children seem to populate the world. As far as you are concerned, however, they might as well live on another planet. And at the same time that you do it all, by the way, you must do your real job. Because if you fail to get that start-up started, or whatever it is that you are really doing, you will be an incomplete person.

The other article of the Doctrine worth noting here is harder to see because it is so transparent in everything about the family life of the 9.9 percent. It has to do with the idea that there is a mom test and that you can ace it. It says: *parenting is a measure of merit*. This really starts to look like a very strange thought, once you step outside of it and look back from the other side of the playroom stuffed with brain-development toys.

Every parent knows at some level that there are acres of parenting that belong to the same category of activity as mowing the lawn. You can screw it up. You can forget to do it. But you can't get graded on a curve that extends all the way up to the 99th percentile of lawn-mowers. Yet the Doctrine says otherwise. It holds that parenting is a business process that operates on the principles of a market-validated meritocracy. Every travel, dining, entertainment, and educational experience of childhood can and should be populated into a spreadsheet and relentlessly optimized for peak performance. Parental productivity can vary as widely as returns on the stock market. The person who dies with the best kids wins. From a world-historical perspective, this is a remarkable belief system. What does it mean that so many people seem to think it is true?

VISIT ANY MODERATELY RESPECTABLE ZIP CODE today and you will see that, like a designer brand infiltrating the local shopping mall, the Menlo Doctrine has come to a suburb near you. SUVs thunder through the cold morning streets, their glassy-eyed drivers hauling scrawny youngsters off to warm the benches at faraway fencing tournaments. Pianos and violins wail under torture at the hands of small children whose passion for music will awaken any day now. Social media pages buzz with plots to game the junior division of the national capoeira championship. Play date snacks crafted from flaxseed and quinoa are policed against long lists of forbidden foods. Cell phone apps track college kids with a degree of geographical precision that only the NSA can rival.[9] Living rooms once lubricated with mixed drinks and sweaty games of charades have been made over into shrines where every childhood epiphany has its photo, trophy, or ball of painted macaroni. Entire homes have been converted into cluttered warehouses for the paraphernalia of childhood. A nation with 4 percent of the world's population that buys 40 percent of the world's toys has to stash them somewhere.[10]

They will tell you that it's bliss from baby's first cries before dawn until the sun finally sets on a glowing college acceptance letter. But they will tell their pollsters that they have never been so stressed and unhappy. They will insist that it's all about sitting back and letting the child bloom like a flower in the meadow. Then they will get back to scraping and chiseling their miniature alter egos like a Pygmalion on uppers. They mean well, for the most part, these new parenting superstars. But they are just a little bit nuts, and not always in a good way.

Consider the case of Yale Law School professor Amy Chua, the tragi-comic author of *Battle Hymn of the Tiger Mother*. In hopes of processing a family crisis brought on by the contradictions in her extreme form of modern, meritocratic parenting, Chua famously depicted a kind of caricature of herself in beast mode. She didn't really mean it when she called her children "garbage" or threatened "to take all your stuffed animals and burn them" if they failed to bring home straight As and achieve concert-master-level violin skills. Except that she sort-of did. In part because the line between self-parody and self-incrimination is so thin, but also because she unwisely packaged modern parenting neuroses in unfortunate ethnic stereotypes, Chua opened up a frothy milk-bottleful of hate. It was like issuing a license to 9.9 percenters everywhere to pretend that the insanity of their own parenting style was the work of alien invaders. The cool dads and the whole grain moms could enjoy a sweet moment of projection. The truth is that we 9.9 percenters are all tiger mothers now.

If you happen to be of a certain age today, you will know that it didn't have to be this way. In my preteen world, the parental units had no idea where we were going when we hopped on our banana-seat Stingrays and headed off into the hills of Southern California. They didn't know about the area we called "Third Field," where you could pop wheelies in snake-infested creek beds. They didn't know about the hole in the fence that led down a cliff to the beach, or about the inflatable raft that we took out to sea through a sewer outlet. We just had to be home in time for the SpaghettiOs. I'm not saying it was ideal; there are some legitimate nutritional and safety concerns. The point is that there is much in the new way of parenting that is neither traditional nor natural.

Sociologists began to document the transformation in the 1990s. Berkeley professor Annette Lareau found that the wealthier, mostly white families were adopting a style of child-rearing that she politely called "concerted cultivation."[11] The various manifestations of the practice came to be labeled child-centered parenting, attachment parenting, helicopter parenting, snowplow parenting, extreme parenting, High Investment Parenting (HIP), hyperparenting, and, in Scandinavia, curling parenting—after the sport where contestants maniacally polish the ice in front of a gliding stone.[12] Supreme parenting, as I will call it, is now the subject of a groaning bookshelf of self-help literature. Some of these books appear intended to provoke parents into still more exalted states of nervous excitement. Others urge them to just take a chill pill. But these books are more bought than opened, because supreme parents are too damn busy to read them.

In short, the ruling values of the 9.9 percent have become the ruling values of American society. In a survey of more than 3,600 parents in all social classes, sociologist Patrick Ishizuka found that, even while actual parenting practices continue to differ significantly across class and race lines, support for "time-intensive, child-centered parenting" ideals is now nearly universal in the United States.[13] Reporting from Brazil, Israel, and India suggests that this new way of family life may one day count as the American 9.9 percent's great gift to the world.[14]

The Menlo Doctrine is now universal enough in the United States that its effects show up clearly in the aggregate statistics.[15] In the early 1970s, according to analysis by economists Matthias Doepke and Fabrizio Zilibotti, college-educated and non-college-educated mothers alike averaged twelve hours per week on child care. By 2012, educated mothers were clocking in at almost twenty hours per week and the uneducated were up to sixteen—even as both groups substantially increased their hours working outside the home. Meanwhile, college-educated fathers more than doubled their load, rising from a measly five hours to eleven hours—or almost as much as "traditional" mothers were putting in during the golden age of housewifery. Even the noncollege men upped their game to nine hours per week. And yet—here again, one glimpses the haunting beauty of the system, from the perspective of those who profit from it—majorities as high as 85 percent of parents surveyed say they don't spend enough time with their kids.

THE DIFFUSION OF SUPREME PARENTING outside the gates of Menlo Park is paradoxical at many levels, starting with the money. Even as it has gone retail, supreme parenting has not gotten any cheaper. At the upper end of the parental-economic spectrum, the statistics on cash flows make the point all on their own. Between 1970 and 2015, the top quintile of the income distribution more than tripled its spending on young children from $3,000 to $10,000 per child per year in inflation-adjusted dollars, while the bottom 60 percent remained flat at $2,000 and below.[16]

FYI: that $10,000 number for child expenses in the upper quintile will look like a warehouse club sale to many families in the 9.9 percent. Here are some more realistic numbers to bear in mind:[17] Travel baseball starts at $3,700 per year. Soccer goes up to $5,000. Volleyball is $8,000 to $10,000. A significant number of ice hockey families report spending $20,000 per year. And don't even talk about horseback riding. The best summer camps run about $2,000 per week. Unless, that is, your budding scientist/community worker is looking for personal development opportunities in Iceland or the Galápagos, in which case a summer of priceless learning experiences might cost as much as small car. All of that, of course, comes before you even start thinking about Nanny's Christmas bonus, private counselors and test preppers, and any tuition at private school, which now runs at $46,000 per year at the best schools—not including room and board.

Not even a pandemic will rein in the budgets of the most supreme of parents. When the coronavirus drove all sensible New Yorkers to escape to the Hamptons—that is, all those sensible enough to own a home in the Hamptons or to have $200,000 in spare change for a five-month rental—the top moms and dads sprang into action. "One woman called and asked if I could install a tennis court right away," a local building contractor told Joe Nocera of Bloomberg.[18] "She said she was afraid the coronavirus was going to cause tennis camp to be canceled, so she needed a tennis court so her kids could play." (Not that the focus on the family meant that there was any letup in self-care for ultimate parents. Dermatologists in the Hamptons also reported an uptick in demand for Botox injections during the Great Escape.)

What happens to the (roughly) 90 percent of parents who believe in the value of parental supremacy but can't swing the spare tennis court, or the ultimate nanny experience? It is by now well understood that the demands of supreme parenting combined with the demands of a typical modern working life make for a perfect sandwich. Parents are getting eaten alive. (Toss in eldercare for grandma and it becomes a club sandwich.)

It makes for some terrifying video. In the underappreciated genre of horror-documentaries, there is a blockbuster lurking in the 1,500 hours or so of footage that UCLA's Center on the Everyday Lives of Families collected in the homes of thirty-two middle-class, dual-income families as they went about the everyday business of putting vitamin-rich food in front of children, dragging them off to supposedly fun activities, harassing them over homework, and wrestling devices out of their bored and twitchy little hands.[19] It is "the very purest form of birth control ever devised. Ever," said one of the filmmaker-researchers, himself a father of two.[20] The research also confirms that married mothers are unhappier than married fathers, and single parents are the most miserable of all.[21]

Surveys consistently show that parenting today causes individuals around the world to become measurably less happy. Out of twenty-two countries studied, moreover, the United States is number one in producing grouchy parents, according to sociologist Jennifer Glass and colleagues.[22] Not coincidentally, the United States ranks last among developed countries in policies on family leave, preschool, child care, and pretty much everything else that might make parenting a financially and psychologically reasonable proposition.

When the Covid pandemic shut down most child care options, policymakers and commentators suddenly noticed that the country has no system of child care and that the economy doesn't work without it.[23] A few months of inconvenience appeared to achieve far more than decades of research in demonstrating that not just the availability but the quality of early child care is critical both for the development of young minds, family stability, and economic growth.[24]

Whether the virus-induced flash of enlightenment can overcome decades of "pro-family" economic messaging is very much in doubt. For the fact remains that—and here again we glimpse the beauty of the system, at least in the eyes of those who profit from it—"American working mothers generally blame themselves for how hard their lives are," as researcher Caitlyn Collins observes.[25] Collins also notes that the United States and Papua New Guinea are the only countries in the world that do not offer paid maternity leave.

AND WHAT ABOUT THE KIDS? Actually, it doesn't have much to do with the kids—and this disturbing fact brings us still closer to the defining mystery of supreme parenting. The point can be read in a rough way straight from the economic data. When income increases, spending on basic goods like food and paper towels tends to go down as a proportion of income. Goods that serve to broadcast one's status to the universe, on the other hand, move in the opposite direction. The richer you are, the greater the proportion of income you spend on Swiss watches and tasteful contemporary art installations. This is what has happened with parenting expenses. At the very highest levels of the game, supreme parenting is an extravagance to be conspicuously consumed.[26] It has become a luxury sport like yacht racing or polo. Winning is hardly the point. Just having your kid show up with a stable of horses and some practiced mallet skills gets the message across.

In a strange way, this is something that supreme parenting has with the fustiest systems of intergenerational wealth transfer. Consider the medieval system of entail, the legal device whereby estates are required by law to pass themselves down whole in perpetuity to a single line of eldest sons (or the next best thing). The nominal point of the system is to lock down the indefinite future of an estate, not just for the one lucky kid, but for a string of grandkids going off to infinity. But why would a medieval lord care what might happen to his estate in one thousand years? The answer is that he knows very well that his power in the present depends on the universal appreciation that his name and glory will remain intact upon his death and that his wishes will be enforced by an heir who is equally robust and equally capable of passing it all down to his mighty heir, and so on. Supreme parenting is like entail in this sense: perpetuating inequality in the future is the means of the crime, not the end. This is why we palpably sense that the battle hymn of the tiger mother has much more to do with the glory of the tiger than the fate of the cub.

So what does it feel like to grow up as a lovingly nurtured Swiss watch or polo accessory—or, for that matter, as the offspring of parents who wish they had a medieval estate but can't quite come up with the mortgage? The science on the subject is not reassuring. It turns out that maybe breeding bonsai-tree children to become résumé zombies isn't so good for their mental health.[27] Supreme parenting can imbue the objects of its obsession with a nasty combination of narcissism, anxiety, and depression. Madeline Levine, a psychologist who plies the supremely rich and anxious pastures of Marin County in the San Francisco Bay Area, saw so much damage in the overachievement community that she filled a book with tales of its self-inflicted woes.[28] In *The Price of Privilege*, she delicately suggests that "some aspects of affluence and parental involvement might be contributing to the unhappiness and fragility of my privileged patients." Summarizing the research literature, she concludes that "upper middle class youth, who are en route to the most prestigious universities and well-paying careers in America, are more likely to be troubled than their middle-class counterparts."[29]

Which brings up another weird parallel with medieval family planning. The funny thing about entail is what it does to families. You'd think it would be good. What family wouldn't want a shield, a castle, and maybe a long string of Ivy League degrees to its name? But entail is actually terrible for families. If you have watched *Downton Abbey*, you will know this to be true. There is no need to follow the twists and turns of a plot that leaves the whole pile to a distant and bewildered cousin, because it comes down to some very simple arithmetic. Entail only works if everything passes down to one single heir after another. To be fair, supreme parenting is spared most (though not all) of the sibling drama associated with the crude inheritance mechanisms of the past. But that is only because it tosses all children into a collective inheritance scheme where the math is brutal for all of them. As Amy Chua's work can attest, the chiseling and scraping required to sculpt the perfect meritocrat generates as much novel-worthy trauma as the scraping and bowing required to land a suitable match at the Abbey. Supreme parenting is a wealth preservation strategy pursued not for the sake of family but at its expense.

If you ask many supreme parents why they do it, on the other hand, you will generally find that the science is always on their side, at least in their own minds. It's all about what the latest research says is good for little brains and little hearts.[30] And yet, if you take a dip into the "research" that makes the social media rounds, you will quickly gather that supreme parenting lives in an ocean of pseudoscience. Even stranger, all of the intellectual detritus points in the same direction.[31] The research always shows that if you play Bach's Orchestral Suites at high volumes, or cleanse diets of certain unnatural foods, or do math puzzles in your head while pregnant, you can turn your chihuahuas into poodles. Fact alert: you can't. Yet the belief persists, because tomorrow, for sure, another study will prove that you've been doing it all wrong and that what you really need to ensure optimal brain development is a horsehair mattress. Or something like that. Whence this will to believe?

If it reduces kids into anxious avatars in a crypto-medieval status competition, messes up families, costs ridiculous amounts of money, is bubbling over with pseudoscience, and leaves most parents miserable—why is it happening? What has gotten into these people? In that book-shelf of parenting cheers and sighs, which necessarily adheres to the formulas of the self-help genre, the finger usually ends up pointing back at the parents themselves. They are the narcissists. Or they are neurotic. Or they are compensating for something that the Woodstock crowd did in the 1960s. Or they need to embrace their inner parenting demon. Or tame it. One can spare oneself much unnecessary reading, however, if one bears in mind that pretty much all such explanations rest on a confusion between cause and effect. The important thing is to understand the causes, and these causes, strange as it may sound, have less to do with what parents today consciously intend to do than with what they consciously try to ignore.

THE REMOTE CAUSE of supreme parenting is inequality. Supreme parenting is very simply what parents do when life in society becomes radically unequal. (Narcissism, neurosis, and other forms of unreason, by the way, are also effects of inequality—we'll get to that.) The connection between parenting styles and inequality is robust enough that it can be detected even with the crude tools of cross-country socioeconomic comparisons. When economists Matthias Doepke and Fabrizio Zilibotti studied parenting around the world, they discovered that variations in the degree of over-parenting across countries could be almost entirely explained through a single factor: "The common denominator in countries where intense, achievement-oriented parenting abounds is a large gap between the rich and the poor."[32]

The causal explanation isn't hard to see. As inequality rises, the landscape of economic hopes and fears gets steeper and meaner. When the people on the hillside look up, they see that they face a long slog to the top. But when they look down—that's when they really freak out. They do everything they can to secure their position for themselves and for their children. They strap the kids to their violins in the desperate hope that this will save them from tumbling down the cliff into a lifetime of pouring Frappuccinos. Pretty soon every kid on the mountain is making screechy violin noises, so the parents go to the store and buy some special math tutoring, rhumba dancing skills, or whatever it takes to stay in place or maybe gain a few inches on the slope. Keep the process going long enough, and you end up with a mountain of children locked in their perches and shrieking for mercy.

In this cacophonous struggle on the hillside, it isn't hard to see, the people nearer the top have a decided advantage over those near the bottom. Quite simply, they can buy bigger and better violins, or whatever it is that ties them and their offspring in place. And that is exactly what they will do. There is no point in shaming them about it. You might as well try to make a mountain flatter by asking the people on it to throw away their climbing gear. Supreme parenting is thus the next best thing to an inheritance mechanism. It is a way for the rich to pass on their riches and the poor to pass on their poverty. To be clear, it's not the only way. We'll get to some of the other devices soon, and they include the old-fashioned method of handing it down in a will and testament. But it is the signature method of the 9.9 percent today.

Now, inheritance mechanisms are not quite the simple things we imagine them to be—entail, for example, is a lot weirder than it looks—but the data suggest that supreme parenting is at least somewhat effective in its mission of freezing society in place. Economists measure the ability of parents to pass along their earnings power with "intergenerational elasticity" (IGE) of earnings, which quantifies the association between parents' relative income level and their children's relative income level as adults.[33] Think of it as a bungee cord connecting your foot to the particular spot on the economic mountainside where you were born. The cord will keep you from falling down very far below your parents' position on the income scale, but it will also prevent you from moving up. An IGE of 1 means that, in a word, you are your parents; an IGE of 0 means that everyone has an equal chance of ending up anywhere on the hillside, without regard to the circumstances of birth.

Over the past half century, IGE in the United States has increased from 0.3 to 0.5. In other words: half of your relative income level is now decided on the day you are born. That compares with IGEs of 0.2 and less in Finland, Norway, and Denmark and a little over 0.3 in Germany and Japan. On this metric, the United States is in a league with countries like Italy, Chile, and Argentina. Contrary to popular wisdom, the land of opportunity is more like the land of the good families and the bad. A closer look at the mobility data also confirms that the stickiest parts of the economic spectrum in the United States are at the top and bottom.[34] It's the children of the bottom decile and, above all, the top decile—the 9.9 percent—that bounce back nearest to their starting point. This decline in mobility—which can be measured in a number of ways[35]—is undoubtedly one of the central developments in American society over the past half century. It marks the emergence of a new, semi-hereditary caste at the top end of the American socioeconomic system.

While the new inheritance mechanism is effective in a statistical sense, it is important to add, that is far from saying that it is a sure bet in any particular case. A substantial degree of mobility still happens—more than enough to fuel the enduring rags-to-riches and the less widely broadcast riches-to-rags stories. This fact is really as familiar as the worry lines that spread relentlessly across the faces of the 9.9 percent. Supreme parenting offers children an edge in battle on the hillside, not a guarantee. Indeed, one may even doubt that the leg-up it offers is necessarily worth the psychological and economic expense it involves. The fact that parents feel they have no choice but to play the game, with the cards in their hand, does not mean that this is a game that they have to like.

In any case, the statistical connection between earnings elasticity and inequality is pronounced enough that it, too, shows up in cross-country econometrics. A few years ago, Alan Krueger, the economist and former chairman of the Barack Obama administration's Council of Economic Advisers, noticed something curious about the international IGE statistics: the higher the inequality in countries, the higher the IGE. Krueger called his graph "The Great Gatsby Curve."[36] It is an apt name: F. Scott Fitzgerald wrote his novel about the collapse of the American Dream in the 1920s, which was also the last time that inequality was as high as it is now. It is customary at this point in the narrative to lament, along with F. Scott, the dying of the Dream. Therefore:

Amen.

But the Great Gatsby Curve points to something more interesting than just another requiem. It is actually about those places where the Dream was incoherent—or, more exactly, misremembered. For example, the traditional theory of the American Dream says that mobility justifies any degree of inequality. Who cares how rich the rich can get, if you have a fair shot of becoming one of them, too? The Great Gatsby Curve says that mobility cannot justify any degree of inequality because mobility is, to some degree, a function of equality.

More than that, the anxious fact patterns surrounding the Great Gatsby Curve (like the knowledge that supreme parenting isn't always fun to play) raise a question about the cardinal value of mobility itself. The problem with mobility-talk is that it takes for granted that everyone must always want what the people at the top already have. But that has never been true. Jay Gatsby himself was quite mobile—that's how he ended up with the party house in West Egg—but he wasn't exactly a model of a life well lived. A society in which one out of ten people turns around at the end of life and takes credit for the wealth produced by the other nine just because he won a talent show does not become equitable by giving everyone an equal shot at winning the competition. And a society in which everybody has an equal chance to practice supreme parenting is not therefore a good society. Contrary to our faulty memories of the American Dream, mobility or its own proves nothing about the justice of a society. Whatever was good in the Dream always had to do with the *kind* of the mobility it produced, not the mere fact that people could trade places.

The important thing to remember is that supreme parenting is the sign of trouble, but not necessarily the trouble itself. Parents do not torture their children and beat down on other people's children because they want to. The injustices they inflict are in direct proportion to the injustice that they perceive in the world. The practice arises both from the lay of the economic landscape and the way in which this landscape is framed and perceived. Interestingly, it is on this last point—the matter of how the underlying problem is perceived (more than the only partly successful efforts to game the parenting system)—that the 9.9 percent makes its signature contribution to the escalating inequality of the new Gilded Age.

LOOK AGAIN AT THE DRAMA of Menlo Mom's parenting adventures, and you may notice that the story comes to rest on a vast, imaginary history of humanity. The unspoken fable goes something like this. The family first came together in a treehouse. Or maybe it was a stone house, *Flintstones*-style. Either way, mom and dad did lots of things to raise and care for the youngsters (most of which, oddly, fell to mom). Then the family discovered that there are other families, and together they formed society. The family was private, society is public. The one answers to the laws of biology, the other to the laws of economics.

This is more or less the story that Margaret Thatcher had in mind when she said that "there is no such thing as society. There are individual men and women and there are families."[37] It is why former intellectuals get paid the think tank pluto-dollars to say preachy things like "the primary responsibility for creating a life of virtue and purpose rests with families and individuals."[38] The point of the story is really just to underscore the first article of the Menlo Doctrine: *you must do it all.*

Histories of humanity are always sketchy, but this one is catastroph-ically inaccurate. So I am going to point to a better fable—not perfect, to be sure, but not catastrophically misleading. It starts with a hard but well-attested fact: human beings are unique among animals in the help-lessness with which they arrive in the world. Their floppy heads come out too big for their flimsy necks, their stubby limbs serve for months mainly to invite stovetop injuries, and years elapse before they learn how to make the macaroni for themselves. Even after they have joined the soccer travel team, their emotional and rational faculties generally leave them unfit to form a viable society without regular supervision. The intensity and duration of the care required to craft useful souls out of these adorable little humans would surely cause any fox or grizzly bear to run for the hills.

The genius of human society, in its earliest iterations, was to devise a culture of care, that is, a system of cooperation spanning an entire community capable of rearing viable members of the next generation. An abundance of evidence from anthropology and archaeology makes clear that this extraordinary achievement was emphatically not a mat-ter of leaving kids alone with mom and a few household appliances in some subdivision of treehouses. For many tens of thousands of years, human societies operated on the understanding that the task of forming the next generation is to be shared among siblings, fathers, cousins, aunts, grandparents, mothers-in-law, the brothers' mothers-in-law, baby-sitters, tutors, mentors, and others.[39]

The siblings' in-laws and the nannies here deserve far more atten-tion than they typically get for one simple reason. They are genetically unconnected to the child. Today we often mistakenly suppose that the nanny came into being as a mother-substitute. In reality, the mother (as we imagine her) came into being as a nanny-substitute. The culture of care came first; and the many subsequent efforts to privatize the delivery of this intrinsically public service and assign responsibility for it to a designated subset of the species came later. Human society properly begins when humans learn to care not just for their kin but for their kind. Thus, one could say, with a certain poetic license, that the nanny stands at the very origin of human society.

A feature of this version of the human story is that it definitely helps to explain an obvious fact about life in Menlo Park. Menlo Nanny is not the inspiring avatar of the culture of care that arises like a songbird of hope at the dawn of civilization. She is there to tell you that our civilization doesn't give a crap about you or your river-swimming twins. Ours is the culture of we-don't-care. How did this fateful change happen? The answer will take us from the dawn of time to birth of the 9.9 percent.

The first of the crimes against humanity is as old as inequality itself. It started with the agricultural revolution, though it achieved a renewed degree of infamy in the industrial revolution. I'm talking about the division of labor by gender. To be fair, the division of labor by gender, in some societies, under conditions of relative equality and simplicity in life options, is one way to solve a cooperation problem, and it is not in itself inherently criminal. Extreme material inequality, however, changes this division into a device for rendering half of the population subservient, squandering its natural variety of talents, and devaluing the very service that it was coerced into performing. The rise of the patriarchy is a complicated story, however, so let's leave this crime for the next chapter.

The second crime against humanity was committed in the process of attempting to correct the first, and it is the one that matters most in explaining the wreckage in the American child care scene today. The modern parenting predicament began to take its present shape around the time that women entered the paid workforce in large numbers. To be clear, the issue was not, as a few reactionaries still fatuously maintain, the mere entry of women into the workforce. Women have always worked. The question was whether they would be permitted to work in the kinds of jobs long assigned to men and to be paid for their work. The answer was that women would be paid for that kind of work—but with a crucial proviso: no one would be paid for the kinds of work that women had previously been coerced to perform.

This extraordinary devaluation of the culture of care was something new. In the high noon of patriarchy, after all, the compensation for care was factored in and paid out of the salary of the "breadwinner," no doubt indirectly and inadequately, along with lots of inexpensive expressions of endearment. In the new regime, the compensation for care has been recalibrated to zero, and the breadwinner wins only enough bread to feed half the family. Thanks to this new dispensation, the entry of women into the paid workforce has served not to raise median household income for couples with children, as one might have expected, but to prevent it from falling. In effect, it has forced couples to work three jobs instead of two for the price of one. Single-parent households have predictably seen their relative income collapse. They have been asked to work two jobs for the price of half a job.

The result has been one of the great transfers of wealth in human history. The winners are those fictional entities that control the economic product of paid human labor—that is, for the most part, the corporations of the world—and the lucky clique of humans who have learned to tap the rivers of cash that flow through them. The losers are those humans foolish enough to get involved in the reproduction and care of the next generation. The system has this further benefit (or cost): by driving losers into a state of desperation, it forces them to sell themselves on the cheap. Heck, it might even force them to spend less time with family, just when the family needs them more. All in all, it's a terrific plan for a society that proposes not to live on the same planet as other people's children.

One lucky group of parents, however, has been able to make it work. The good people of Menlo Park now have at their disposal a system that would have been the stuff of dreams for the old patriarchs: a pool of subservient, gender-oppressed labor that can be purchased on the open market, without the need even for those cloying expressions of endearment; constant affirmation from the world economy about just how smart and valuable they are; and plenty of cash. Better still, they have the means to keep most of these advantages well under wraps. This is what equips them for their real mission, which is to convince the 90 percent that the plan is working. Unless it's not, in which case, that's on you.

THE PRACTICAL SOLUTIONS to the piece of the inequality puzzle that has arisen from the devaluation of care are not hard to see. Most industrialized countries have figured out that adequate family leave policies, publicly supported child care, and universal preschool make for more happier parents, better kids, and a stronger economy. As a matter of fact, the United States figured it out during World War II, when the federal government offered a highly successful public child care option. But that program was scrapped out of the usual fears about communism and anxieties about empowering women.[40]

The obviousness of the solutions is the most striking fact about them. The remarkable thing about the inequality that is shredding American families is not that it exists but that we pretend that it is coming to us from outer space, or wherever the laws of economics are to be found. It isn't. We are doing this to ourselves. Hoarding the resources that give children a leg up, quietly slamming doors on the opportunities of other people's children—these are not good things. But they are just the beginning of the work that the 9.9 percent perform to perpetuate the system. The real damage flows from the validation that comes with the concealment of these injustices. That concealment is the actual foundation for the definitive article of the Menlo Doctrine, the article that says that parenting is a solo exercise performed by superparents living in treehouses. The task of the paid-up members of the 9.9 percent is to preach that article, so that aspiring members of the club will internalize the demands of the class of fictional beings that dominate the economic landscape. It is our way of saying that we should all love these almighty manifestations of human economic power so much that we will shape and mold our own children to their needs. We will do it all, and we will expect nothing in return except that our little ones be considered as promising candidates for servitude, too.

Why We Get Along So Well
with the Other Sexes

One of the things that make the various Princeton University student and alumni publications so much fun to read is the stream of letters from the old guard that blow in from time to time like jets of prehistoric cave-air from your crazy uncle. It's like having Thanksgiving all year round. Back in the early 1980s, the grunting noises came from a group of "concerned" alumni, all men, who had not yet fully processed their outrage over the admission of women into their sacred quadrangles for the first time in 1970. But in 2013, the blast from the past came in from one of members of that first generation of Princeton women.

Susan A. Patton, a graduate of the great class of 1977, had a message to deliver to the young women of Princeton. She offered it in person first, at an on-campus gathering with students, and then she wrote it down for *The Daily Princetonian*, the student-run paper.[1] "For most of you," her missive reads, "the cornerstone of your future and happiness will be inextricably linked to the man you marry, and you will never again have this concentration of men who are worthy of you." She goes on to say that men like to date downward in age and are inexplicably unimpressed with the intellectual capacities of their partners. So, put on your hot pants, Freshwomen, and find a man now—or die![2]

The howling lasted long enough for the Princeton Mom, aka the Princeton Momster, to get a book deal.[3] Her message was "mind-blowingly retro," ran a typical response.[4] The assumptions about heteronormativity and female subordination were indeed spread as thick as clotted cream on a raspberry scone. The underlying sociology was ill-informed: Patton overlooked the fact that the median age at which elite college graduates marry is now around thirty—by which point most college crushes have faded into an archive of mortifying texts. And maybe, as some readers unkindly suggested, there was a whiff of bitterness coming from the cave. Was Patton, a divorced mother of two Princeton graduates, blaming her unhappy marriage on the fact that she herself had failed to snag a fellow Tiger?

And yet, setting aside the hoary gender assumptions, the demographic slips, and whatever axes were getting sharpened, the stubborn fact remained: Princeton Mom spoke truth. As a matter of fact, plenty of the people on the ground have been living her truth. A moment's glance at the *New York Times* wedding section will settle the question beyond doubt.[5] Here, clicking through pages almost at random, are some typical entries:

"Ms. K___, a feminist since she was old enough to understand the concept of gender equality, met Mr. M_____ . . . when both were undergraduates at Princeton." You go, girl!

"The bride and bridegroom graduated magna cum laude from Harvard, where they met." Do the summa cum laudes marry the summas, too? There are levels within levels!

"Ms. T___ . . . was an undergraduate summer intern from Yale, and Mr. F___, . . . a postdoctoral fellow representing Brown, when they met." Yale digs Brown—now that's diversity!

OTHER STRANGELY BACKWARD-LOOKING THINGS have been happening in these gender-forward times. Tune in to the right music streams and you'll see what I mean. Country music really has been getting worse. This is not just cosmopolitan condescension talking. A study tracking more than eight hundred weeks' worth of Billboard hits from 1983 to 2016 finds that country songs "increasingly depicted women as sexual objects instead of employed equals" and shifted toward

representations of men as "providing women with alcohol, transportation, and places to hook up."[6]

Though country music hasn't yet caught up with the misogyny of rap
and some other forms of popular music, the destination seems clear.[7]
In the old days, country heroes might sing about how mama tried to
keep it all together in the lean years or how good it feels to build a home
for your darling. The more recent trend is moving in the direction of
Dierks Bentley's catchy 2014 hit, "Drunk on a Plane." A Country Joe is
stood up at the altar and decides to fly solo to Cancún with the honey-
moon tickets. A "stewardess" who "is somethin' sexy" offers him some
"mile-high flight attention." After knocking back a few mini-whiskeys,
he starts partying with the hot and excitable passengers in the aisle.
Pretty soon the whole plane is a celebration in the sky. As the scene
wraps, the voice-over croons that Joe is looking forward to returning
home and telling the woman who trashed his marriage-market value
to "kiss my ass."

It goes without saying that Country Joe's ideas about women and
gender relations hardly make him unrepresentative of a large segment
of American voters. Anyone who was awake in 2016 knows this. There
is no need here to relive the reality show of pussy-grabbing, porn-star
payoffs, beauty pageant walk-ins, and campaign T-shirts demanding a
commander-in-chief with supersized, demonstrably active, red-white-
and-blue testicles. Surveys confirm what the winning candidate himself
made clear with his own words: that hostility toward women ranks
almost as high as party identification in predicting which way individuals voted.[8] It's hardly a coincidence that the era of the Trump-voter is
also the golden age of the male supremacist group.[9]

The development here is more durable than one particularly vile
political leader. To a degree unprecedented in American political history, Americans have come to vote their gender. Statistically speaking,
the Republican Party is the party of (white) men, and the Democratic
Party is the party of everyone else.[10] In 2016, a mere 32 percent of white
men could bring themselves to pull the lever for Hillary Clinton.[11]
Curiously, Americans also vote by marriage—though not in a direct
way. While marriage and divorce rates are roughly comparable between

supporters of the two parties (adjusting for age), the same is not true of the states and regions where they happen to live. Democrats tend to live in places that practice what Republicans call "family values." The homeland of the Republican Party, on the other hand, is the wasteland of the American family.[12]

Any survey of the gender landscape in twenty-first-century America will only come back with a fistful of similar paradoxes. On the one hand, the debate over human rights, and women's rights in particular, seems to be over. The ideal of gender equality has never been more widely embraced and practiced than it is now. On the other hand, regressive efforts to control women's fertility and otherwise put them in their place remain alive and well. Meanwhile, crucially, the economic trajectory of women has stalled.[13]

Women make up 62.8 percent of minimum wage workers in the United States, 27 percent of the top 10 percent in income, 11 percent of the top 0.1 percent, 5.4 percent of the Fortune 500 CEOs, and 2 percent of partners in venture capital firms. Women hold nearly two thirds of all college debt,[14] earn about 49 percent as much as men on average, have one third as much in retirement savings, and are 80 percent more likely than men to retire in poverty.[15] As a rule, being a single woman with children—whether never married, divorced, or widowed—is among the worst choices you can make, statistically speaking, if you are aiming for the 9.9 percent.[16] Not unrelated: over the first decade and a half of the twenty-first century, the participation of women as a whole in the paid workforce in the United States fell by three points, after rising consistently over the preceding four decades, and even while continuing to rise in other developed countries.[17]

The political side of the paradox in this post-sexist world is more striking still. On the one hand, the formal and informal barriers to power continue to fall, at least for some women. On the other hand, gender rage—mostly directed at those women who step out of line—is the lifeblood of American politics. What passes for "the national conversation" often sounds like a shouting match in an abusive relationship. Considering not just the presidency but the composition of the Supreme Court, one could plausibly argue that misogyny is part of the governing ideology of the United States. It's enough to make you wonder what happened to the arrow of time. Unless you happen to live in the land of the 9.9 percent, where the many sexes are almost ready to forget that there was ever any reason to fight.

YOU HAVE PROBABLY MET Ultramom and Ultradad, or a version of them. (I want to assure all of my friends that they are among my *other* friends.) They could live in any major American city (but let's just say it's New York). There's a nine-in-ten chance they are white (so they are white). They need not be heteronormative or binary-identified (they probably are). They are not into any country music after early Merle Haggard. The two important things to know about them are, first, that they are quite enlightened about gender equality issues, and, second, that they would count as a very good match in Princeton Mom's understanding of the term.

As far as gender equality goes, their ideas are clear and eagerly expressed. They believe that their contribution to social justice consists in the purity of their thoughts and actions whenever they interact with representatives of any known identity groups. They are scrupulous in their effort to divvy up their own luxuries and they are very careful with their pronouns. They take for granted that sexism is the grotesque legacy of an earlier generation, and that supporting gender equality is as straightforward as distinguishing the future from the past.

The Ultras have at least four brand-name degrees between them and both have logged time in those PowerPoint-based occupations that are impossible to explain to the older generations. They would look good in one of those *New York Times* wedding announcements. This is the other, Princeton-Mom-ish side of their story, of course, but it doesn't often come up in conversation. It's like the plumbing in their well-appointed loft: always there, but only talked about when something has gone wrong. The curious fact is, however, that you need to understand something about this side of their story in order to understand the other—and perhaps to make sense of life in the post-sexist world of twenty-first-century America.

The thing that is going on in those wedding announcements, technically speaking, is "assortative mating"—meaning "like mates with like." There really is nothing intrinsically objectionable about it at an individual level, apart from maybe a certain lack of spiciness. Ultramom committed no crime in marrying Ultradad; and you just don't want to picture Ultradad picking up a barmaid at the speakeasy, or whatever the modern equivalent would be. It's also doubtful that a program to pair up Ivy League graduates with high school dropouts would do much to advance social justice. But the fact that everyone is behaving well enough doesn't mean that the process turns out happily ever after for all.

The first thing to know about assortative mating is that it isn't a constant in human society.[18] It increases as a direct function of rising inequality. The explanation is obvious. The bigger the gap between the rich and the poor, the greater the reward for marrying well—and the harsher the punishment for choosing love over money. So the haves pair up with the haves, and the have-nots make do with the leftovers. At the same time, the orbits of rich and poor move farther apart, so the odds of love ever bumping into money go down. Taking romantic life into campus was in this respect, as Princeton Mom intuited, a stroke of genius. In the dining halls at the right universities, future earnings power only bumps into future earnings power.

An OECD study that covers cohabitation as well as marriage patterns confirms that assortative mating has risen faster in the highly unequal United States than in other developed countries.[19] The data further reveal that this kind of mating is not just an effect of inequality but a contributing cause. As much as one third of the increase in household income inequality in recent decades (the estimates vary depending on various measurement assumptions) is attributable to the fact that money mates with money and broke mates with broke. The practice is to some extent a consequence of the privatization of care already discussed. You can't marry the nanny anymore, so the trick is to marry someone who can split the cost of the nanny with you.

The second thing to know about assortative mating is that it is not a version of Noah's Ark. That is, it does not mean that everybody in society marches onto the boat of life happily matched with a socioeconomic equal partner in marriage. Assortative mating sorts some people into marriage and other people out of marriage altogether. This fact, too, is plainly visible in the demographic data. While people with college degrees have been getting married and staying married in roughly constant proportions (after a transitional blip in the 1970s), the proportion of working-class adults in marriages plummeted from 57 percent in 1990 to 39 percent in 2020, while the proportion among low-income adults crashed from 51 percent to 26 percent.[20] Meanwhile, among women with high school education or less, the rate of births out of marriage shot up from 20 percent in 1970 to 60 percent in 2012.[21] A critical and telling exception to the education-marriage link is the case of Black women with college degrees, who are less likely to be married than white women without college degrees, for reasons traceable back to the racial wealth gap and incarceration politics.[22]

Over the past several decades, many hands have been wrung over the breakdown of the American (working-class) family. Among cultural conservatives in particular, it is an article of faith that the calamity is all due to the decline in religion, if not to the lascivious behavior of bohemians in the 1960s or of un-straight people in San Francisco. Sure. The fact of the matter is that the parts of this story that are not about money are just rounding errors. The bottom line is that rising inequality, through innocuous mechanism of assortative mating, and abetted with structural economic shifts that are themselves the consequence of inequality, has turned marriage and a stable family life into a luxury good.

The final thing to know about assortative mating is that it's not simply a matter of one bank account falling in love with another (or one bad check bouncing off another, as the case may be). There is another form of capital involved, and it comes with its own, very distinct methods of exchange and regulation. It used to be called class, though today we don't talk about it, because we're still pretending that class does not exist. Whatever you call it, this other capital differs from the old kind in a number of ways, but the most important is this. Money is a leveler, in a certain sense: my dollar is just as good as yours. But class amplifies differences. It takes the smallest grains of variation and works them up into impassable mountain ranges. This is something that the Ultrapartners have discovered on their own.

IN THE FIRST YEARS OF THEIR PARTNERSHIP, not improbably, the Ultrapartners experience some major plumbing failures, as it were. When the eldest child turns four, they apply to all of the finest preschools in New York—which, if you believe in whispers, are thought to guarantee a path straight to the Ivy Leagues, Goldman Sachs, and a classic six on the Upper East Side—but they are rejected from each and every one. Statistically, this is no surprise: the schools admit as few as 10 percent of applicants, and the percentage is that high only because they limit the number of applications they will even consider.[23] And, to be clear, it is the parents who are being judged, not the child. That's the way the system works. Even so, the pain is real. Then, to add to the woes, one of the Ultras starts colliding with ceilings in PowerPoint land and, one leave of absence at a time, transitions almost imperceptibly from an office worker to a domestic worker focused on the preschool admissions project.

At first, she (okay, 80 percent of the time, it is the mother who experiences this premature career transition)[24] is defensive about her choice. This leads her to talk a little too loudly about the various "pro bono projects" and "start-up concepts" she is allegedly pursuing. If there is a patriarchy developing here, it's going to happen over her dead body. As the hard-won triumphs in her new occupation accumulate, however, she eases up on the posturing and embraces her mission. Besides, Ultradad is now on track for a window office in cubicle land, and he is earning more than double what upper-middle-class professionals think is an acceptable income. Why fight it when you are so blessed?

Ultramom becomes *that* parent—the one who knows when to set the alarm for the early morning line for the school that quaintly insists on using an old-school clipboard-sign-up sheet, how to fine-tune the little one's skills for navigating those merciless interviews masquerading as group play dates, and whom to approach with what offerings on the school board. Soon the Ultra loft is teeming with indigenous-textile knitting instructors, math-themed board games, Mozart-themed videos, and ongoing calligraphy projects. Drawing on her experience in corporate branding (or whatever it was), Ultramom crafts a brand for the child and the family. (They are The Exotic Arts & Crafts Family.) A year of intensive labor later, the Ultras hit kindergarten pay dirt: admission to a school that will shepherd the eldest directly into that classic six. This proves to be the first of many glories to come.

Ultramom happens to be riding a small but telltale trend at the upper reaches of the working world. To see it, one needs to look more closely at the curious decline in female participation in the paid part of the American workforce. Half of these "dropouts" (as the unfortunate term has it) cite the lack of child care options as the reason for not seeking paid employment, and most are women of high school education or less.[25] When economist Joni Hersch examined the data on the smaller number of college women who drop out, however, she discovered something surprising.[26] Women who graduate from selective colleges are significantly more likely than those from nonselective colleges to hang up their office shoes and stay home. So the "dropouts" are actually coming from both the bottom and the very top of the economic spectrum, while the middle keeps showing up at the office.

According to the (supposed) laws of economics, this makes no sense. The individuals with the highest earning power are voluntarily moving toward the lowest end on the scale of economic being. According to the gospel of merit, it is blasphemy. These people are taking the "human capital" that they had purportedly accumulated at great expense in the finest universities and squandering it on work that the market has clearly assigned to people who didn't do so great on standardized tests. Even the usual theories of self-alienation would appear to be at a loss. Can one really maintain that the high achievers from selective colleges, so rich in gender theory courses and consciousness-raising exercises, are more likely than their nonselective peers to subscribe to "traditional" ideas about female subordination? If you know something about Ultramom, however, you know very well that these paradoxes prove only that the laws of economics, the gospel of merit, and the theories of culture are often full of the stuff that the nanny puts in the Diaper Genie.

What Ultramom knows that the economists don't is that in her new career she is accumulating real wealth for her family, in any meaningful sense of the term, even if Ultradad happens to be the one collecting the paycheck. What Ultramom knows that the high priests of the meritocracy are loath to admit is that the merit of those fine schools has much less to do with starting salaries than it does with imparting the skills and resources that permit the accumulation of this other, better form of wealth. Ultramom's greatest assets are the easy air with which she can walk through the walls of one exclusive institution after another, her mastery of the language in which the rulers of the corporate universe converse, her extensive contacts with the starship commanders in that same universe, and her familiarity with all of the presentational details that they don't tell you about on the website.[27] She is an accumulator of small things, of those telling details here or there about how this or that part of the world works, and she is quite capable of assembling this basket of nuances into a juggernaut that will blow every rival family's life raft right out of the water.

It's all very modern, and it's all early-nineteenth-century at the same time. Were it not for some of her rhetoric and the fact that there is still some probability that she could be male or have some other gender identity and/or skin color, Ultramom would not be out of place in a Jane Austen novel. In Jane's world, the male protagonists usually have the money, but that doesn't mean that the female leads are poor. They are short on cash, of course, which is why they are out there on the hunt. But, as every lord worth his feudal income knows, they possess a degree of wit, erudition, manners, and powerful friendships that is costly to produce and more than worth its weight in finely crafted corsets.

An important thing to acknowledge about the kind of wealth that Ultramom and her fictional alter egos are accumulating, however, is that it is not necessarily of the kind that shows up in the gospel of the free market and miraculously leaves everybody better off. The thing about class, it almost goes without saying, is that it usually involves some degree of struggle. Its purpose is not to produce wealth but to decide who gets to keep it. Although the "capital" it produces can sometimes help toward socially useful ends, much of it counts as wealth only within the alternately competitive and collaborative games that the 9.9 percent play among themselves to determine who will lay the greatest claim to the fruit of other people's labor. It is on this account that occupational blindness is typically one of the defining characteristics of class membership. Why pay attention to those other parts of humanity that aren't in the game at all?

Jane Austen, for all the insight in her writing, offers a useful illustration of the point. Her myopia is evident in the mathematical shortcomings of her novels. The typical male lead in an Austen novel, such as the moody Captain Wentworth in *Persuasion*, has an income from an inherited estate of about £10,000. That would be roughly 500 times the GDP per capita in early-nineteenth-century England. Yet the typical Jane Austen novel has a population of about a dozen major characters. Where are the other 488 villagers who till the Captain's fields and whip up his buttermilk scones? Nowhere near the pages of the novel, that's for sure. Austen's heroines wouldn't marry them any sooner than they would marry a door knob.

This is one of the less appealing things that Ultraparents have in common with Jane. There are certain kinds of people whom they just don't see. They don't see them even when they are serving up coffee, cleaning up the apartment, or stuffing that Diaper Genie. It perhaps should have been mentioned that the Ultrapartners, very much like our friend Menlo Mom, make liberal use of nannies, in order to allow Ultramom to focus on the high-value-added aspects of child cultivation. And they do offer warm embraces to their nannies, frequently calling them "a part of the family." In fact, they seem to figure that the loving kindness is part of the nannies' compensation—until they are eventually cut loose. For the Ultrapartners, the nannies are rarely remembered once one has moved on to the next room.

As it is with Ultraparents, so it will be with the Ultrachildren. The Ultras are systematically making sure of that. Over a bottle of sensibly priced rosé, Ultramom peers far into the adolescent future and congratulates herself again on her eldest's educational fortunes. One of the advantages of the new school, as she sees it, is that the other children will grow up into acceptable dating material. Here she taps her finger on an essential aspect of assortative mating. In the fictional universe of modern economic ideology, assortative mating can be made to look like a natural process emerging from a free-mating market in which individuals drive the process by making rational choices intended to maximize their pre-existing mating preferences. Sure. Ultramom knows very well that this is bullshit. My great-grandfather, for that matter, knew it, too. Assortative mating means taming one's desires—and other people's desires—in accordance with social requirements. If people don't limit their own choices, then their parents will do it for them. They might even try to restrain their children's consciousness altogether, leaving them in the dark about the existence of the external world. Class is what happens when you don't marry the girl from the speakeasy.

Love has almost always been an equalizing force in human society. It is a wild card that mixes up hierarchies of money and power. Its pulverizing impact is built into the basic math of reproduction: after a certain number of generations, everybody is descended from everybody. That's why the defenders of property are always policing relationships, often with the help of frustrated priests and icy-veined matrons of society. It's why the headiest romances usually involve star-crossed lovers or impulsive escapes to the big city. Charlotte Brontë probably understood this better than Jane Austen. Her lords sometimes do run off with the nanny. Class does not reproduce itself by selling memberships to rational buyers in the sexual marketplace. It generally extends itself by constructing the choices available to others—typically starting with the offspring. Like a virus, it spreads because it calls forth agents who have both the desire to impose it on other people and the power to do so. Class uses family, not for the family's sake, but for its own sake.

The invidious form of wealth that goes into producing class is of course a very human phenomenon, and no one should expect or want it to disappear from human experience. We all know that life without it would be less fun and movies would certainly be less amusing. The most important thing to know about the process of class formation and separation, however, is in some ways the most obvious. Like the assortative mating that is its best-known instrument, class division grows as a direct function of economic inequality. It is also quite indifferent to the moral declarations of the people involved in the process. If inequality wants to play the gender card, it will be played.

There is something still more disturbing, though harder to articulate, about this familiar connection between inequalities of money and inequalities of class that has blossomed anew with the rise of the 9.9 percent. As the enforcement power of privilege over other people grows, so, too, does the enforcement power with the mind itself. This is the side of Ultramom that makes me wonder most. The branding narratives that she has developed to sell her children and her family to the world, amusing as they are, have almost no connection with any observable reality. The Ultras might as well have been The Rescue Scuba Diver Family or The Jazz and Tango Improvisation Family. These are just incidental fictions to be used and discarded in the accumulation of those small things that matter. That's why you can tell the story of Ultramom's life, catching all of the essential twists in the plot, and yet say nothing at all about her actual character, her actual relationship with her partner, the distinctive attributes of her individual children, or much of anything else that would ordinarily make life meaningful. This is what happens to people in times of rising inequality. They empty out their insides and start chasing whatever fictional versions of themselves serve the system best.

Class is often taken to be a way of grouping people according to some understanding of their rational economic interests. But this really only applies to classes considered from the outside, or insofar as they are conscious of themselves. The defining features of class from the inside generally have to do with the absence of consciousness and the insecurity of membership. This combination of anxiety and absence of consciousness is really just an invitation to unreason. It is a way of disorganizing society, not organizing it. Contrary to popular perception, class does not make people smarter; it produces a small group of people who are deluded about the sources of their good fortune and a large group of people who are deceived about the sources of their misfortune. All of this follows in a deductive way from the fact that all humans belong to the class of humans, which alone can provide the basis for rational action. Such was the view of those philosophers who played

the decisive role in the creation of the American republic. But let's set
the philosophy aside for now and consider what it all means for those
who can't quite afford the luxury of a marriage like that of the Ultras.

MANY OF THE CONSEQUENCES for those who find themselves on
the other side of the game of assortative mating are too well known to
belabor. Single parents are far more likely to be poor and significantly
less likely to score well on happiness surveys. Their children, as Isabel
Sawhill of Brookings points out, "do less well in school, are less likely to
graduate, and are more likely to be involved in crime, teen pregnancy,
and other behaviors that make it harder to succeed in life."[28] When they
grow up, those same children, statistically speaking, go on to reproduce
the disadvantage from which they emerged. The single most significant
predictor of the low social mobility in a commuting zone, according
to a study led by Raj Chetty, is the rate of single-parent households.[29]
    It gets more curious when you see that this other side of assortative
mating is very far from gender-neutral. Single parents are overwhelmingly female—especially single, low-income parents. The divergence
starts with an obvious biological difference, but a closer look at the data
indicates that the subsequent work is done through the compounding
power of inequality. Single mothers stay single because—in their collective judgment, which we may accept as statistically indisputable—a lot
of men today make for unappealing marriage partners. As MIT economist David Autor and colleagues explain, rising inequality combined
with a declining manufacturing sector, growing job instability, and
incarceration resulted in "the falling marriage market value of young
men" from 1990 to 2014.[30]
    How do the men take it? Ask Country Joe. There is nothing very
surprising about what these men do in response to these circumstances,
nor is there anything uniquely American about it. The objectification
of women in American country music differs little from the objectification of women in the youth culture of Mozambique, where research
demonstrates that young men in economically precarious situations
"put a greater emphasis on heterosexual virility."[31] The objectification

of women in these circumstances, moreover, is not driven entirely by the demand from men. When marriage becomes a luxury good and an investment strategy, humans of all genders will gleefully participate in the game of self-objectification. The phenomenon is not only predictable, but clearly associated with economic inequality. Across counties, regions, and countries, one study shows, those areas with the highest degree of inequality also top the charts in the prevalence of sexy selfies shared on phone networks, cosmetics sales, and other measures of the objectification and hypersexualization of women.[32]

How do those who succeed in the assortative game against the odds—that is, those who make it without having access to the Ultra lifestyle—respond to these developments? In many different ways, naturally, but with a decided tendency to get defensive. They come down hard on perceived threats to family stability. They don't do well with deviants of any type. They tend to have little sympathy for the failures gathering all around them. Statistically speaking, they are much more likely to find religion, especially if that religion offers clear instruction on how the genders are supposed to behave. All of this can be read from the simplest demographic comparisons between America's red states and blue states: high inequality correlates with both higher porn usage and higher church attendance, with both higher divorce rates and higher levels of "pro-family" belief.

How does all of this gender anxiety play out in the politics of a modern democracy? This is where things get really interesting. Start with the obvious but often overlooked fact that the leader of the economic-conservative party is very likely to be male; the leader of the social-reactionary party is almost always male, and the authoritarian leader who unites social and economic conservatives is typically not just male, but superlatively male. He is a "strongman." He is definitely not "gay." He prizes those women who perform stereotypical femininity unstintingly. To the disempowered men, he offers a model of the virility they wish to have in themselves, a conviction that they have a right to property in women, and the prospect of exacting revenge against those women who do not follow the rules. To disempowered women, he offers the model of a strong provider, the hope for security in a world not organized for their benefit. To the defensive couples that make up much of the middle of society, he offers protection against the loose (or empowered) women and effete men who threaten this precarious order of the genders on which their own sense of security depends. This is the reality not just in Trump's America but in Putin's Russia, Erdoğan's Turkey, Orbán's Hungary, Bolsonaro's Brazil, and in countless other instances from the past.

Of course, supporting a strongman usually turns out to be a very bad way to achieve widespread marital bliss or feelings of gender security. But this fact itself points to something crucial about the way in which inequality exploits gender anxiety to shape the political order. Inequality produces a disempowered population that turns to politics not for solutions but for show—for the symbolic reenactment of grievances and concerns, or just for entertainment and distraction. At the same time, to state the obvious, inequality creates powerful and wealthy forces that seek to advance their interests, often against those of the general public. Thus, inequality not only generates gender conflict in everyday life, but also produces the actors that are all but certain to amplify and exploit it for political gain. Inequality always invites the politics of the irrational.

This is why the defining political alliance in the United States over the past four decades has been that between economic and social conservatives. At the superficial level of declared political principles, this alliance has always been hard to explain. Why would the apostles of the free market join forces with people determined to restrict the freedom of people in the bedroom? Why would the self-proclaimed saviors of the family want to work with those who are destroying the economic security of families? According to the unspoken logic of inequality, however, it all makes sense. The free market crowd monetizes the destruction of families and then shares some of the wealth with the holy rollers, who convert the resulting gender rage into their own political power, which they share back with their unlikely partners. It's a win-win for everybody except for those who happen to be members of human society.

There is nothing particularly new or American about this process. Nor is it something that comes straight from nature. It is a version of what human societies have been doing in some form or other more or less since the agricultural revolution. In order to understand it, it is helpful to return to that unspoken history of humanity that lies embedded in the stories that people like the Ultrapartners and Country Joe rely upon to make sense of their lives.

"PROGRESS," WROTE CHARLES FOURIER IN 1808, occurs "by virtue of the progress of women toward liberty, and decadence of the social order occurs as the result of a decrease in the liberty of women."[33] Fourier, who is credited with inventing the word "feminism," also believed that progress would one day make the world's oceans taste like lemonade. At least he was right about the rights of women. Maybe the most remarkable fact about human history over the past two centuries is the extent to which gender equality has been reliably associated with improvements in human health, wealth, happiness, political stability, and many other good things. Some facts of history are so obvious that even crackpots can see them. Sometimes, the crackpots are the only ones who will say them.

Fourier's fact is now a central feature of the self-understanding of the 9.9 percent, or at least of many of its representatives. Only, today it comes with a certain, problematic simplification. Even in the handy quotation above, Fourier recognizes that, while gender equality always supports progress, history does not always move in the direction of gender equality. In the story that the Ultrapartners tell themselves, however, the arrow of history usually points in the hopeful direction. Gender inequality, as they understand it, is the result of some antiquated way of thinking. It is a personal prejudice, most likely rooted in the defects of human biology, and it must fade away in time. But none of that is true.

It may help to recall a second, no less obvious fact of history, complementary to Fourier's fact but all too often overlooked. The rise of gender inequality did not precede but rather followed the rise of general inequality among humans. To be clear, by gender inequality I do not mean biological differences between males and females, which exist in nature, precede civilization, and can account for some degree of gender difference, division of labor, and inequality in any society. The point has to do with the massive inequalities between man and woman that show up, for example, in the oldest books of the Bible: "Thou shalt not covet thy neighbor's house; thou shalt not covet thy neighbor's wife, nor his manservant, nor his maidservant, nor his ox, nor his ass, nor anything that is thy neighbor's."[34] Whatever the physiological differences between male and female, there is nothing in nature that can explain the reduction of half the species to a form of property to be listed along with, in no particular order, houses, slaves, and donkeys. The archaeological evidence suggests that gender differences in early human societies, though likely real and not negligible, were not even remotely of biblical proportions, and the anthropological evidence suggests that the same is true of hunter-gatherer societies.[35]

In short, massive gender inequality, like massive inequality in general, does not exist before or outside civilization. It is a human invention, not an artifact of nature, and it dates from around the beginning of large-scale agricultural civilization, not before. This basic fact seems worth bearing in mind when we consider the realities about gender relations in twenty-first-century America. If gender inequality arose with general inequality, then it can return with it, too. It is not a legacy of the past but an artifact of the present. Misogyny, or the hatred of those women (and other deviants) that threaten to destabilize the gender hierarchy, is not a natural disposition in human beings of any gender. It is a means of enlisting many members of society of any gender in policing the gender order that helps keep the economic order in its place. The point of the subjugation of women, in the final analysis, is not for all men to triumph over all women in a war of the sexes. It is also for some men and women to triumph over other men and women. Misogyny is back now—not in all aspects of daily life, but on our screens, and in the driver's seat of an out-of-control political bus—because power always makes use of useful tools.

In this unraveling of an unequal human society through gender dysfunction, the individuals who succeed in the 9.9 percent life plan have a peculiar, central, and somewhat melancholy role to play. Their achievement in demonstrating that a liberal, relatively gender-equal, care-centered way of life, far from spelling doom as the priesthoods of ancient rulers and modern think tanks have long warned, creates vibrant families and a vigorous society remains a significant historical accomplishment. But they have built this liberated world on an island of privilege. The attempt to isolate gender inequality and solve for it as if it were an independent variable in human society, in the final analysis, is something worse than a misunderstanding. It is a way of ignoring the surrounding ocean of inequality from which it emerges. And ignoring the cause is really just a convenient way to perpetuate the effect. The compartmentalization of justice is another form of injustice. As a rule, liberation for the few is usually a prelude to the subjugation of all.

It follows from the deep and often hidden connections between gender inequality and general inequality that no lasting progress on gender justice is possible without economic justice. Some of the necessary economic reforms will have to do directly with women, or with the kinds of labor that reliably fall in disproportionate ways on women. Recognizing and paying for the value of care is one place to start. But some of the most important reforms may not have much to do with women at all. Probably the best way to turn Country Joe into the kind of guy you'd want to have in your country is to find him a decent job.

Why We Are So Highly Educated

C an capitalism teach the world something new? William (Bill) McGlashan Jr. thought it just might. A few years ago, McGlashan was relaxing under the Caribbean sun on billionaire Sir Richard Branson's private island when he hit upon the idea for an "ethical venture fund." He immediately shared the concept with Branson, the rock star Bono, eBay mogul Jeff Skoll, and a few other billionaires who happened to be lazing around the island.[1] "We can take this beast called capitalism and help direct it in a way that is productive," he later explained to the *Financial Times*.[2]

With Bono and the band of billionaires on board, McGlashan swiftly raised $2 billion in commitments for the Rise Fund, a new kind of financial venture dedicated "to achieving social and environmental impact alongside financial returns."[3] The fund has made major investments in the education sector, where it hopes to use the magic of capitalism to develop new technologies that will render the old ways of human-to-human teaching obsolete.[4] McGlashan's personal role in the venture, by his own estimation, had to do with the "ethical" part. As a partner in TPG Growth, an established and successful private equity firm, he explained to *Barron's*, his job was to bring to the effort "a level of integrity and discipline" that it needed.[5] "We need to hold ourselves humbly accountable," he told the conference-goers at Davos, where he participated on a panel with Bono.[6]

A graduate of Yale and the Stanford Business School (dad went to both institutions, too, as it happens), McGlashan did time at Mitt

Romney's Bain Capital on his rise through the ranks of private equity finance. In 2017, he ascended to the edges of public consciousness as an invited speaker at *Vanity Fair*'s characteristically exclusive and self-congratulatory New Establishment Summit.[7] The following year he finally arrived at the World Economic Forum in Davos. He lives in the prime 9.9 percent bedroom community of Mill Valley, California, with his wife, Marie, who "stays up on health issues surrounding pesticides and chemicals, especially when it comes to what to feed my family," as she explained to local media.[8] The McGlashans send their children to a selective private school in the area, the Marin Academy, where tuition runs $48,000 a year and where Bill himself served until recently as a trustee.[9]

At the peak of his career, right around the time he was high-fiving fellow mini-titans at Davos, McGlashan turned his attention to a more personal aspect of the question about the future of education under capitalism. The time had come to find a college for his eldest son. McGlashan seemed to think that the right place for the young man was the University of Southern California. But there was a problem. USC is extremely selective, and it looked like the odds for the son were not good.

McGlashan turned for help to a private college consultant named William "Rick" Singer.[10] Together they appeared to work on an out-of-the-box solution to the problem. As the FBI would later tell the story, McGlashan funneled $50,000 to a "philanthropy" fund controlled by Singer, who allegedly arranged to have someone "correct his son's answers after the test was completed."[11] The son scored (or at least was recorded as having scored) an impressive 34 out of 36 on the ACT, rocketing him into the 99th percentile of all test takers.

But that wasn't enough. As McGlashan knew very well, a great test score alone won't land a spot at a place like USC. You need a narrative. You have to demonstrate some special talent, a compelling focus of interest, and, most importantly, an arc of personal development that ends in some sort of redemption. Otherwise you are just an ordinary high achiever, and your odds of saying you went to a place like USC are low.

Singer came up with the narrative. The boy was going to be a star athlete. This, he promised, would get him "accepted before he even applies."

"I'll pick a sport and we'll do a picture of him, or . . . we'll put his face on a picture, whatever whatever," Singer said. "I've already done that a million times."[12] They settled on football. The fact that the boy did not play football was apparently no objection. Neither was the fact that his school, the Marin Academy, didn't have a football team. We'll make him a kicker, Singer suggested. Kickers don't have to be big, plus they are in high demand.

"He does have really strong legs," McGlashan volunteered. "You could inspire him. You may actually turn him into something. I love it."[13]

They just needed a photograph of the boy kicking a football. Which did not exist. No sweat, Singer said. All dad had to do was to supply a photograph of the boy outdoors, and his head would be photoshopped on the body of some random high school football kicker.

The price of the plan, Singer added, was now $250,000. The money would go to Singer's "philanthropy" fund—potentially picking up a nice tax deduction along the way—and from there, as anyone with any functioning neural systems might have surmised, most of it would move into the pockets of a friendly university coach. Thanks to his experience as a social impact investor, McGlashan knew all about philanthropy.

"I would do that in a heartbeat," he said, when he heard the $250,000 price tag.

Of course he would. At that price, he knew, it was a steal. This was a point that Rick Singer was eager to emphasize with every greedy little breath. If you are really rich, he explained to all of his multimillion-aire clients, you can skip the hassle of fixing tests and photoshopping your kids. You can just pay cash money. The only problem is that the price has gone up, way up. Back in the day, meaning in 1998, Charles Kushner offered a mere $2.5 million in promised donations to snag a spot at Harvard for genius son Jared.[14] You'd be lucky to get the same deal for $5 million, or even $10 million now.[15] Singer's pitch was that he had opened up, in his words, a "side door." This was a discount special. It would be of interest not to billionaires but to the people who try to hustle billionaires on their private islands. That's what inequality does—it shrinks the circle of joy and adds to the crowd on the outside fighting to get in.

Now, dad had to go and get those photos. McGlashan realized he would have to search through his son's phone. But he wanted to do it without letting his son know. He asked Singer for assurances that the son would not discover anything about their plans. Because, presumably, nothing says "I love you" like shielding your kid from the knowledge that he's not quite up to faking his own way through life.

"Pretty funny," McGlashan said into his wiretapped phone. "The way the world works these days is unbelievable."

In March 2019, the FBI rolled out the indictments. McGlashan, along with fifty-four other parents and accomplices, were swept up in "Operation Varsity Blues" and hit with a variety of criminal charges. The stories differed in the detail but not in the substance. These were families that loved everything about their children—except for the fact that the kids were so obviously not what the parents wanted them to be. Maybe the most haunting words on the McGlashan tapes are: "You may actually turn him into something."

These were families who knew what they wanted even before they knew exactly what it was. One fine day, fashion designer Mossimo Giannulli emails his wife, the actor Lori Loughlin, to say that they've got to do something if they want their daughter to get "into a school other than ASU." The next day, they head out of the house with Super Soakers loaded with cash and start busting through the law (both have since pled guilty).[16] There is no indication and little reason to believe that Loughlin and Giannulli knew anything about the educational offerings at Arizona State University at the time.[17] The Varsity Blues files contain scarcely a mention of the mostly public, non- or moderately selective universities that actually educate 97 percent of all American college students.

It was all quite unbelievable, just as McGlashan said—and McGlashan himself would shortly provide evidence as to how much more unbelievable the world could get. The great majority of the parents and others charged with crimes (as of this writing) pled guilty. It was all on tape, after all. Not McGlashan. Notwithstanding the long hours in which he was recorded making all of the sounds that ducks make when they are doing ducky things, McGlashan insisted that his intentions were pure.

Even more astounding, he would build his defense around the argument that his dealings with Singer, understood in the right context, were part of a perfectly legal plan to use his money and influence to purchase a spot for his son at USC.

At the very time he was meeting with Singer, he claimed by way of self-exculpation, he was also reaching out to two of USC's trustees and had already secured a spot for his son on a supposed VIP list—a list of rich people's children who, according to legend, are all but guaranteed admission unless they are certifiably feral. You see, buying your way into a selective university, unlike bribing your way in, is quite legal—and it's *especially* legal if you have the money, as McGlashan apparently does, to hire a white-shoe law firm to make the point for you. In short, McGlashan's defense strategy was to throw his entire social class under the bus, as it were, and prove that collectively they really are as arrogant and entitled as people think they are. Unbelievable indeed, the way the world works these days.

Yet sometimes the real crazy sits right at the silent center of a story, in the black hole where all of the incoherent assumptions of the plot go. The Varsity Blues files contain scarcely a mention of precious child's research interests, the faculty they might work with, the wisdom they might gain, or any of the other fine things that show up on the glossy brochures for the universities that they were so desperate to break into. Change USC to LVMH and the entire crime spree reads like a shopping trip for designer handbags that got out of hand. This void at the center of the story seems especially poignant in the case of the man who identified himself as the ethical force behind the Rise Fund. At the very moment that he was mobilizing the gods of capitalism to rescue the global system of education, William McGlashan was approaching the education of his son with all the ceremony of a bumbling shoplifter. Among families seeking admission to the finest educational institutions in the country, it seems, the actual, um, education is pretty much the last thing that anybody cares about. How did we arrive at a point where getting an education has nothing to do with getting an education?

"THE AMERICAN WAR IS OVER, but this is far from being the case with the American Revolution," wrote Benjamin Rush in an Address to the People of the United States published in January 1787.[18] The first order of business was to perfect "new forms of government" for the modern world's first democratic republic. That was the immense task to be taken up in the Constitutional Convention planned for later in the same year. As far as Rush was concerned, the next critical item on the agenda, surprising as it may seem today, was to establish a "federal university."

Rush was far from alone in his strenuous advocacy for a national center for higher education. Joining him in the cause were George Washington, John Adams, Thomas Jefferson, James Madison, Benjamin Franklin, and Noah Webster, among many other early leaders of the republic. In his Farewell Address of 1796, Washington reiterated the call for a national university—and privately chastised Alexander Hamilton, the man who was putting words into his mouth, for not having given the idea still more prominence in the speech. The national university never came to pass—the resistance from "small government" southern conservatives was too much, even then—yet it represented a profound commitment to a certain vision of education in realizing the promise of America. It was an intrinsically public vision of education, and it rested on at least three guiding principles.

The first principle of the vision is that education is an investment not just that individuals make in themselves but that a democratic republic makes in its citizens. Thomas Jefferson, who put forward vigorous proposals for the public funding of primary schools in Virginia, told his old teacher George Wythe that any tax paid in support of schools "is not more than the thousandth part of what will be paid to kings, priests, and nobles who will rise up among us if we leave the people in ignorance."[19] John Adams, who differed with Jefferson on many other issues, emphatically agreed: "The whole people must take upon themselves the Education of the Whole People and must be willing to bear the expenses of it."[20]

A second piece of the vision, central to the idea of the research university, is that the advance of knowledge has an intrinsically public and democratic character. In his first Address to Congress in 1790,

Washington named the general principle when he said that "knowledge is in every country the surest basis of public happiness."[21] The pursuit of truth through open inquiry and basic research, according to this line of thought, is a public good in the first instance because its potential contributions are, by their nature, not knowable in advance and are therefore not reducible to any merely private quest for profit within existing systems of exchange. It is a public good in the second place because much of the knowledge it produces—like the knowledge of how to live a good life—belongs to that category of knowledge that spreads across society and confers benefits widely without ever becoming the object of exchange. Finally, on the basis of the deeper principle that reason necessarily serves to advance justice and equality, the advance of knowledge through the research necessarily lays the foundation for cooperation across society. The pursuit of truth is thus a public good in a democratic society because it necessarily makes for a better democracy—one that is more prosperous and more just at the same time.

A third guiding principle embedded in the founders' vision for higher education in particular in a democratic society is the idea that "merit"—the defining idea of the 9.9 percent—has an intrinsically public character. The idea of merit starts with the premise that higher education must be selective, as not every individual is fit for higher-level coursework. But the original concept of merit adds that the criteria for the selection must answer to the public, not the private, mission of higher education. Merit is not merely a measure of an individual's economic worth or "human capital," as economists today presume; it is also the measure of an individual's obligation to serve the public. Jefferson sums it up well: "Those persons, whom nature hath endowed with genius and virtue, should be rendered by liberal education worthy to receive, and able to guard the sacred deposit of the rights of their fellow citizens, and . . . should be called to that charge without regard to wealth, birth, or other accidental condition or circumstance."[22]

The remarkable fact about the American system of higher education, considered in the very broad sweep, is that, despite many setbacks, imperfections, and periods of stagnation, the system evolved for a very long period toward rather than away from the founders' vision for education in a democratic society. Some of this progress resulted from the diffusion among the public of the democratic idea of education. But the spread of the democratic idea of higher education also depended crucially on conscious and forceful policy on the part of federal and state governments.

A case in point is the Morrill Act of 1862. Justin Smith Morrill was one of the longest serving senators in history, and yet he is rightly remembered for a single big idea. He wanted Americans to have access to practical forms of higher education, and he wanted the federal government to pay for it out of its enormous treasury of real estate holdings (many of which, as it happens, had been acquired forcibly from native populations)[23]. In the 1850s he was unable to overcome the resistance of southern conservatives who loathed any form of "big government" that did not advance the interest of slaveholders. Senator Clement Clay of Alabama denounced Morrill's plan as "one of the most monstrous, iniquitous, and dangerous measures which have ever been submitted to Congress."[24] But in 1862, with Abraham Lincoln in the White House, southern opponents on the other side of the battlefield, and the republic in the process of reestablishing itself on the basis of principles first articulated in its Declaration of Independence, Morrill finally got his act. In 1890, in the teeth of Jim Crow, Morrill pushed through a second act that extended the land-grant system to the southern states. The two Morrill Land-Grant Acts ultimately involved the transfer of more than 17 million acres of federal land and spurred the establishment of sixty-nine universities that now enroll 4.6 million students.

In the aftermath of World War II, the federal government once again was the catalyst of a major paradigm shift in the system of higher education. Between 1944 and 1956, the Servicemen's Readjustment Act of 1944, commonly known as the G.I. Bill, sent 2.3 million veterans to college. In the peak years, these veterans accounted for half of all college admissions in the nation. The college attendance rate of young white men (the principal intended beneficiaries of the program, like most such welfare programs at the time) exploded from 6 percent in 1940 to 18 percent in 1947, and has continued to rise since (as have, belatedly, the rates for college-age individuals who are not white or male).

In 1965, the Lyndon Johnson administration expanded access to higher education with Educational Opportunity Grants, which in 1972 became the foundation for the Basic Educational Opportunity Grant Program, later known as the Pell Grants. The federal government now deploys about $20 billion per year to help about 7 million low-income students pay for college. Research has consistently shown that this financial aid for higher education "likely pays for itself several times over" both publicly and privately.[25]

At the same time, the federal government crafted a further, critical leg of support for the university system with its expansion of federally funded research programs, which now account for roughly $30 billion per year of university budgets. The economist Mariana Mazzucato offers compelling evidence that this publicly supported research generates many of the scientific and technological advances that private companies later exploit for the benefit of their shareholders.[26]

From the founding of the republic to the end of the twentieth century, in brief, the trajectory of higher education in America migrated in one direction: from private to public and from elite to universal. The movement was sometimes halting and always hobbled by profound racial injustice, but it was (mostly) nonpartisan and it drew its energy from the overwhelming desire of ordinary Americans to improve themselves through education. For a time, in a sense, it laid the foundation for a new kind of 9.9 percent—an elite defined not by property but by the public idea of merit.

This remarkable transformation can be read out of the most basic statistics. In the first years of the republic, essentially all higher education was private, and as of 1897, 80 percent of college students still attended private institutions. By 1940, the proportion was down to 50 percent.[27] At the end of the twentieth century, the polarity had been reversed, with 80 percent of students in public institutions and only 20 percent in private. Today the system of higher education has 19.9 million students (of all types), 4 million employees, and 4,300 degree-granting institutions.[28] For all its flaws, it remains a tremendous engine for social mobility, economic prosperity, and the advance of knowledge. It is still, on balance, one of the great forces for good in the world.

The people who engineered the critical postwar transformation of the American university system were well aware of the public character of its mission. In 1947, the President's Commission on Higher Education, commonly known as the Truman Commission, declared that "higher education must inspire its graduates with high social aims" and that "teaching and learning must be invested with public purpose."[29] In commencement addresses and mission statements to the present, comforting echoes of this message can still be heard. But the Truman Commission also issued a warning. Where access to education is unequal, it noted, in what must now count as prescient words, "education may become the means, not of eliminating race and class distinctions, but of deepening and solidifying them."

IN THE NEIGHBORHOODS WHERE the 9.9 percent roam, the critical plot twist in the Varsity Blues movie was not that wealthy families are deepening and solidifying class distinctions by using their money and influence to gather up spots at elite universities. It was that some of them were crazy enough to use illegal means to do so. Didn't they know that there are other ways to accomplish the same goal without going to jail? Or—really scary thought—is the competition now so intense that the legal methods won't work anymore?

These are the weighty considerations that appear to be troubling the Ultraparents when I catch up with them over the customary bottle of sparkling rosé in a suburb of Washington, D.C. (or some other city; let's just say they moved). Ultramom and -dad are proud of their eldest, who is now coming into the college application home stretch. The "narrative thing," Ultradad confesses, has been a tough nut to crack. "What does it mean for a sixteen-year-old to have a 'passion' for social justice?" he wants to know. But they are feeling cautiously optimistic now. I get the feeling that they think they are finding their angle.

The key to the elite college game, as experienced 9.9 percenters like the Ultras know, is the narrative that ties a young person with good academic standing into an individual deemed worthy of admission. Here is where the law-abiding elements of the 9.9 percent diverge from the Varsity Blues parents, and not in an entirely healthy way. True, the rank and file can claim moral superiority over the Varsity parents, who, after all, turned out to be criminals. Yet the Varsity parents displayed a certain kind of transparency in their actions. They did not actually believe that their children were water polo gods or talented football kickers (though McGlashan seemed to waver: "He does have really strong legs!"). They acted on the assumption that the whole merit business is a sham. The ordinary 9.9 percenters, on the other hand, want very much to believe in the merit of their offspring and the justice of the system—even as those children achieve results out of all proportion to what any reasonable statistics of merit would allow. The burden of the 9.9 percent is not merely to perpetrate fictions on the outside world, but also to spin the stories to themselves.

At the right dinner parties today, you may be required to hear out some of these narratives. You may be invited to scroll through some proud photo albums, for example. Maybe one of the them shows a young man in the prime of his high school years relaxing with smiling locals in a dusty village somewhere in West Africa, holding up some angular doll-figurines made from old coke bottles and colorful beads and manufactured with his assistance as a trained doll-engineering volunteer. Or maybe you'll be shown some photos of a young woman teaching indigenous people in Brazil how to paint with watercolors. There will be nothing photoshopped about these photos. That would be gross. On the other hand, staging the shots did take lots of planning and tens of thousands of travel dollars, not to mention a spare summer and a lot of parental foresight. But isn't that more sensible than wiring the money to Rick Singer's fraudulent charity? Plus, it might even be true that these young people have an earnest desire to bridge the divides in a broken world.

If you're not sure which village to save, as Ultramom points out to me, you can always hire a summer expert for $5,000 who will guide you on how to create the best summer experience for your child. The experience itself will only cost you only another $12,000 or so.[30] Although the options are often quite exotic, not all of them take place overseas. Some of the priciest enrichments are glamping-updates on the traditional New

England summer camp. In case you are in doubt about exactly what the money buys, apart from sushi-making classes and farm-to-table s'mores at camp, the promotional material usually lays out the deal in living color. "Campers attend some of the most prestigious colleges and universities," says one website. "[Our] camps find their staff at many of these same schools. The connection between camp and college is very strong." For those who still don't get it, there are photos down below of gothic structures emblazoned with the names of Harvard, Yale, Princeton, Stanford, Duke, Brown, Columbia, and Wake Forest.[31]

A glass or two into that bottle of bubbly, the Ultraparents start dishing on their fellow private school parents. Ultradad relates the legend of "Montana Boy." The spawn of a New York investment banker and a San Francisco management consultant, he was, as his own parents could see, in a highly disadvantaged geographic slot. The colleges like to say that they take students from all fifty states, which heavily favors applicants from states forty-six through fifty at the expense of the top five. So dad has declared that the second home out in Big Sky Country is the family's primary residence. He flies the kid out to the "family farm" on every break and has lined up a local internship at one of the parks. He even bought him a cowboy hat. It's hard to know how much truth there is to the story, but there is no doubt that the Ultraparents believe it to be true.

Then there is Hero Girl, Ultradad whispers. The kid has a certain reputation for trouble. One summer night, she and her friends are experimenting with substances on the beach, and one of them goes into convulsions. The rest of the gang runs away from the scene as fast as their stoned little legs can take them, but Hero Girl makes a moral choice. She calls an Uber and takes her incapacitated buddy to the hospital. The ER doctor says that a bad batch of drugs has been going around and people are dying. Fortunately, Hero Girl acted just in time. Bingo! All that she has to do is show her face at a few substance-abuse-prevention meetings, and she is the leader of a reform movement. The college application essay practically writes itself.

If you're still having trouble coming up with a creative narrative in which to package your child's authentic self, well then, as the Ultras point out, that's what independent college counselors are for! The Ultras went through several counselors before finding one that fit. Counselors are perfectly legal, and they usually don't cost anything like the $250,000 that the Varsity Blues parents seemed eager to drop in a heartbeat. In fact, basic college counseling "packages" start around $10,000. A former employee (now an Uber driver) of the aptly named Ivy Talent consulting firm (which appears to be focused on wealthy families in China) has told me that the base price there was $20,000 and that it was not unusual for clients to spend about $50,000. Sometimes the numbers do get out of control. In one case, a counseling firm charged a family $1.5 million for successfully placing their daughter into an Ivy League college. But even that stupendous sum was perfectly legal. Indeed, we can be confident it was legal because the firm sued the parents in court when the family failed to pay the second installment.[32]

As a matter of fact, as the Ultras know from experience, if you haven't gotten into the counseling game when the kids are about three years old, you expose your child to the grave risk of falling behind. New York parents of a certain type routinely drop $375 an hour ($12,000 to $25,000 for the "package") with advisers on preschool and kindergarten admissions to the so-called Baby Ivies.[33] If you've reached the college application level and you're still not there, your best bet might be a rush job with a four-day application boot camp at $16,000.[34] But you'd better hurry—the one held in Boston in 2019 was so oversubscribed that it had a waitlist and was held at a secret location to keep out the gate-crashers. Oh, and the price for next year has gone up to $18,000. "We've literally had reporters and competitors try to stalk us," the program director told *Boston Globe* reporter Beth Teitell. One of the parents, who happens to work in the financial services industry (surprise!), dismissed the idea that boot camp was about buying a way in to college. "There are misconceptions that having someone help organize things is somehow giving a leg up," he told Teitell. Self-awareness, as ever, is an optional extra in this demographic.

Of course, you can always make use of the free counselor at your local public school—joke alert!—after she sees the four hundred other students whose concerns are more life-threatening than not getting into colleges that reject lots of people.

Ultradad has covered the other big variable in the process: the tests. It turns out that gaming the standardized tests is also, within limits, manageable without risking a stint in striped pajamas. Paying a weirdly youthful-looking tennis instructor $50,000 to ace your kid's ACT, as a number of the Varsity Blues parents did, is obviously icky. It's also pricey. At the top end of the market, the test-prep gurus charge $750 per two-hour session. So you could do a year's worth of weekly lessons and still save some change, and not go to jail. True, the test-preppers generally can't take your kid from a 24 to a 34—only the evil tennis guy can do that—but maybe that's a good thing. What is your 24 going to do when she gets to college and finds herself in a roomful of 34s?

Some of the most significant hurdles in the race to college don't cost much at all to jump over. You just have to know that they are there. You have to know that the colleges track in-person visits, for example, and give you points for taking the tour. That's why they have you sign in when you arrive. It might also help to know that you don't actually have to take the tour; you just need to sign in. That way you can duck out to a coffee shop rather than go through another round of poster-student-tour-guide patter and the usual jumble of gothic buildings. Or maybe you can fit in another couple of colleges on a short trip. Ultramom assures me with a wink that this has been done.

Then there is the matter of what one might call counteroffensive operations. The Ultras go quiet on me, but if you've kept up on the private school news that got pushed aside for the Varsity Blues event, you will know what this means. Elite colleges tend to limit their intake from any particular high school. Therefore—let's face the Darwin—getting *your* kid in means keeping *their* kids out. The counselors at private schools can do the math, too, and this adds another layer of jockeying for individual families. In order to maximize the total haul of elite university admissions, private schools actively guide and limit their students' applications to colleges. So families have to get on the school's list for top colleges before they can even apply to a top college. The game gets rough enough that, at Sidwell Friends, an elite private secondary school in Washington, D.C., two of three college counselors walked off their jobs in protest and the head of school felt compelled to issue a stern letter to parents. Evidently, the parents needed to be told that the "circulation of rumors about students," "verbal assault of employees," recording phone conversations with counselors, and calling them from blocked numbers to pass along dirt about other people's children are really not cool.[35]

Somewhere near the bottom of the bottle, Ultramom confides that her eldest has been the target of abuse and harassment at school from a fellow student. Demeaning words were exchanged. Ultramom is frustrated and upset, and every administrator in the school knows it. Fortunately, the school has come down hard and fast on the situation. The offender has been required to keep their distance and to undergo anti-bullying education. The Ultrachild, who is a thoughtful and articulate individual, appears to have recovered. Naturally, you start to express sympathy and concern.

But then you detect a glint of excitement at the edge of Ultradad's frown. They have found their narrative! Even more remarkable, the Ultrapartners believe in the moral of the story, or at least in enough of it to get on with the job. Because even if, in a momentary fit of self-awareness, they acknowledge the merit of their child consists principally in having at their back an extraordinary parental and educational support squad capable of locating that winning narrative in a pile of disorganized teenage experiences, still it remains a form of merit. Now there is no time to waste. Ultramom has already reached out to national anti-bullying organizations, and Ultradad is gently coaching the child on speech ideas. What college would not want a spokesperson for the victims, one who has direct and bitter experience of the reality of struggle, and who can give voice to the voiceless?

IN HIS SUCCESSFUL 1966 CAMPAIGN for governor of California, Ronald Reagan decided to run against the California university system. One of his signature promises was to clean up "the mess at Berkeley," which he described as a place for "beatniks, radicals, and filthy speech advocates" who indulged in "sexual orgies so vile that I cannot describe them to you."[36] Paradoxically, the California university system was by most accounts one of the great success stories of the emerging middle-class welfare state. But Reagan was riding a wave of big money and highly racialized, white middle-class resentment to power, and the counter-cultural symbolism of the university system made it too tempting a target to ignore. In retrospect, the assault on the democratic promise of higher education in America may be said to have started when the money-power discovered how much political power might be mined in the fear and loathing of the white middle classes for Black people, sexual deviants, snotty college kids, and their weirdo professors.

Once in office, Reagan set in motion the cycle of tax cuts, university budget cuts, tuition increases, and endless culture war against academia's alleged hostility to American values that have become familiar features of the American political landscape in the second Gilded Age. Considered in its totality, the agenda that has guided American higher education over the past four decades may be called the "Great Reprivatization." The motivating idea behind the agenda is the belief that education is a private good that trades in accordance with every one of the prejudices of economic dogma. Educating citizens has no public purpose beyond satisfying the desires of the particular parties involved: a student in need of training and an institution willing to supply it. Producing knowledge can only matter insofar as it produces private profits. The merit of individuals can be measured entirely in their ability to make money. Government at all levels should therefore remove itself as much as possible from the higher education business. Although the agenda was and often still is wrapped in the flag and presented in the rhetoric of freedom, it is very nearly the opposite of the vision of America's founders for education in a democratic society. And yet this new, perverse idea of education laid the table for the version of the 9.9 percent we have today. Indeed, legitimizing and sustaining the new system has in some sense become the life mission of the 9.9 percent.

Following Reagan's election to the presidency in 1980, the Great Reprivatization was soon encoded in state budgets around the nation. Even as enrollments continued to climb, the states slashed funding for universities from 15 percent of state expenditures in 1990 to 9 percent in 2017. In the first fourteen years of the twenty-first century, state funding per student collapsed by nearly 30 percent in inflation-adjusted dollars.[37] The deficit, by design, fell on students. Between 1989 and 2019, tuition at public four-year institutions more than tripled in real dollars, while tuition at private nonprofit institutions (which started from a much higher base) more than doubled.[38] In 2018, for the first time in history, tuition surpassed government funding in a majority of state university systems.[39] In the same year, student debt soared to a total balance of $1.5 trillion. The share of students defaulting on loans climbed to 16 percent in 2016 (after which the Department of Education stopped measuring).[40]

The cuts in funding amounted to an assault not just on students but on university-based research. Between 2011 and 2017, government spending on research slipped by one-quarter as a percent of GDP, and the United States slid to number 28 out of 39 OECD countries on research spending as a percent of GDP.[41] In the drive to funnel tax dollars back to the wealthiest Americans, the Trump administration seized every opportunity to slash research budgets still further. Who needs more biomedical research when the rich need yachts to buy in order to keep themselves motivated? Most of the consequences will play out over decades to come, but with the Covid pandemic some of the damage came due almost immediately, when the underfunding of the Centers for Disease Control and Prevention and of vaccine research in particular magnified the crisis.

The Great Reprivatization's assault on public higher education was accompanied with a parallel, equally massive assault on public secondary and primary education. Much of it was organized by inaction as much as through conscious policy. As economic segregation spread across the American residential landscape, the system of local funding for public education effectively privatized primary and secondary schools without firing a shot. The price of admission to a good public school was simply slipped into local property values. In urban districts and other places where this mechanism of soft reprivatization failed to produce the desired segregation of education, the local 9.9 percent opted for the old-fashioned variety of private schools. Indeed, private school tuition soared as waves of wealthy refugees from the urban public school systems flooded in. In the not-so-good neighborhoods, meanwhile, teachers were pushed to the wall and down the status hierarchy, while the schools themselves began to look increasingly like the corrections system—with which they were in fact increasingly interconnected. Dostoevsky, it turns out, was only half right. To assess the condition of a civilization, you need to consider not just the state of its prisons but also the state of its schools.

The Great Reprivatization also did not leave untouched the (supposedly) public sector of the university system. Especially at the top end, the public universities began to look and smell more like private institutions. They went on recruiting expeditions to wealthy, mostly white neighborhoods out of state, where the 9.9 percent could be counted upon to pay full freight.[42] In hopes of chasing the prestige of the elite colleges, they began to reject many more in-state applicants. They filled up mailboxes around the country in search of still more applicants to reject, with a view to acquiring the many good things that come to universities that lower their admission rates. Along the way, they embraced the managerialist vision of the triumphant corporate world, reducing much of their teaching staff to the quasi-serf-like status of adjunct professors and rewarding the heroic administrators who succeeded in squeezing the labor force and the rich donors with equal vigor.

Cuts in public funding were significant enough that appreciable numbers of Pell Grant–eligible students were left without places at a university. The "free market" soon came up with an answer to that problem. The for-profit universities came into being in order to siphon the trillion-plus dollars in taxpayer-funded education benefits that public universities are unable to claim. But these marvels of the free enterprise system spend less than half of your tax dollars on instruction. Instead they splurge on advertising so that they can collect still more of your taxpayer dollars.[43] The credits they offer, according to Michael Itzkowitz, are often deemed so worthless by other schools that as many as 94 percent are not transferable.[44] Studies now confirm that students coming out of for-profits have worse labor market outcomes, more debt, and a far greater likelihood of defaulting on loans than their counterparts at public institutions.[45] Trump University—which in 2018 settled claims of fraud from students for $25 million—was no accident. Under Trump's secretary of education, Betsy DeVos, no effort has been spared to ensure that this "free market" Petri dish for parasites may take shelter under the full protection of the government.

As the Great Reprivatization unfolded, the burdens fell hardest on the disadvantaged, and especially those disadvantaged by racial identity. The states that have implemented the largest cuts in university funding are mostly those with the largest populations of nonwhite young people: Louisiana, Alabama, Nevada, Mississippi, Florida, Georgia, and North Carolina. As Michael Sorrell, president of the historically Black Paul Quinn College, has suggested, this likely isn't a coincidence.[46] Why pay for the education of people who don't look like you?[47] People of color are still less likely to go to college, more likely to go to a nonselective college, more likely to go to a for-profit institution, and more likely to default on student loans. Ten years out of college, Black people have twice as much debt as white people.[48]

During the Great Reprivatization, even as the money drained out of the door of public institutions of higher education, the rising tide of inequality had the effect of channeling vast public subsidies into the coffers of the old, elite, private institutions. As the rich grew richer, their alma maters grew richer with them. University endowments totaled $567 billion in assets in 2017—up almost four times in *real* dollars since 1993—and about half of that bonanza was in the hands of just twenty-three big names.[49] Harvard, Yale, Princeton, and Stanford alone add up to a magnificent $120 billion. Giving to universities in 2017 totaled $43.6 billion, with Harvard and Stanford both hauling in more than $1 billion apiece.[50] Investment income added another $46 billion or so in 2018.[51] Those contributions and the income they earn mostly escape taxes, which is a nice way of saying that they come with a huge public subsidy. When Trump booster and "anti-government" hedge-funder John A. Paulson donated $400 million to Harvard to establish the Harvard John A. Paulson School of Engineering and Applied Sciences, for example, he actually donated something closer to $270 million—and then passed along to Harvard the $130 million (or so) reduction in his tax bill received from the government he detests.[52]

The combined $90 billion or so in contributions and investment income on university endowments equates to approximately $30 billion in subsidies from the public to the nation's wealthiest universities.[53] Economist Richard Vedder estimates that Princeton alone receives a taxpayer subsidy on the order of $54,000 per student per year—while the average Pell Grant recipient gets $4,010.[54] And this doesn't count the massive break on property taxes that universities typically claim at the expense of municipal taxpayers. The total taxpayer subsidy for endowed nonprofit universities would be enough to double the amount of money the federal government spends on the 7 million recipients of Pell Grants, or to reduce all student tuition payments to public universities by one third. That, apparently, is just how much the private schools are worth to the public.

The process through which the Great Reprivatization squeezed out the founders' democratic vision for higher education took place too slowly, and in too many locations, to admit of a single defining moment or leader. Yet the substitution of one vision with another achieved a kind of literal clarity in 2015 in a symbolic battle over the University of Wisconsin's mission statement. For more than one hundred years, the university, which was one of the first beneficiaries of the Morrill Act of 1862, had embraced the "Wisconsin Idea." First articulated in the Progressive Era, the Wisconsin Idea says, in essence, that universities exist to serve the public good through the advance of knowledge and understanding. Under the remarkable governor and senator Robert M. La Follette, the Wisconsin Idea supplied the foundation for progressive economic and political reforms that were later adopted across the nation.

But in 2015, the Koch brothers–backed, Republican governor and presidential candidate Scott Walker delivered a $300 million budget cut to the university system along with some edits to its mission statement. The edits tell the story (ADDITIONS; ~~deletions~~):[55]

The mission of the system is to develop human resources TO MEET THE STATE'S WORKFORCE NEEDS, to discover and disseminate knowledge, ~~to extend knowledge and its application beyond the boundaries of its campuses and to serve and stimulate society by~~

~~developing~~ DEVELOP in students heightened intellectual, cultural, and humane sensitivities, scientific, professional and technological expertise, and a sense of purpose. ~~Inherent in this broad mission are methods of instruction, research, extended training and public service designed to educate people and improve the human condition. Basic to every purpose of the system is the search for truth.~~

To Walker's dismay, some number of Wisconsinites apparently still believed in the Wisconsin Idea, and they fought back. The governor backed down on the word changes—deleting "the search for truth" did seem gratuitous after all—and he put cut a demonstrably false story that the proposed changes were the unintended result of a "drafting error."[56] The budget cuts, however, remained, and the Great Reprivatization continued apace.

The year after Walker's assault on its "Idea," Wisconsin was one of the tipping-point states that delivered the electoral college to Donald Trump. The program that Reagan initiated in the summer of 1966 had arrived at its natural end state. White, non-college-educated voters went for the Republican ticket by a two-to-one margin, even while the rest of the population went the other direction.[57] It wasn't just the lack of education that distinguished Trump voters but the experience of living in education deserts. Counties with the lowest average levels of education swung for Trump even harder than lower-education voters themselves.[58] The evidence also makes clear that the attack on higher education has become a very effective tool for mobilizing Trump's Republican Party. A 2019 Pew survey showed that only 33 percent of Republican-leaning voters say that colleges have a "positive effect on the way things are going in the country," compared with 67 percent of Democratic-leaning voters.[59] The view among the so-called populist conservatives appears to be that the stupendous evil of political correctness on campus is such that it would be preferable to have no higher education at all than the kind of higher education we have today.

Republican leaders like Scott Walker understand that they can enhance their power still further by weakening the university system and turning what is left of it over to private operators collecting on government-backed student debt. That way, their friends make more money—and their voters become even less educated. From the perspective of those concerned to maintain the existing concentration of wealth, that is the real beauty of cuts to the education system. In most situations, when you take away a public good, the public eventually gets upset. But when you take away their education, they don't know what they are missing, because it often takes some education to appreciate the value of an education. This is what gives the situation of the 9.9 percent its somewhat tragic quality. They are the designated winners in a system that is designed to demolish the education on which their success, such as it is, depends.

THE RESULTS OF the Great Reprivatization are now in. The American system of higher education in its present form is one of the wonders of the world. Two things about it in particular make the world wonder, and one of them is its price tag. The Great Reprivatization did not bring the legendary efficiency of the free market to higher education. On the contrary, it produced the most expensive system of higher education in the history of the universe. According to an OECD study, the United States spends $30,000 per student per year on higher education, or about twice as much as any other developed country.[60] The American system is so expensive, in fact, that government here spends more on the highly privatized education system, as a percent of GDP, than government does in many countries that provide public higher education for free.[61] While every other country spends most of its education money on teaching, moreover, the United States alone spends more on administration.

U.S. spending on higher education is extraordinary compared not just with other countries but also with its own spending on early, primary, and secondary education.[62] Per student, the U.S. expenditure on primary and secondary education is 39 percent higher than the OECD average as of 2020, which puts it roughly in line with its higher GDP per capita. But in higher education, the United States sits 95 percent above the OECD average per student. Research leaves little doubt that spending in the early years of education largely bakes the cake of childhood development, providing the highest return in terms of increased social mobility and improved individual outcomes. Higher education is really just the icing on the cake. But in America, the educational dollars flow toward the cherry on top. Why? Because the money is going for *our* kids, not *theirs*.

At the small number of hyperselective universities that stalk the fever dreams of the 9.9 percent, the Great Reprivatization has brought tuition to levels that defy any merely economic explanation. The list price all-in for a four-year degree at an Ivy-plus university (that's the traditional Ivy League plus the University of Chicago, Stanford, MIT, and Duke) is now about $350,000. This is more than six times the median annual wage. It is more than the price of the median American family home. It is more money than the most Americans will ever possess at any time in their life. This is the price of the credential that is said to be the ticket to the American Dream. Yet, as the antics of the 9.9 percent confirm, the very top universities are charging well below what the market will bear. The Varsity Blues parents were eager to spend upward of $250,000 simply for the privilege of paying another $350,000 in college expenses. The Ultraparents of the world often spend far more than $350,000 on their private schools, SAT tutors, admissions counselors, and other experiences. Only a lingering sense of decency can explain the private universities' failure to capture all the profit potential that the Great Reprivatization has laid at their feet.

To add to the wonder, there is little evidence to suggest that, setting aside the tiny clutch of cherries at the top of the system, this spare-no-expense-charge-what-you-can philosophy has resulted in a superior quality of education. "Spending per student [in the U.S.] is exorbitant, and it has virtually no relationship to the value that students could possibly get in exchange," a director of the OECD study concludes.[63] Indeed, college-educated Americans perform worse than their peers in fourteen other developed countries in various tests of educational attainment.[64] Americans often look at global university rankings and tell themselves that the United States dominates the world in higher education, but as Kevin Carey of New America points out, this is because they confuse two very distinct ideas. It is true that "of the best universities [in the world], most are ours."[65] It is not true that "our universities are, on average, the best."

Even as the expenses rose and quality stagnated, moreover, the character of the education American universities were peddling changed in some profoundly unhealthy ways. With so much money at stake, students and parents insisted on "practical" education that would lead directly to a high starting salary. Homer, Shakespeare, history, philosophy, and the rest of the humanities lost out while STEM subjects surged. The biggest winners were the "business" disciplines—a supposedly practical field of study that has remarkably little practical value, apart from signaling a desire on the part of the student to submit to the corporate value system in exchange for decent pay (there will be more wild claims on that point in a coming chapter). The drive toward the pseudo-practical was especially pronounced at the lower-income end of the educational spectrum, and so the university system was divided in this respect, too, between an elite sector in which students were still encouraged to think holistically and critically about the major social and political challenges of the age and a growing mass encouraged to think of their education in vocational terms and not ask questions.

Which takes us to the second thing about the American university system that must make the world wonder: its extraordinary effectiveness in reproducing the social class system. The Varsity Blues parents may have gotten caught, but the Ultraparents have positively crushed it. In America today, how much your parent(s) make is by far the most important predictor not just of whether you go to college but also of what kind of college you go to.[66] While 78 percent of children in the top quintile of the household income distribution go on to higher education, only 32 percent of the bottom two quintiles do. About four fifths of the students from the top quintile who go to college come out with a bachelor's degree, but only about one third of those from the bottom 40 percent do. Of those who go to college, 69 percent from the top quintile go to selective institutions, but only 26 percent of bottom 40 percent do. Multiply all of these filters of relative advantage together, and the result is that children born near the top are about 15 times as likely to acquire a bachelor's degree from a selective college as those from the bottom. For those at the very top, the advantage is even more extreme. According to a study led by Raj Chetty, children of families in the top 1 percent of the income distribution are 77 times more likely than children of bottom quintile to attend an Ivy-plus college.[67]

Visit any of the premier colleges around the country and the parking lots full of shiny new cars and the goose-down winter wardrobes will tell the story. At Yale, Wake Forest, and Georgetown—all three of which figured in the Varsity Blues scandal—more than 70 percent of students come from families in the top quintile of the income distribution, and fewer than 8 percent from the bottom two quintiles put together. The card-carrying members of the 9.9 percent alone account for about half of all students at the most selective colleges.[68] To their credit, the universities at the very top have taken great pains to share the bounty with growing numbers of low-income, first-generation, and minority students. Among students admitted to Princeton's Class of 2024, 20 percent are from low-income households, 17 percent are the first in their families to attend college, and 60 percent will apply for some level of financial aid. One of the unintended consequences of the effort to recruit low-income students is to leave a void in the middle of elite college populations, which now throw together children from the two ends of the spectrum and leave out many of the kids born in between.[69]

The pattern of stark socioeconomic difference continues on the other side of college. Ten years after enrolling, the median Ivy League graduate takes home $70,000, while the median graduate from all other colleges earns $34,000.[70] The top 10 percent of graduates from all the others hits the Ivy median of $70,000, but the top 10 percent from the Ivies makes $200,000. A study of 4,512 board members of Fortune 500 companies shows that about 30 percent graduated from a handful of elite colleges representing a tiny percentage of all students, and about 14 percent had degrees from one institution: Harvard.[71] Another study shows that the earnings impact of an elite undergraduate degree persists even after an individual attains an elite postgraduate degree—meaning that two fancy degrees are better than one.[72] A 2017 study concludes that "earnings differences attributable to college selectivity are striking."[73]

On these two dimensions of wonder—the extraordinary expense and the extraordinary inequality—the only thing that can compare with the American system of higher education is the American health care system (on which more later). Both systems cost almost twice as much in the United States as in any other developed country, and yet both underperform the other countries in net results, delivering lower life expectancy along with an epidemic of ignorance. Both reward the rich and punish the poor, doling out exceptional service to the few and crushing debt burdens to the many. Both serve to perpetuate the fraud that the United States is the wealthiest country on earth. The massive bills paid for education add to paper GDP even as they subtract from anything that deserves the name of wealth. Higher education in America, like health care, has evolved into a tax that the many pay for the benefit of the few.

The twin marvels of expense and inequality in higher education are often treated as separate and discrete problems, to be palliated with efficiency measures over here and admissions tweaks over there. But they are really just two aspects of the same problem. The cost of higher education is untethered from any educational reality because education is not its most profitable product. Access is its most profitable product, and the education is more like a side benefit (often accompanied with tragic knowledge of the predicament in which its possessors find themselves). Higher education in America is the toll booth for the American social class system. The system charges whatever people will pay to get to the front of the line in American life. The greater the inequality, the more that people will pay. The Great Reprivatization was thus both the consequence and an enabling cause of rising inequality.

STILL, THE MONEY DOES BUY SOMETHING, and one thing you can take to the bank is that those cherries on top do offer an exquisite campus experience. In fact, given the immense welfare payouts from their publicly subsidized endowments, America's top colleges are undoubtedly delivering more than $350,000 worth of fun and learning to their students. The best colleges offer dining options that put your typical gourmet market to shame, and they care for the souls of their charges as if they were handling heirloom china. The deans' offices are teaming with "happiness officers" and "wellness coaches" and various counseling services to make sure that those who get in will get out with a degree and a smile. Really, if the goal is to breed in young adults an aristocratic sensibility of entitlement to constant nurture from a world organized around their well-being—well, then, mission accomplished! And those campuses—so beautiful! The well-tended lawns and majestic oak trees, the grand old buildings, the state-of-the-art gymnasiums with their rock-climbing walls and deluxe squash courts—so inspiring! At Princeton, I have stood in awe before the freshly built gothic quad of Whitman College, which converted one of the fortunes of the dot-com era into one of the largest orders for white Italian limestone in recent history.

It would indeed be pleasant to imagine a world in which the glories of America's finest universities serve to mark the privileges that an enlightened society might accord to those who promise to contribute to the advance of knowledge. The pursuit of truth, however, is the luxury of a more equal society. Truth is useful for a democracy, but an oligarchy thrives on its opposite. The beauty and goodness of the best universities has an illusory quality. As the reward for elbowing one's way to the front of the line goes up, customers are willing to pay more. Colleges add to their services without limit in order to sustain the illusion that it's all about the education.

The results of the Great Reprivatization are now so clear that they raise a fundamental question—not about what has happened, but about what has not happened. Why are people putting up with this? Where is that national university that George Washington promised? As a matter of fact, a public option at a national level, backed up with a credible system for selecting the most promising young scholars and matching them with educational providers selected according to transparent forms of accreditation, would bring both greater cost discipline and greater justice to the system of higher education. Couple it with a more coherent program of national service and we would have a system that works for all youth. Compel the private universities to use their public subsidies for the public good, and provide public universities with the funding they need to actually serve the public—the solutions aren't necessarily easy, but they aren't rocket science either. Here, however, is the last sting of inequality. It forbids that we even discuss such ideas, for fear of offending the rich who provide us with so many blessings. Like a scorpion surrounded by fire, as one narrative about the self-destruction of the Confederate States of America has it, an unequal society injects the venom into its own brain, the better to speed the descent into mindlessness.

WHEN NEWS OF Operation Varsity Blues hit the internet, the screens lit up with anger (and not a little glee). Much of the attention settled on a pair of minor television celebrities caught up in the scandal. Anger can be useful, but in this case it was misplaced. Inequality did not happen because the 9.9 percent began hoarding places at selective universities. The 9.9 percent began hoarding because inequality happened. It was inequality that made the 9.9 percent clear-eyed and crazy at the same time.

In the end, it is the lucid insanity of the Varsity Blues players that lingers. Consider the case of Jane Buckingham, the author of, among other works, *The Modern Girl's Guide to Sticky Situations* (you can't make this stuff up). In 2012, Jane coauthored a *Time* magazine article with her then husband, the management guru Marcus Buckingham (author of *First, Break All the Rules*—really, it just keeps giving).[74] In that piece, the couple demonstrated keen awareness of the perils of supreme parenting. "Millennials have been raised by 'helicopter parents,'" the Buckinghams intone. "Sheltered from critique and failure, members of this generation ooze unearned confidence at the office" and "expect a promotion just for being on time to work." Yet in 2018, Jane thoughtfully planned a fake ACT test at home for her millennial son so that he might be sheltered from the knowledge that she had agreed to pay $50,000 to have someone else take the real test on his behalf elsewhere. You would almost think she knew what she was doing. Maybe she just couldn't help herself.

"I know this is craziness. I know it is," Jane tells the felonious college consultant Rick Singer, in one of those transient moments of self-awareness that seem to characterize our class. And then—one can almost imagine the made-for-television scene reenacted in the gravelly voice of an 8mm horror-film villain—"I need you to get him into USC."

Why Our Neighborhoods
Are the Best

Henry George's first epiphany took place one afternoon in 1869 as he walked from the "good" side of New York City to the "bad" side.[1] On Fifth Avenue, he strolled past ostentatious mansions where the new rich were so rich that the old rich had no choice but to marry them. Upon arriving at the Lower East Side, he entered a filthy maze of tenements where the streets ran with urine and the sewers regularly exploded from the accumulation of noxious fumes, where a dozen adults might sleep nose to toe in rooms without windows and one in ten children died in infancy. "The squalid misery of a great city appalled and tormented me, and would not let me rest," he later wrote to a friend. On that day, as he stood amid the pleading faces and nauseating stench of poverty in the city, he solemnly records, "a thought, a vision, call—give it what name you please" came to him unbidden.[2] "Every nerve quivered. Then and there I took a vow."

George himself had lived on both sides of the divide. He did not need to be told what it felt like to be so poor that you had to stop a stranger on the street and demand money to feed your newborn child and her mother. He also knew what it was to find a home and a place in the great affairs of society, to publish papers that thinking people read and that the well-to-do feared. What stayed with him was the mystery of that division in human experience carved into the brutal geography of the city. "It is as though an immense wedge were being forced, not underneath society, but through society," he declares in the book that made him famous.[3] "Those who are above the point of separation are elevated, but those who are below are crushed down. This association of progress with poverty is the great enigma of our times." The vow he took on that day in New York was to never rest until he had explained the problem of the age and discovered its cure.

George's second epiphany took place in the following year on the other side of the country. He was riding a horse in the hills of the California coast, where cows grazed on windy pastures, when he asked a passing teamster about the value of the local land. The man replied that he didn't know for sure, but that there was a fellow nearby who was offering his patch of dirt at the incredible rate of $1,000 an acre. "Like a flash," said George, the answer to the enigma of progress and poverty came to him. The value of land, he concluded, held the key to understanding the troubles of the age.

Like any single explanation to all the world's problems, George's analysis rushed quickly past many complicating details. Yet it grabbed a surprisingly large handful of the truth along the way. And the power of his insight has not diminished as much as one might have expected. Consider the fact that he happened to have his second epiphany while trotting along the eastern shores of the San Francisco Bay. One thousand dollars for an entire acre! If only he knew.

UP AND DOWN THE CALIFORNIA COAST, the signs sprout at the intersections every weekend afternoon. Sometimes five or six fight for space on one corner, pointing this way and that to the nearby open houses. Around 1 p.m., the traffic picks up noticeably as the cars move on from one once-in-a-lifetime opportunity to the next. The real estate agents greet every visitor with a hardened smile. The shoppers stomping through the properties are mostly looky-loos. They've come for the intelligence, or maybe for practice, or maybe because few things say as much about you today as your taste in real estate. Sometimes it can feel like they are all playing a giant, open-air game of Monopoly.

Something odd is happening at the jumbo end of the American Dream, something that makes ordinary people behave with unexpected pizzazz. Under normal circumstances, the sensible, middle-aged couples that cruise the open houses in the good neighborhoods aren't the kind of people who will be popping the $1,000 champagne bottles in nightclubs. Some of them probably still snatch shampoo samples from hotel bathrooms. But when it comes to refurbishing their dream home, they will insist on chilling their grapefruit juice in a built-in, restaurant-grade, walnut veneer refrigerator system that costs as much as a Harley-Davidson Fat Boy with a 1,868cc engine. Then they'll install the marble-plated steam-shower and claw-foot bathtub set that goes for about the price of a three-bedroom home in Ohio. The magic words "resale value" can justify almost any indulgence. It really is like Monopoly. You're not buying those little green houses for your own comfort; you're counting on passing the bill along to other people.

For the paid-up members of the 9.9 percent, the right home in the right neighborhood has come to stand for so many things that it almost counts as the answer to the riddle of the meaning of life. It is an exercise in self-branding, a means of educating the children, a way of crafting a certain kind of family life, and, let's not forget, an investment strategy and retirement plan. In the right neighborhoods, the right home is like a laundry machine. You put in a load of wealth and privilege, and it comes out smelling minty fresh. In the best zip codes, even the old plywood homes have the glow of a life tastefully lived. The upper end of the real estate market is in this respect a lot like the upper end of the higher education market (and the two curiously overlap in certain towns). What's inside the buildings matters much less than what the address on the title says about you.

If you look at the numbers, it starts to make sense at ground level, at least for a minute or two. In certain neighborhoods, the real estate market has turned house-sitting into a viable career option. According to estimates from Zillow, the median home in San Francisco appreciated in value in 2018 at a rate that, spread out over the workweek, equates to $60.13 per hour.[4] In San Jose, the payoff was $99.81 per hour. Those numbers will get you into the 9.9 percent without ever having to leave your bed. It's kind of like landing on Park Place or Boardwalk: you can relax and watch TV as the money starts rolling in.

The only catch with the house-sitting plan for financial security is that you have to own the house you sit in to make any money at it. In 74 percent of housing markets in the United States, the average wage earner cannot afford the median home price—and in 76 percent of markets, the home prices are growing faster than wages.[5] The way to get into the market is to be in it already or to have a lucky roll of the dice. Or, much more likely, have your parents open the door for you.

Homeownership has become such a central part of wealth formation that some analysts believe it may account for most of the increase in wealth inequality.[6] The great real estate game determines not just where people will sleep at night, but how much spare cash they will have under the mattress and what sort of challenges and opportunities they will face in the morning. The biggest winners are not the 0.1 percent, whose wealth is concentrated in financial assets like stocks, but the 9.9 percent. In fact, we could almost rename the 9.9 percent as "the people of the right zip codes." The losers are everybody else. The relative decline in home values at the lower end, combined with low homeownership rates, is one of the main reasons why half of American households in 2020 have lower net wealth than the median household did in 1970.[7]

What you don't want to be, in the great board game of the American housing market, is either a renter or an owner of the wrong kind of property. That's kind of like landing on "Go To Jail"—or wasting cash on properties that don't give you a monopoly. While the median home-owner has a net worth of $195,400, the median renter has $5,400.[8] One in four renters spend more than half their income on rent. Households that spend more than 50 percent of income on rent spend 35 percent less than the typical household on food and 74 percent less on health care.[9] As Princeton sociologist Matthew Desmond points out, evictions have become a routine occurrence in modern America, throwing people out of bad situations and into desperate ones. Many millennials waited too long to be born and then racked up massive debts on their education; so they face catastrophically lower rates of homeownership than boomers.[10]

Many people of color compounded these errors by failing to inherit a home or to choose parents wealthy enough to pony up for a down payment. This is one reason why almost 60 percent of African Americans are renters, compared with fewer than 30 percent of whites.[11] Another reason is that, thanks to racially structured policing and incarceration policies, a disproportionate number of Black males of home-buying age have literally spent time in jail. Another reason is that owning a home while Black is statistically not as profitable as owning while white (more on that in a coming chapter).

This growing division between rich houses and poor houses would be one thing if those houses were all rubbing elbows on the same street. But they are not. In the reality version of Monopoly, as in the game itself, the nice properties and the not-so-nice have been moved to different neighborhoods, far enough apart that they can't see each other. That's part of the point. Contrary to popular myth, American neighborhoods are not divided by culture, with blue latte-sippers on one side and rock-ribbed, red-meat types on the other.[12] They are divided by wealth, or, more exactly, by who has a chance of making it and who does not.

Some of this sorting-by-dollars plays out on a national scale. There are opportunity deserts like Detroit,[13] where only 1.9 percent of households have incomes above $150,000 and the median home value is $36,293,[14] and gilded epicenters of the 9.9 percent like San Francisco, where families making $117,400 are now classed as "low-income."[15] The median home in San Francisco would buy a neighborhood consisting of 39.8 homes in Detroit.

But the differences within metropolitan areas are more significant. Pew research shows that the share of low-income households living in majority-low-income neighborhoods rose from 23 percent in 1980 to 28 percent in 2010, while high income concentration went from 9 percent to 18 percent.[16] In Houston, forty years ago, middle-class neighborhoods—where the average income was within 25 percent of the citywide average—housed about two thirds of the population; now they represent only one third of the city.[17]

In a nation whose middle class is evaporating, moreover, the side of the split that matters most is not the isolation of the poor—though that is a problem—but the segregation of affluence, or the "secession of the successful," as former Secretary of Labor Robert Reich aptly puts it.[18] The rich don't choose to live with their fellow rich because they smell better. They do it for the same reasons that they choose to be rich in the first place. Rich neighborhoods are better neighborhoods, and they are better not just in proportion to their wealth but—and this is the defining paradox of Monopoly in both its real-life and board game versions—out of proportion to their wealth.

The great housing game is a way for the rich to get richer and the poor to get poorer—even as it encourages everyone in the comfortable belief that these two trends have nothing to do with one another. The miracle of space is that it promotes forgetfulness. It allows the lucky few to pursue stainless steel projects in tasteful living without ever having to think about where the wealth comes from. You really don't need to know about the people who come in by bus (unless they're bringing in a virus). Where those people go back to is anybody's guess.

Rising inequality has delivered two very different American Dreams. One is a fantasy ever more detached from reality; the other feels more like the quiet dread of an unwanted envelope or an unexpected knock on the door. Anyone who has access to a listings website can know this. Surprisingly few people take it to be anything other than an act of nature. One individual whose ideas could explain more than most was Henry George.[19]

HENRY GEORGE'S LAST DAY OF SCHOOL took place when he was fourteen years old, and by eighteen he had gone off to sea. As a printer and later a journalist, he acquired no formal training in economics. Yet at the age of forty-one, he published a 563-page beast that set out to shatter the presumptions of the discipline of economics—and that at the very least gave it a good kick in the pants. George first sent the draft out under the sales-killing title *Political Economy of the Social Problem*, and all the publishers turned it down. He changed the name to the more enticing *Progress and Poverty* and self-published it in 1879. It went on to be translated into thirteen languages and outsell every book but the Bible for several glorious years in the 1880s.

In his book, George at first follows Adam Smith and David Ricardo in dividing the economic world into three factors of production: labor, which generates wages in exchange for work; capital, which generates returns on investments; and land, which generates rents out of nothing but titles to land. In George's scheme (like Ricardo's, to some degree), the problem child is not capital, as it is for socialists. Rather, the bad guy (at least potentially) is land. As a local economy grows, according to George's analysis, landowners are able to demand higher rents from both labor and capital simply for living and operating around a particular point in space. This extra rent comes not from any improvements on the land or other useful activity on the part of the landowner. It merely amounts to extracting unearned income by virtue of having a kind of monopoly over a particular point in space. It comes at the expense of those who, through labor and capital, are responsible for actually producing wealth. "Private property in land is robbery," he concludes. "It has everywhere had its birth in war and conquest, and in the selfish use which the cunning have made of superstition and law."[20]

Since there is only one problem in the world, in George's mind, there is only one solution. "We must therefore substitute for the individual ownership of land a common ownership," he declares. Recognizing that seizing everybody's land titles and throwing them into a communistic pile is not going to happen without a great deal of unpleasantness, however, George proposes an easier and more effective way of establishing a de facto common ownership of land. Simply tax properties at a rate of 100 percent of the "unearned increment" or rent they generate. In such a world, home builders would still be free to profit from building homes, farmers would be free to profit from raising crops, and factory owners would be free to profit from making widgets in factories, but all of them would be removed from the business of land speculation, as any gains or losses due to changes in the value of the underlying land would be shared among the general public. Technically, George's proposal is called a "land-value tax," but his growing army of supporters took to identifying it, in quasi-messianic terms, as "the single tax."

The land-value tax is such a simple and economically coherent idea that even anti-tax conservatives have trouble mustering a cogent attack on it. Milton Friedman, the high priest of libertarianism, called it the "least bad" tax, noting that insofar as it returns an inherently public good back to the public, the land-value tax does not distort economic activity in the way that an income tax, for example, does. The editors of *The Economist* are left to oppose it only on the grounds that it might be a chore to implement—an objection that surely would kill off the income tax, too, if it were to be taken seriously.[21] The crucial philosophical point that shines like a gem in George's proposal—and that the defenders of property and their ideological champions in the economics faculties have long sought to obscure—is that taxation is not, in principle, a matter of taking wealth from those who supposedly created it and distributing it to those who did not. On the contrary, rightly done, taxation in a democratic society is a matter of returning wealth to those who are ultimately responsible for creating it.

The idea is simple enough, in fact, that it can be explained in the form of a game that is intelligible to the average nine-year-old. That was the insight that moved one of George's more impassioned followers, a young woman named Elizabeth Magie, to invent *The Landlord's Game* in 1903, six years after George's death. The daughter of a freethinking abolitionist, Magie first attained notoriety when she placed an ad offering her services as a slave. The exercise drew attention to the cause of women's rights, though it also elicited a number of creepy proposals. In *The Landlord's Game*, players move around a square board accumulating properties along with railroad interests and utilities, creating monopolies, charging rent to each other, and collecting $200 when they pass Go. If that sounds familiar, it should. Unfortunately, as Magie would soon discover, inventing the game we call *Monopoly* and securing monopoly rights over the distribution of that game were two very different things—a point that George himself would surely have appreciated.

THE TRAGEDY OF THE AMERICAN DREAM is that it made the most sense when it was least understood. In the decades following World War II, the United States experienced a housing boom with few parallels in history. The homeownership rate increased from 43.6 percent in 1940 to

61.9 percent in 1960—only about 3 percent below where it sits in 2020.[22] Most of the growth happened on the crabgrass frontier, as the share of the housing stock located in suburbs soared from 19 percent in 1940 to 44 percent by 1990.[23] In the course of the suburban boom, homeownership became a part of the political religion of the United States and the undisputed setting of the American Dream. Owning a home with a garage on a leafy street, the dreamplan said, taught self-reliance, created happy families, and bred responsible citizens with a stake in their communities. These truths seemed so self-evident that many people took suburban homeownership as the natural end state of the human species. Who wouldn't want the lawn, the in-home parking, the washer-dryer, and the wholesome neighborhood of white picket fences?

The dream came with more than the usual allotment of illusions. Without massive public subsidies for the automotive infrastructure combined with active sabotage of public transportation, the suburbs would have remained prohibitively remote. Without racially motivated "white flight" from urban centers, those distant cow fields would have remained populated only with cows, and without racist policies they would not have remained white. The most intractable of the illusions had to do with aura of self-reliance that enveloped the husband and wife in their castle on Elm Street. The housing boom of the postwar period always pretended to be an expression of the pioneering spirit of hardworking individualists. Yet it was principally the consequence of the most significant welfare program in American history, one that was targeted with unerring precision at the hearts and wallets of the white middle class.[24]

In the postwar Dream period, federally funded financial and tax incentives (including changes in mortgage regulation, G.I. Bill provisions, allowances for the deduction of mortgage interest and property taxes, and omission of imputed rents) accounted for 40 percent to 45 percent of the increase in the homeownership rate.[25] That comes before considering the contribution of the highway expansion program, in which the federal government covered 90 percent of the cost of making it possible for white people to live with other white people in otherwise remote locations. As the economy boomed and other people's incomes rose, moreover, home prices naturally increased. For the freshly recruited legions of the middle class, the housing boom was in effect an equalizing, share-the-wealth program that converted economic growth into welfare payments for homeowners. It reinforced the growing equality in incomes, the growing empowerment of workers in the workplace through unions, and the growing access to quality primary, secondary, and higher education. In its highly racialized, morally compromised, and deeply self-deluded way, the American real estate game played a central role in the creation of a (mostly white) middle class whose power and breadth had few parallels in history.

Beginning around 1980, however, the great real estate welfare program shifted down and then quietly, without really drawing much attention to the fact, slipped into reverse gear. In its present form, the real estate system in America today transfers wealth from poor to rich, from young to old, from Black to white, and from the future to the past. The great reversal of the American real estate machine—from dream-maker to dream-killer—can be read out of the aggregate statistics.

During the postwar Dream period, an essential factor in ensuring that the system worked to the benefit of the middle class was the compression in home values. In 1930, homes at the 90th percentile in value were worth 11 times those at the 10th percentile.[26] From 1950 to 1980, when the housing boom was in full swing, that ratio fell by almost half, to below 6. Combined with the extraordinary rise in homeownership rates, this narrowing of the value spectrum meant that the largest part of the hidden, homeowner subsidy went to the expanding middle class. It also meant that home value appreciation happened on a broad base of the market.

Starting around 1980, however, the top decile of homes began to pull away from the rest. The changes, it is important to add, had little to do with relative differences in the size or quality of houses. It wasn't a matter of extra rooms or better bathroom fixtures in the fancy homes. Rather, the differences are mostly about the relative value of location. By 2012, the ratio of values between the 90th and the 10th percentile was back up to 10, or very close to its 1930 peak. The timeline of inequality in housing prices falls into the same U-shape that characterizes graphs of income

and wealth concentration trends over the past century.[27] As a consequence of this change, the crypto-socialist-homeowner-cash-machine
of the middle-class welfare state morphed into a laundry machine that
began to funnel money and resources away from the middle and toward
the top—or more exactly, the 9.9 percent.

Government of the sort that engineered the postwar housing boom
might have shifted the outcome. But the story of the great reversal of
the real estate engine is also one of government by omission—a form
of government that in some ways defines the era of rising inequality.
Unfortunately, one of the features of governing by not governing is
that few people can see it, and so most Americans have formed an
utterly inaccurate impression of how the so-called real estate "market"
actually works.

If one mentions the words "government" and "housing" in polite
conversation today (generally not a good idea), the words "taxes" and
"poor people" are likely to make an appearance in short order. Yes, we
want to help, the response will come, but aren't we doing enough already?
The funny thing is that government works much harder to help rich
people make money off their homes than to help poor people find shelter.

According to the Center on Budget and Policy Priorities, the federal government spent $190 billion per year on housing assistance of
various sorts, as of 2015.[28] But 60 percent of this amount corresponds
to the mortgage interest deduction, which benefits only the 7 million
or so households with more than $100,000 in income. The bigger the
house, the more they get. A further $32 billion per year goes to covering
the exclusion of capital gains taxes on inherited homes. An uncounted
additional amount pays for the capital gains exclusion on home sales.
All but a few rounding errors of these amounts land in the pockets of
the 9.9 percent—every year.

The chump change left over for affordable housing, sadly, does
remarkably little to ameliorate the housing crisis.[29] One piece of it goes
into subsidizing the construction of quality apartments in low-income
neighborhoods. The organizing idea is that the purpose of housing is
to supply low-income families with refuge from the weather and good
kitchen appliances. This idea is bonkers. In fact, the point of housing

today is to provide opportunity. As studies make abundantly clear, opportunity comes with a new or better neighborhood, not a new refrigerator.[30] Another piece of the affordable housing budget goes into housing vouchers. But these vouchers are often all but impossible to redeem outside the same, underserved neighborhoods where recipients already live, and so they, too, have the effect of concentrating disadvantage.

The drive to subsidize wealthy homeowners at the expense of the general public is so well entrenched in the American political system that it appears to be one of the few forces capable of transcending the partisan divide. A perfect illustration of this point is the debate about federal income tax deduction for state and local taxes, commonly known as the SALT deduction, that arose in response to the 2017 Tax Cuts and Jobs Act. A quirk of the American taxation system that arose more by inertia than design, the SALT deduction has become, in effect, one of the quiet ways in which all taxpayers subsidize those wealthy taxpayers who pay for those local schools and services to which only the wealthy have access. Although the 2017 Act was a characteristic atrocity perpetrated by the party of the rich against the rest of society, more out of spite against blue states than principle, it included one surprisingly progressive provision: a $10,000 cap on the SALT deduction. That cap turned out to be a $137 billion tax increase on the wealthy.[31] According to estimates from Brookings, about 25 percent of the increase fell on the 0.1 percent, and all but a few pennies of the rest hit the 9.9 percent, most of them residents of the best neighborhoods in the bluest cities like New York and San Francisco.[32] Suddenly, Democrats found a tax cut they could get behind.[33] Senator Chuck Schumer of New York went so far as to pitch the idea of restoring the SALT deduction as a form of Covid relief. For anyone who toured the abandoned apartment buildings in the extremely SALT-y neighborhoods of Manhattan's Upper East Side or Brooklyn's Park Slope, whose residents fled en masse to their second and third homes in the country during the pandemic, this suggestion was good at least for some comic relief.

The most significant subsidy of all for homeownership, however, does not show up on any of the books because it is built into the way we think about property and taxation. If you own a house and rent it to some Jack, that rental income is naturally taxed in the way that all investment income is taxed. If that Jack owns the house in which you live and rents it to you, then he pays tax on that rental income, too. But now if you and Jack get together and agree to buy each other's houses, the tax on the rent will magically disappear. Nothing will have changed about your living situation or Jack's, your wealth or Jack's, your use of local services, or anything else of material consequence—but you and Jack will have more money, and the public treasury will have less. Why? Because you and Jack have discovered that our tax system is quietly in love with homeowners and loves to hate on renters.

From a theoretical perspective, it should not matter to a taxing authority whether you rent a property to someone else or to yourself. Indeed, when the government measures GDP, it goes to the trouble of measuring this "imputed rent" and counting it as income, since otherwise national income would shift arbitrarily as housing units switch between owner-occupied and rented. But when it comes to paying income tax on this virtual stream of income, poof!, the gloriously free market returns and the IRS melts away.

Imputed rent now stands at a stunning $1.5 trillion per year, or 8 percent of GDP.[34] The last time it was this high relative to GDP was around 1930. The failure to tax this imputed rent on the same basis as actual rent does not impact all members of the public equally. It favors homeowners over renters, and the bigger the home the better. Estimates of the distributional impact of this nontax vary, but they start around $110 billion per year and go up from there.[35] That's $110 billion moving from the pockets of those who can't afford big homes to those who can. The OECD has recognized what is happening and recommends taxing imputed rental income.[36] Some countries, like Holland, have done so at least partially. Conservative commentators like Bruce Bartlett admit that they can't find many reasonable objections to it.[37] Which of course leads them to conclude that it can never happen here.

SOMETHING HAPPENS TO PEOPLE when the Dream comes true. Homeownership, it has long been said, has the marvelous effect of making people put down roots in their communities. The evidence shows that homeowners' first priority, as they joyfully plant themselves at the center of a community of fully realized fellow citizens, is to pour as much concrete as possible over those roots.[38] The way to keep values up, everybody comes to understand very quickly, is to prevent other people from moving in. Especially "those" people. In some of the more expensive areas, even the long-term renters like to get in on the game of slamming doors on outsiders.[39]

The effect is so pronounced that it can overwhelm whatever remains at the local level of the notorious passions of partisan polarization.[40] Venice Beach, for example, is a happy community of canals and boutiques on the hipper shores of the Los Angeles area that went about 90 percent for Clinton in the 2016 election. But when a city councilwoman showed up at a town meeting with a plan to establish a temporary homeless service center on an empty bus parking lot, residents started to chant "Lock her up!" In Long Beach, residents otherwise known for enlightened attitudes on race questions staged an "anti-crime" march to express their outrage at similar attempts by local government to grapple with a homelessness problem that appeared to involve no crimes at all. Over in the charming, upscale Ballard neighborhood of Seattle, a plan to raise a tax to fund the creation of a homeless shelter brought forth what one journalist called an "organized mob" for "Two Hours Hate."[41] In San Francisco, ecologically correct residents routinely use environmental regulations to burden, slow down, or stop unwanted housing developments.[42]

The comments sections in public forums (I went there so that you don't have to) offer a window on how homeownership alters consciousness, and in particular the consciousness that other human beings exist and have needs. In reaction to zoning proposals that would have added housing density to one fashionable California neighborhood, some reader responses could veer toward the genocidal: "There is not necessarily a shortage of housing but an excess of people. Just because you want to live somewhere doesn't mean you can."

The charms of the not-in-my-backyard movement, or NIMBYism, are sometimes thought to be universal to the human condition. In fact, they grow in power and impact with rising inequality. They grow with inequality both because there is more money at stake and, more importantly, because local power is a function of local money. According to Brookings, the deployment of zoning and land use regulations to curb growth has risen in tandem with inequality.[43] In a study of ninety-five metropolitan areas whose conclusions will surprise no one who has ever attended a public meeting in a wealthy neighborhood, researchers found that areas with high concentrations of wealth have more restrictive land use regulations.[44] America's wealthiest neighborhoods have been so successful in capturing the legal and local governance processes that they have actually managed to decrease the density of occupation in the most desirable locations. Under rising inequality, in short, local governments have been turned into agents of nonconstruction.[45]

Why exactly does the sun appear to shine brighter in some neighborhoods than others? The first thing to know about good neighborhoods is that they are usually located near a giant cash machine: the local tech monopoly or financial oligopoly. More optimistically, we could say that in the modern economy, high economic productivity happens in clusters or "hives" where a certain density of know-how, networks, and human interaction yields high levels of economic activity and innovation. Thus, the wealthy neighborhoods tend to fall on transportation corridors or in easy reach of the leading urban centers.

Once the neighbors are in control, of course, they work to keep density low and squeeze every undesirable person out to some other, undisclosed location. That's why the not-so-good-neighborhoods, almost by definition, are the ones that force their residents into long commutes across opportunity deserts. Ample research confirms what many Americans relearn every weekday morning, that long commutes are associated with increased stress levels, health problems, likelihood of divorce, and bad things in general. According to Harvard economist Nathaniel Hendren, commuting time is a better predictor of social mobility than education quality, family structure, and local crime rates.[46] One of the oddities of rising inequality has been the emergence of a class of "extreme commuters." As of 2016 there were 4 million people living ninety minutes away from work—or more.[47]

The other, big thing that the good neighborhoods have going for them is their schools. The dismantling and reprivatization of America's system of public education has been happening one privileged neighborhood at a time. Ten of the top thirteen ranked public elementary schools in California on niche.com are located in the Palo Alto Unified School District, as are two of the top four public high schools in the state. They are free and open to the public. All the public has to do is buy a home in a neighborhood where the median home value was $2.8 million in 2020. Six of the top seven public high schools in Maryland are in Montgomery County, and most of those are in the Bethesda area, where the median listing price for homes in 2020 was $1.2 million. Meanwhile, 9 million students in America, or one in five, in 969 districts, "live virtually across the street from a significantly whiter and richer school district."[48] They have, on average, $4,207 less per student in funding.

In 1972, activists brought the matter to the Supreme Court, arguing in *San Antonio Independent School District v. Rodriguez* that the school financing system effectively allows the state to discriminate against low-income children. This is quite plainly true. But the Supreme Court had fallen into the hands of Nixon appointees, and it narrowly beat back this challenge to the social class system in America. The author of the Court's 5–4 majority opinion was the recently appointed Lewis Powell, fresh off having written a memorandum for the U.S. Chamber of Commerce in which he plots out the agenda for corporate domination of the U.S. political system that laid the foundation for rising inequality in our time.[49]

In some neighborhoods, the privatization has taken the form of a renaissance in old-fashioned private schooling. Although the share of students in private schools has not changed significantly in the aggregate in the era of rising inequality, the share of wealthy students in private schools has gone up substantially.[50] Not coincidentally, the tuition at nonsectarian private schools has increased even faster, rising from $4,120 in 1979 to $22,611 in 2011 in constant dollars. "US schools—both public and private—are increasingly segregated by income," Harvard's Richard Murnane and Stanford's Sean Reardon conclude.

A case in point would be New Haven, Connecticut, the hotbed of the meritocracy according to recent authors based at Yale. People of means and merit in New Haven generally avoid the local public schools, which serve an overwhelmingly Black, low-income student body. So it is not surprising that tiger mom Amy Chua, a professor at Yale Law School, sent her children to an elite private school in town as she was composing her *Battle Hymn*. Her employer, meanwhile, paid a laughable $4.9 million in local property taxes on its $2.5 billion land portfolio, thanks to its tax-exempt status.[51] Beating up on your own children to make them play the violin, it turns out is only the louder half of the story of tiger parenting. The silent half is living in a place where other people's children don't have a shot at playing the violin at all.

Maybe the best thing about good neighborhoods is that they are not bad neighborhoods. The effects of living in underserved areas are so well known, and so dismal, that they hardly need to be stated. Research consistently shows that bad neighborhoods really are bad for children above all.[52] In one particularly telling study, children from a randomly selected group of families who moved to wealthier neighborhoods were more likely to go to college, to get married, to have higher incomes, and to live in higher-income neighborhoods themselves than the peers they left behind.[53]

The geographical concentration of wealth brings many additional advantages for the lucky few beyond better schools and commutes. It supplies residents with social capital, in the form of networks that can help deliver valuable internships for the kids and open up business opportunities with prospective clients and employers. It delivers better security, nicer parks, and other public amenities. Maybe the most underappreciated benefit it delivers is the rush that comes with the exercise of power over one's local fiefdom.

In a study of a characteristically snitty spat over school-catchment boundaries in an elite public school district, sociologists observed that "parents frequently employed their professional expertise to directly challenge . . . officials" and "drew on elaborate interpersonal networks."[54] "Behind their challenges lay a sense of entitlement," the researchers conclude. Local power is better than any other buzz. It gives everyone who possesses it a lasting feeling of autonomy, self-determination, and democratic spirit. It's also a way of pillaging everyone and everything outside the zone without ever appearing to be anything other than an upstanding member of the community.

The outcome of the process is visible in skylines and landscapes across the country. In leading urban centers like Manhattan, luxury apartments up in the stratosphere sit empty even as the population migrates away in search of more affordable housing.[55] Ryan Avent, a columnist for the *Economist*, aptly describes the process as a "flight to stagnation."[56] As economist Enrico Moretti and others have pointed out, this is bad news for the economy.[57] Workers are fleeing the areas where they can be most productive and moving into the land of permanently lowered wages, all because the rent is too damn high. In the land of the 9.9 percent, we like to pretend that every neighborhood has a chance to become a good neighborhood. The reality is that our neighborhoods are so good precisely because the other neighborhoods are not.

WHEN HENRY GEORGE LOOKED AROUND to see who was driving the wedge that lifted some and crushed others, he was sure he saw the weapon wielded in the hands of a land speculator. It was an understandable simplification. The railroad companies then were doing what the tech monopolists are doing now: snatching up pieces of the public good and ransoming it back to their fellow citizens with a snicker.

In the final chapter of *Progress and Poverty*, which contains most of the passages that impressed themselves on the mind of his time, George situates his analysis in a framework more expansive than the land question. From the beginning of human history, he argues, the basis of progress itself is the human ability to secure freedom through collaboration. Reason binds us together and sets us free at the same time. "Civilization is co-operation," he writes; "Union and liberty are its factors."[58] As societies grow richer and individuals specialize, however, some individuals learn how to game the system to their advantage. They accumulate wealth and power, and then they use these advantages to increase still more their relative advantage. Rather than work to build a better society, the elites invest their efforts in status competitions with one another. They compete for spoils rather than compete to produce.

Progress halts and "petrification" sets in. "What has destroyed every civilization has been the tendency to the unequal distribution of wealth and power," he concludes.

The farther George goes down this road, the clearer it becomes that "land" is about a lot more than land. When George, echoing Thomas Paine, says that "the earth belongs to us all," he increasingly deploys "the earth" as a metaphor for all that we have in common. He could also call it "air," "water," or "bandwidth," on the understanding that the earth's atmosphere, hydrosphere, and its available electromagnetic spectrum, too, are resources that are in principle available to all humans, exist in limited supply, and yet are sometimes improperly claimed for exclusive use by the few. His real concern is with the tendency of humans to latch on to certain monopolies and use them to extract wealth at the expense of society. His insight is that all systems of exchange, left unchecked, produce these accumulation points of monopolistic advantage, and that the problem starts with a confusion between legitimate objects of exchange (such as the right to work a piece of the earth for a time) and illegitimate objects of exchange (the earth itself).

In a series of essays in Frank Leslie's *Weekly* in 1883, George fires off broadsides on monopolies of every kind. "The big mill crushes out the little mill. The big store undersells the little store til it gets rid of its competition," he inveighs, and then goes on to point the finger at monopolists in telephones and telegraphs.[59] He slams the "gospel of selfishness" (now called Social Darwinism) championed by Herbert Spencer in England and William Graham Sumner in America. He warns of the emergence of an aristocracy in America just like the ones in Europe, dedicated to the preservation of its own wealth. He also shows how government has been captured, and how systems of taxation "have been imposed rather with a view to private advantage than to the raising of revenue." He grasps clearly that the kind of formal, political equality championed by libertarians easily becomes a guise for further exploitation. "It is not enough that men should vote; it is not enough that they should be theoretically equal before the law. They must have liberty to avail themselves of the opportunities and means of life; they must stand on equal terms with reference to the bounty of nature," he writes.

The editor of the series, Frank Leslie, yanked the plug just as George was getting warmed up. It was all too radical for one of the most popular periodicals in the country. Still, some part of the message got through. Although Georgism as a coherent political movement faded after his death, George's ideas grew in strength as they blended into the progressive currents of thought emerging in the new century. Among the many prominent figures who acknowledged their debt to his work were Albert Einstein, Bertrand Russell, Leo Tolstoy, Upton Sinclair, George Bernard Shaw, and that obscure feminist and part-time game designer named Lizzie Magie.

Soon after its invention, *The Landlord's Game* developed an eager following among socialists, progressives, and other people who just enjoyed playing fun board games.[60] It caught on in Atlantic City, among other places, where fans substituted local names for the properties traded: Boardwalk, Park Place, Baltic Avenue, and so on. One of the people who enjoyed many evenings playing the game, now informally known as "Monopoly," was an unemployed engineer named Charles Darrow. Recognizing the commercial potential, Darrow packaged up the game as his own invention and licensed the rights to Parker Brothers. The company, aware of Magie's prior claim, bamboozled her into giving up her rights in exchange for $500 and no royalties. They assured her that this was the best she could get for a socialist game—everyone knows that communists don't like to pay for things. Having secured a monopoly on Monopoly, Parker Brothers and Darrow went on to claim a stream of millions of dollars in rents that lasted for decades. Darrow concocted a heartwarming story about how he invented the game in his own basement during the Depression to entertain the family while he was out of work. He became an American folk hero, while Magie spent her last years working as a typist in a government office, where she developed a reputation as an eccentric old widow who talked a lot about games.

In Magie's version of *Monopoly*, however, there were two ways to play the game. The first is the one we know and love, where the winner takes all. The other way is intended to teach the impact of George's land-value tax. Under the alternative set of rules, when players acquire a monopoly in properties, they are obliged to pay the money into a common fund that is then distributed to all players. Building prosperity thus makes everybody richer. The game ends when the least-rich player has doubled their original stake. It's very educational, but it doesn't exactly make for an exciting game. This was something that Darrow and Parker Brothers saw clear as a dollar bill. It's much more fun when the opportunity of a lifetime is just around the corner and the winner gets to stomp all over the losers. That's the way the actual American real estate market is organized. If it were a game, it would be a lot more fun, too.

To get practical: one way to slow the inequality spiral is to stop the laundry machine. A home should be a place to live, not an investment strategy or a weapon of class warfare. A neighborhood exists to build communities, not to segregate and isolate them. Local control of local resources is a fine thing, but space is not a local resource. Neither is the education of schoolchildren. Neither is access to opportunity. Henry George was basically right. We need a land-value tax, or at least a tax on imputed rent. We need to make zoning answer to the needs of the whole economy, not the predilections of a few lucky squatters. The earth belongs to us all.

— 6 —

Why We Believe in Merit

In one of the photos in the newspaper spread, the sun rises over the dunes of a Central Asian desert to reveal a collection of stylish white tents connected in a lattice of red carpets. Another photo shows a procession of camels against the blue sky. The most striking image has hundreds of young professionals lined up on the rim of a crater gazing into a bonfire below. You get the impression that they are participating in some strange spiritual ceremony that might end awkwardly for one of the audience members.

The press on McKinsey & Company's 2018 retreat was predictably unkind, and it wasn't just because of the tackiness of the Silk Road reenactment.[1] The global consulting giant had rather brazenly decided to hold its celebration of itself four miles from an internment camp where the Chinese government confines and indoctrinates ethnic Uighurs. The public was perhaps appalled to learn of McKinsey's strategic commitment to serve corrupt and authoritarian regimes, not just in China, but also in Russia, Ukraine, Saudi Arabia, and really anywhere that can afford to pay the fees.[2] At around the same time, the public also caught up on the fact that McKinsey had made a habit of supplying its services to opioid manufacturers and U.S. Immigration and Customs Enforcement.[3]

For me, on the other hand, the news of McKinsey's Central Asian escapade evoked an unexpected sense of familiarity, like looking at other people's photos of an old vacation spot. True, the desert luxury/

internment camp scenario was more imaginative than the consulting retreats I attended, which were set in more conventional venues, like Jamaican horseback riding resorts and Napa Valley golf spas. Still, I look at the people on the rim of the crater and I see with surprise that they are perpetuating a way of life that, contrary to my earlier expectations, is only becoming more rich and powerful, more elaborate and fixed, and more like itself over time.

Over the past two decades, about one out of seven Ivy League college graduates have gone straight into consulting, and one of four elite MBA graduates have done the same. Roughly similar numbers have stampeded into investment banking, which is different from consulting mainly in that the money is bigger, the hours are still longer, and the social impact even more doubtful.[4] As both industries have grown—management consulting alone now employs about 700,000 people[5]—they have expanded their recruiting to cover all elite and aspiring-elite colleges, not just the Ivies. Given that the typical consulting career flames out after two years and investment banking doesn't last much longer,[6] these firms now burn through an appreciable fraction of all the aspiring members of the 9.9 percent. We now live in a world where the first job that the best and the brightest take is to tell other people how to do their jobs, and the first skill that they master is scraping together the sentence fragments and pie charts that go into the typical PowerPoint presentation.

They come for the money, of course, and more than that, the prestige. They leave—if they should be so lucky—with a certain, troubling insight into what it is that our society values. This is the vanguard of the 9.9 percent, the hardened shock brigade of the meritocracy. If you want to know where we are going, you need to know something about where they already stand. Above all, you need to know something about the way they think—and what they try to avoid thinking about.

WHEN YOU FIRST TAKE UP A JOB in management consulting or in any of a number of other, equally mysterious occupations that employ the best of our decile, it can feel as though you have stepped into a new dimension of the economic universe. Suddenly you find that all the dollar signs are followed by a random zero or two. One minute, you think that $100 is the price of a big night on the town, and the next minute your boss is dropping $1,000 on camel rentals and much more than that on the after-dinner drinks. Your old self sees $10,000 as a lifetime savings goal, and suddenly you're looking at $100,000 as a starter salary and you're bumping into people in the next tent over who are vocally unhappy because they're making only $1 million. To your friends back in flatland, you'll still offer your words of wisdom for the price of a cup of coffee. But once you project those words on a glowing screen, your clients will be expected to pay something closer to the median value of an American family home per month. It is as if you are gazing down upon a miraculous gusher of warm, green cash spewing skyward out of some hidden spring in the earth.

Then it starts to get complicated, and maybe even a little uncanny. Sometimes in those first weeks and months, as you are grinding through the nighttime hours wrestling bits of so-called data into presentations designed to satisfy the momentary urges of some mini-Napoleon who seems to enjoy kicking down even more than kissing up, it occurs to you that these people aren't *that* smart. Or maybe they are *too* smart for the work, which is more like a game of checkers played out on a board that seems infinitely long and wide. You look around and realize that your bleary tent-mates are actually taking a twisted pleasure in not going home, or in not having much of a home to go to. You get the feeling that what distinguishes them from the rest of humanity is not so much their A+ talents as an almost superhuman tolerance for punishment, and maybe an unspoken dread of falling off the narrow and treacherous path that brought them to the rim of the crater.

Then it hits you that life around the gusher is ridiculously expensive. You spend twice as much for half the space, and you accumulate innumerable necessities that weren't necessary before. You start to wonder if it really is money coming out of that hole in the ground or just some odd form of accounting that adds zeroes as you arrive and lops them off when you try to leave. As you join in the strange excesses like overpriced desert barbecues and amateur horseback riding, you get the sense that these fleeting moments of high living are being done in a certain spirit of revenge, but you're not entirely sure against whom or what.

After a while, however, assuming you stick around long enough, the weirdness of the gusher fades into the background of life, and you no longer really notice it. You start to think that this just is the universe, and what you left behind is a rounding error. You gradually lose the ability to distinguish between success in jostling into position and the value of things snatched out of the air. You come to believe in your power to convert desert sand into flowing rivers of green. The gusher starts to feel like a rock of absolute certainty: I make money, therefore I am. I am a contributing part of global GDP. I am the reason why airports, smartphones, and minibars exist. Eventually you figure you can smell a gusher. You don't actually need to see it. You can detect its presence in the behavior of other people, and maybe even in yourself. You look back only rarely, through dark shades of contempt, on the immense hinterland to the rear, where the gushers have long gone dry.

Then one day, you glance up at the daytime sky for the first time in years. You discover that your fountain of joy is actually just spillover from an immense gusher off in the distance, far out of reach, a blossom of cash so massive that it looks like a mushroom cloud. You look around and realize that your luxury tents might just be a form of internment, too. Gushers tend to make people unreasonable. This glimpse of the irrational is probably the most useful intuition with which to begin an anthropology of the life-forms that emerge in the vicinity of a gusher.

AFTER SOME PERFUNCTORY and unconvincing apologetics about how its impeccable ethical standards practically oblige it to serve needy authoritarians everywhere, McKinsey focused its response to the unwelcome press coverage of its Central Asia camelback adventure on a curious detail of the reporting.[7] In the course of its story, the *New York Times* had pointed out that one of McKinsey's former consultants happened to be the son-in-law of a very senior and superlatively rich Chinese government official. Another consultant, the paper noted, was the daughter-in-law of a top Ukrainian oligarch (indeed, the pre-Trump-impeachment president of Ukraine). McKinsey found the imputation—that its consultants are selected on any account other than their sheer meritorious awesomeness—absolutely intolerable. The firm fired back with a robust defense of the individuals in question and an impassioned declaration that all of its associates are subject to "a rigorous, meritocratic assessment process." You may doubt McKinsey's commitment to advancing democracy around the world, but you may never question its fidelity to the ideals of the meritocracy.

As a founding partner of a management consulting firm 80 percent of whose other partners had graduated from McKinsey, I think I can say something about that "rigorous, meritocratic" process thing. The process at my firm included a number of crucial vetting procedures borrowed straight from McKinsey. One of them was variously called the "beer test" or "Des Moines Airport test," which in my recollection was brought over by an uncharacteristically amiable ex-McKinsey partner.

The scenario: Your flight is canceled and you are stuck with the candidate for endless hours in the only bar at the Des Moines airport. Do you still wish you had hired this person? The actual question behind the question is: "How likable is this person?" Which is usually a variant of the more fundamental question: "How much does this person remind me of me?" Which may be one reason why consulting firms have historically tended to hire a lot of people who look like Brett Kavanaugh.

The beer test, sadly, comes with an expiration date. Once people learn about it, they start prepping for it. Pretty soon there are online courses on how to ace it. Then everyone knows how to fake their way through the Des Moines airport. This is why people near the gusher are never who they say they are. They hollow themselves out and then replace the insides with the narratives that score better. They become résumé zombies. Human ingenuity having its limits, they start to look alike on paper. They even start to talk alike. That's when you notice the army of merit-bots looming on the horizon. Upon detecting the advancing army of highly qualified beer drinkers, the keepers of the meritocracy must therefore devise new and more demanding tests. As the circle shrinks, the definition of merit must be revised and tightened.

On the delicate matter of hiring the sons- and daughters-in-law of Chinese billionaires and Ukrainian oligarchs, the meritocratic process in fact works very smoothly. In my old firm, we frequently hired the scions of local dynasties. Indeed, we did so pretty much every time we opened an office in a new country. That's because we often hired them secondhand from McKinsey itself. And just like McKinsey, we stayed true to the Creed by meticulously including within the definition of merit the virtue of "being the scion of a local dynasty." One criterion we did not apply in hiring, curiously, was: "having survived McKinsey's meritocratic selection process." This turned out to have little predictive value.

But I digress. Before anybody says anything bad about the meritocracy, it is vital to remember what is very good about it. Properly understood, meritocracy stands for the principle that power should be accountable to rational standards and open to public scrutiny. It is not a doctrine about how everyone gets what they deserve, as many people today seem to think, but a necessary postulate of a liberal political theory. It says that wherever individuals are in a position to exercise authority, they should be there in virtue of their publicly demonstrable fitness for the position and the contribution they may be expected to make to the common good, and not as a reward for being born well, golfing with the boss, or cutting a deal with the president. It simply means choosing the best people for the job, to the extent that that is possible, according to transparent methods and criteria.

Meritocracy in this valuable sense is the opposite of corruption, and it is as essential to a modern, liberal democracy as its antithesis is to an oligarchy. It is a founding ideal of the American republic, and it played a vital role in the creation of a robust middle class in the United States and elsewhere during the Great Compression of the middle decades of the twentieth century. It is a version of the very American ideal that Jefferson articulated when he compared the "natural aristocracy" grounded in "virtue and talents" with the "artificial aristocracy founded on wealth and birth."[8] It is in this sense, however, an essentially limited or negative doctrine, making a claim not about the origin of wealth but about the importance of placing a check on unaccountable power.

But in the land of the 9.9 percent, "merit" has come to mean much more than a check on the corrupting effects of power. Merit today is the first (and often the last) answer to the question about the source of all the money that gushes through the upper reaches of the economy. It is a doctrine about the distribution of wealth, and it says that rewards in our society are (or ought to be) handed out in exact proportion to the talent and effort of individual brains. It says not just that the most meritorious person in the room gets to lead the team, but that she *is* the team, and that everything of value that it produces comes straight out of her stash of merit and is therefore entirely hers by natural right. All of the green goodness gushing out of the desert sands, it assures us, is nothing but the liquefied brain-sweat of the individual people gathered around the gusher. This is our ten commandments and our $e=mc^2$ wrapped up in a golden paycheck. It is how we say: *we earned it.* Or just: *mine!* The merit myth—which ought to be carefully distinguished from the much more limited idea of genuine meritocracy—is the origin myth of the 9.9 percent.

Economists often dress up this doctrine of merit as the idea of "human capital," effectively embedding in a putatively neutral economic concept the dogma that individual productivity varies in direct proportion with natural assets and investments in individual brain capacity. Popularizers like David Brooks spread the same dogma thickly with stern warnings about "the skills gap" that separates the educated wheat of the economy from the sad people who drift like chaff past a shiny machine that has no need for their labor.[9] Charles Murray does the same with morbid, racialized talk of a "cognitive elite" that interbreeds and takes over the economy (which makes it sound almost like a prelude to a eugenics program).[10]

Even many of the harshest critics of the system seem to have absorbed the underlying doctrine. According to Daniel Markovits, author of *The Meritocracy Trap*, meritocracy gets its start when "massive prior investments in training" generate an "immense stock of human capital" that "sustains enormous wages for superordinate workers." According to Harvard philosopher Michael Sandel, the problem with meritocracy is that it imbues the most productive members of society with an obnoxious confidence in themselves, leaves the unproductive people feeling sad, and robs us all of our commitment to pursue the common good. All of which sounds righteous enough—except that it takes for granted the underlying theory that brainpower is the measure of productive potential.

It is a bold theory, this doctrine underlying the merit myth. On second thought, it is manifestly preposterous. If you have spent more than a few days at the office, you can probably identify by name a number of living refutations of the merit myth. This is obvious not just from the abundance of bozos, but also from the sizable population of individuals who perform admirably in positions of authority and yet have no distinguishing abilities or talents beyond what their position conveys. Only the most fervent believers in the 9.9 percent can really go along with the bizarre and offensive suggestion that paychecks in this world line up with brain-sweat. Even a cursory, street-level acquaintance with the statistics already considered in previous chapters of this book should be enough to make the merit myth look ridiculous. You can't really believe in the merit myth without also being a racist, sexist, ageist, xenophobe, or genetic determinist convinced that rich people have a unique ability to pass along their merit-genes.

There is yet another level of preposterousness in the brain-sweat theory that will be familiar to probably everyone who has done time in PowerPoint land. The theory takes for granted that there is some necessary connection between the specific nature of the "merit" that individuals obtain and the reward that comes to them. It isn't just any old skill or talent that is supposed to entitle you to claim the prize, the unstated premise of the merit myth says, but the skill or talent in doing whatever it is you are supposed to do. But in the land of the 9.9 percent, "merit" has come to mean a youth spent proving to the world that you are capable of writing a beautiful sonnet on the nature of courage, that you can master a musical instrument to near-citywide prizewinning levels, and that you can do all this while managing a varsity sport and organizing meaningful community service projects. And the prize for all this merit appears to be a lifetime of office nights curled up with computer spreadsheets and presentations populated with fictitious numbers and manipulative jargon.

Let's call this the orchid-compost paradox. The meritocratic system of the 9.9 percent hothouses orchids, and then stuffs them into the compost piles of an extractive economy. To put the matter in a slightly different vocabulary: a remarkable aspect of prestige in the modern meritocratic system is its fungibility. Prestige in human society is not necessarily a bad thing—it's how we signal that this or that person or thing is of special value—but somehow we have landed in a system where prestige accumulated in, say, mastering abstruse doctrines of ancient marble players is thought to make for the ideal investment banker.

When I contemplate my own adventures in business, I confess that the brain-sweat theory of merit sometimes causes me to make involuntary snorting noises. My personal "immense stock of human capital" before becoming a partner in a management consulting firm consisted of a doctoral degree in nineteenth-century German philosophy and a couple of summers at the nastier ends of the fast-food and home construction businesses. How that "massive prior investment" in nearly unreadable philosophical capital and bad food accounted for the "enormous wages" I collected as a "superordinate worker" is surely a mystery that only Hegel could unravel. As a general rule in business, I found that the less time my meritorious colleagues had spent studying "business," the better they were at it. They got better still the farther away their studies took them from anything that could plausibly be construed as a "prior investment in training." And however good they were, their goodness always only explained a small part of the good things they produced with other people, for that goodness always derives much more power from where people sit than what they are.

Back in 1755, Jean-Jacques Rousseau could write, without fear of contradiction, that the suggestion that "strength . . . wisdom or virtue are always to be found in individuals, in the same proportion with power or riches" is "a question fit perhaps to be discussed by slaves in the hearing of their masters, but unbecoming free and reasonable beings in quest of truth."[11] What a difference a couple of centuries makes! Not long ago, Bill Gates was invited to play chess with Magnus Carlsen, the reigning world chess champion. Why? Because Bill Gates is about million times

richer than the average American—so he must be a million times better in chess. (He lost in twelve seconds.) In a recent interview, Warren
Buffett, the billionaire investor who has attained oracle status, joked
that he would be interested in receiving a blood transfusion from one
greater than he, namely, the almighty Jeff Bezos.[12] This is not funny,
Warren. This is not the way that free and reasonable beings converse.

When the British labor leader and politician Michael Young came
up with the word "meritocracy" in 1958, he famously coined the term
in the spirit of satire.[13] Surely no one would actively embrace the idea
that wealth and power in society are distributed precisely in accordance with this "merit" thing. Couldn't everyone see that the point of
merit is to hold power accountable, not to supply yet another excuse
for unaccountable power? As Young himself lamented in his last years,
the joke was on him.[14]

The question with which any anthropology of the gusher must
begin, then, is just this: Why are so many people so convinced of a
theory that is so palpably wrong? What exactly makes us think we are
so smart? More generally, how did the 9.9 percent manage to turn a
sensible, foundational postulate of liberal democracy into a preposterous
doctrine concerning the distribution of wealth? The purpose of such
an investigation of the mind of the 9.9 percent is to shed some light
on the actual origins of the kind of meritocracy we have today, and
the results, I think, will have practical implications. The reigning view
among those who live by the code of the 9.9 percent, seconded by all of
the gurus and most of the critics, says that meritocracy is the cause of
inequality. We're just too damned smart for the world to handle! But a
proper investigation will show that the merit myth is an effect of rising
inequality, not the cause.

Before elaborating on that argument, however, it is important to
explore a little further one particular aspect of the merit myth. It has to
do with the "sweat" part of the brain-sweat theory—that is, the extraordinary work ethic, not to say workaholism, that seeps through every
pore of the stories that 9.9 percenters tell about themselves. This part
of the story is so familiar today that we forget just how strange it is. It
is perfectly possible, after all, to imagine a world where the reward for

being smart is that you don't have to work so hard. The need to sand away the unsettling edges of this reality of life in the 9.9 percent today is so great that it motivates a whole subgenre of speculative myth making about the origins of the insane work ethic of modern times, much of which invokes imaginary religious and cultural narratives, and almost all of which may be safely confined to the genre of bedtime fiction.

AFTER THE BEER TEST—assuming you pass it—comes another, critical, ongoing evaluation procedure in that rigorous, meritocratic thing. It is a continuation of the beer test, in a certain sense, only now it involves a variety of Kool-Aid. I prefer to think of it as the "absence-of-life" test. The point is to demonstrate that you cannot conceive of a meaningful existence outside the firm. The best way to pass the test is never to leave your desk during waking hours, even if this means impersonating a potted plant. Just to be sure, you'll want to send out some lengthy emails when you get "home" at 2 a.m. If you do plan to pursue extramural friendships, get married, or have children out of firm-lock, make sure to clear it with your real family first, in the office, maybe in between meetings.

The absence-of-life test, of course, is all about the sweaty side of the merit myth. To be a member of the vanguard of the 9.9 percent is to imagine that one belongs to a cadre of laborers distinguished not just by their hypertested intelligence and exquisite training but by their inhuman capacity for brain-busting hours of on-screen toil. "The rich increasingly, and now overwhelmingly, owe their massive incomes to selling their own labor—to long, intensive, and exceptionally remunerative work," explains Daniel Markovits, who weirdly seems to think that restating the dogmas of the meritocracy amounts to critiquing them.[15]

This disappearance of human life into the working life of the 9.9 percent is now significant enough that it has left discernible traces in the aggregate data.[16] Back in 1980, the highest-income men, not surprisingly, worked almost four hours less than the average worker. The point of having the extra money, it was widely agreed, was to golf. By 2005, however, the higher-income men were putting in almost three hours more than average at the office. A similar pattern is observable among workers with high educational attainment. Between 1995 and 2010, men with a college degree gave up 2.5 hours in leisure time and women college graduates lost two hours per week—even as their compensation stagnated. At the professional services firms that now mark the culmination of a successful Ivy League career, the numbers, though mainly available through anecdote, are undoubtedly much more alarming. Bankers used to be famous for cruising off to the links at 3 p.m. and reaching for the martinis at 5 p.m. Now, at top financial services firms, fifty-hour weeks count almost as vacation time. Among consultants, the standard expectation is closer to sixty or seventy hours. Associates at law firms and hedge funds routinely log ninety or one hundred hours—and more, if one counts the after-hours screen time. In 2013, a young investment banker named Moritz Erhardt worked three days and nights in a row, returning home only to shower and change—and on the third day, he died.[17]

And yet, to state what would be obvious to any sentient potted plant, the most remarkable aspect of this extreme work ethic is not how productive it is but how unproductive. One study confirms that productivity starts to drop after fifty hours of work per week, and after fifty-five it approaches zero.[18] At around seventy hours, the negative health effects are alarming enough that the CDC treats the practice as it would an infectious disease.[19] Internal research at audit firm EY shows that employees who take more vacation time perform better at work—and yet 40 percent of American workers do not use all their vacation days.[20] Exactly why the free market would tolerate such inefficiencies is a subject best left for a later chapter (hint: it ain't free). The important thing to note here is the order of causes. The paid-up members of the 9.9 percent do not earn high pay *because* they work long hours, as confused commentators seem to think; they work long hours because they have high-paying jobs.

The extra hours, as those who have taken the absence-of-life test know very well, are performative. They are there not to get something done but to prove a point. The obvious part of the point is to manifest the unconditional, strip-me-naked-and-tie-me-to-the-grindstone level of commitment that an employer with access to streams of gusher money may demand in exchange for sharing those market rents with you in particular as opposed to the next fanatical overachiever on the list. It's the less obvious part of the point—the one intended to convince oneself—that is more concerning. This is the part that involves saying—and believing—that "this Kool-Aid tastes great!"

For a growing segment of the 9.9 percent, the new class motto appears to be: "Thank God It's Monday!"[21] The strange development in the office zeitgeist, as one wag noticed, was ably captured in the message carved in the cucumbers at the water station in a WeWork office: "Don't stop working when you are tired. Stop when you are done!" (Really, as one wit pointed out, who needs metaphors when the cucumber in the water is literally telling you to drink it now!)

To add to the mystery, the passion for toil afflicts many individuals whose prospects for redemption at the office are sadly unrealistic. As writers such as Erin Griffith and Derek Thompson have observed, the religion of "workism" is rampant among millennials in particular—the worst-paid generation in recent history. At leading professional firms like McKinsey, it hits young associates hardest, and yet the vast majority of these associates will not make partner and thus, though assured of membership in the middle ranks of the 9.9%, will have difficulty crawling into that last 0.9 percent of glory at the top of their class.

THIS IS A SITUATION THAT SEEMS TO BE begging for an old-fashioned, French existentialist critique. Jean-Paul Sartre (who believed that there is no philosophical problem that cannot be solved with a filter-less cigarette and a stiff espresso) anticipates the issue with his description of a waiter-impersonating-a-waiter at the local café.[22] What exactly is so disturbing about this overly waiterly waiter? His voice is too eager, his demeanor too rigid. "His movement is quick and forward, a little too precise, a little too rapid." He is trying to turn himself into "some kind of automaton"! He is a free being by nature—as he demonstrates by his very own choice to impersonate a robot—and yet he is attempting to turn himself into the zombie instrument of a superior power. This, says the superior power (embodied in this instance by Jean-Paul himself, sitting grouchily at his corner table in the ill-fitting overcoat) is what it means to act in "bad faith." Today, Jean-Paul would not need to take the elevator down to the company café. He could wander the cubicles, where these self-subordinating waiters are all bumping into each other like robots as they eagerly serve up their ingratiating PowerPoint slides. At Amazon headquarters, famously, they are known as "Amabots."[23]

The emergence of this new sensibility did not happen overnight or by accident. A brief detour away from the café and into the eerie, Möbius strip trajectory of management theory over the past century helps make this clear. In the middle decades of the twentieth century, after Frederick Winslow Taylor threatened to reduce manual laborers to mindless drones with his fanatical efficiency studies of (supposedly) scientific management, a humanistic strain of management thought arose out of a desire to remind everyone that humans are, well, human. This school achieved a kind of popular breakthrough in Tom Peters and Bob Waterman's 1982 blockbuster, *In Search of Excellence*, which, in Peters's summation, conveys the message that "treating people . . . as the natural resources may be the key to it all." *Excellence* hews closely to the formulas of the self-help genre, which means that it passes off a list of eight platitudinous exhortations as a set of surefire principles of success, and then insists that you, too, can be rich/famous/an excellent corporation if you will just put your mind to it. (Frankly, Napoleon Hill had said it all before in his 1937 title: *Think and Grow Rich*.)

It was all harmless stuff, easy enough to laugh off, and it made for an excellent graduation-day gift. As the critics soon noted, the "research" on which the book was based did not rise far above fortune-cookie levels, and the forty-three companies that it exalted as paragons of excellence began to underperform the market almost immediately upon being named.[24] Peters himself had the sense to acknowledge that the vaunted principles of success, true to the self-help method, were basically "motherhoods." (In a frank moment, he used the word "baloney."[25]) But the person who got the last laugh, as it turns out, was a young man who happened to graduate from high school in the same year that *Excellence* was published: Jeff Bezos.

In the early twenty-first century, as Amazon began to consolidate its dominance of the online retail sector, the company distilled its founder's wisdom into a list of fourteen principles. Amazonians (the ones in air-conditioned office towers, not the ones in the warehouses who don't have to fake the robot thing because everyone is pretty sure that they are robots) are now schooled in this corporate catechism. Some of them reportedly take the doctrines home and teach them to their children. Yet the most memorable of these principles read as if lifted from some subconscious memory of Peters and Waterman's book. *Excellence* demands "a bias for action" and Amazon demands "a bias for action." *Excellence* urges "staying close to the customer," and Amazon preaches "customer obsession." *Excellence* promotes "productivity through people," and Amazon wants to "hire and develop the best" people. Maybe the key to it all is the principle that *Excellence* calls "autonomy and entrepreneurship" and Amazon translates as "ownership."

Self-help is always ultimately about taking ownership of your own life, of course, and that sort of self-ownership is almost always a beautiful thing. But when the demand for self-ownership comes down at you like a ton of packaged goods from the person who actually owns the company, it takes on a rather different color. The way to become a successful Amazonian is to shuffle off your birth identity and act as if you were the owner of the firm—even though you are not, in fact, the owner but the owned. Now that you are the "self-owner" in this virtual sense, you will have no tolerance for those employees who fail to take ownership. This is why Amazonians police one another in a process they call "purposeful Darwinism."[26] It may also explain why, when they move on to other firms, they are often described as "Amholes." Owners also obsess about customers because, let's face it, obsessing about suppliers would involve thinking about people who supply labor, and that's just costly.

Considered in the broad sweep of management history, the ideological achievement of Amazon and its kindred leviathans is to have transformed the human relations school of management thought into a white-collar version of Taylorism. The new efficiency mantra is about optimizing the professional soul, channeling its needs and desires so as to minimize disobedience and maximize productivity. It operates in parallel with the more traditional, blue-collar Taylorism with which Amazon engineers every movement and bathroom break of its warehouse workers in order to turn them, too, into the happy instruments of world domination. Let's call it "The 15th Principle" and tack it onto Amazon's fourteen. It says:

Work hard so that you can work harder!

Maybe the surest sign that the 15th Principle has run amok and destroyed some aspect of consciousness in the new, white-collar world of the 9.9 percent is the dialectic of narcissism and despair that rages through many modern workplaces. Up at the commanding heights of the feudal corporation, the process of self-objectification has delivered tremendous rewards to a lucky few, and the few consequently find it all but impossible to distinguish their actual worth from that of the fictional beings that have amassed so much perceived merit. Sometimes they go out and hire people just to remind themselves of how great this person that they are impersonating really is. This is why modern offices often fill up with a category of workers who may as well be called ego whisperers.[27] Since the whisperers only make one hundredth what the CEO makes, you can actually hire several of them and still make a profit, so long as they add that extra margin of ego-satisfying productivity at the peak.

Then there is the inexplicable fear that seems to course through the cubicles. Step into one of the offices of McKinsey or Amazon, or any other firm that makes use of the absence-of-life test, and you can almost smell the paradox. With your eyes you will take in some of the most advantaged people in the world: the gifted, the talented, and the lucky, the beneficiaries of the best educational experiences and the finest parenting, impeccably dressed and coiffed, gathered around the most tasteful office furniture, and sheathed in dazzling layers of self-confidence. And yet, with your other senses, you will detect a malodorous miasma of anxiety and insecurity, of superstition and self-disgust. It's not enough to make you pity them (their paychecks will cover plenty of therapy, after all). But it has to make you wonder. It's almost as if they work so hard just so that they can feel crappy about themselves.

The lead partners of consulting firms, by the way, understand this self-subordination thing well. They are well into the "meta" level of this particular development in organizational psychology. To paraphrase a comment passed along from Roland Berger, a McKinsey alumnus who built up his own large consulting firm, consulting is really a branch of the lemonade business. You find anxious overachievers and bring them in with what they think is a lot of money and a few tokens of prestige. Then you squeeze them like lemons and toss out the rinds.[28]

It is worth emphasizing again just how anomalous this lemon-tree aspect of life in the meritocracyis. The traditional view, memorialized in stories about the kind of summer vacations that we no longer have the time to enjoy, said that the point of having wealth was *not* having to toil. As a number of students of the current madness have already noted, this is the commonsensical assumption that the brilliant economist John Maynard Keynes did not even bother to articulate when in 1930 he famously forecast that the fifteen-hour workweek was just a few generations around the corner. What else could be the purpose of automation? "For the first time since his creation, man will be faced with his real, his permanent problem: how to occupy the leisure," said Keynes.[29] It turns out the permanent problem is more about what to do with that bucket of lemon rinds. Which underscores the mystery of the merit myth all over again: if we are so smart, how did we manage to enslave ourselves?

Faced with this enigma of the lemon tree, those contemporary critics who manage to rise at least an inch or two above the prevailing dogma typically fall back on religious fables to explain away the paradox. The crazed work ethic of modern meritocrats goes back to crypto-theological doctrines purportedly descended from a particular line of northern European Protestants or some such group allegedly responsible for modern capitalism. Max Weber is the grandfather of all such narratives, though latter-day epigones have never been in short supply. There is a certain circularity in these fables: they explain one set of strange beliefs in terms of another. There is also something thoughtlessly ethnocentric about them: now that versions of the meritocratic system are spreading through East and South Asia, can we still chalk it all up to a handful of uptight Dutch Calvinists? Fortunately, these stories can be set aside with some further investigation, for it turns out that they simply confuse cause and effect. The deranged work ethic of the 9.9 percent is mostly the consequence of the economic conditions from which it arises, not the cause. It is one of the ways in which inequality makes us all unreasonable. In order see how this happens, however, it is necessary to take a deeper look at the mathematical foundations—more exactly, the mathematical absurdities—of the merit myth.

ONE OF THE THINGS YOU LEARN as a management consultant is that humans aren't very good at math. A big part of the business is just doing the math others can't do (or more often, for interesting reasons, won't do). Another thing you learn: if you turn the mathematical tables on the management consulting business itself, it more or less self-combusts. I mean, the math that consultants use offers a great way to understand why the business as they like to describe it on campus and to less well-informed clients cannot actually exist. As a matter of fact, at my old firm, we built a business that succeeded, for a time, by betting against the mathematical misperceptions at the heart of the consulting business. The important point here, though, is that the same mathematical misperceptions are the crooked timber out of which the merit myth is constructed in the first place.

Let's take a closer look at some open secrets about addition and subtraction at a firm like McKinsey. Say you start with the 40,000 young people who apply to Harvard every year—a bright, ambitious, and mostly wealthy group that are likely to have the intellectual gifts and drive for work that a consulting firm might seek. Right away you vaporize 38,000 of them because they didn't get into Harvard. Amazingly, about half of the special 1,600 or so of those who matriculate and graduate from Harvard choose to enter the consulting job interview process. But the typical firm makes offers to only about 1 in 20 candidates. So now you're now down from 40,0000 to 40. But the meritocracy doesn't stop once they pass through the door. After two years on the job, one in every three of these extraordinarily meritorious individuals is "counseled" right back out the door. Two years later, another round of expulsions reduces the numbers in similar proportion. The culling continues until, ten years in, you are left with a single winner.

Now take a look at the financial rewards, which follow an even more extreme curve in the opposite direction. Your winner will be making (order of magnitude) $10 million per year. One or two also-rans will be on $1 million. The people at the bottom of the pyramid will get about $100,000. What happens to the other 39,960 people is anybody's guess, but it probably starts below the median national income, or roughly half of what those young consultants get on their first day of work.

According to the merit myth, the world-class genius at the top of this scheme has 10 times as much "human capital"—or works it 10 times as hard—as the humans one step down the pyramid. He (about 90 percent of the time) has 100 times as much of the right stuff as the ones who took the job just 10 years previously, each of whom must have considerably more whatever-it-is-ness than the 1,000 hopefuls they beat out from the Harvard applicant pool. This is evidently what some partners at McKinsey have come to believe. In press reports on the firm, there is always a McKinsey man who stands up and says something along the lines of: "This is the greatest collection of talent that the world has ever seen!"

Now you have a choice. Either you believe McKinsey Man. Or you figure that he is full of the stuff that cash-camels dump all over the deserts of Central Asia. Now, to be fair, if you were McKinsey Man, that stuff left in the sands would shine with the luster of a thousand suns. Because you would have been told every quarter every year since you were about thirteen years old that you are the sparkle in the teacher's eye, and you will have proven yourself more brilliant than thousands of competitors in one stuff-polishing competition after another. On the other hand, the math doesn't really care about your need for affirmation. The numbers are the numbers. The merit myth has a math problem.

In order to see exactly where the math goes bad, it's helpful to distinguish two ideas that are often wrapped up in one in any conversation about meritocracy. The merit myth promises both that the best people will rise to the top and that rewards will be commensurate with merit. When people complain about the injustices of the meritocracy, they're usually focused on the first of these promises. They rightly worry that many good eggs were tossed out in the slog up the pyramid, and they obsess about the injustices of the various selection processes. When champions of meritocracy defend their world, they, too, focus on the selection mechanisms, though they insist that the competition was mostly free and fair. Both concentrate on the question: who wins? But it is the other part of the meritocratic promise that raises a mathematically more challenging question: How much do they win?

If an individual's personal merit is to predict and produce wealth, it must be measurable in some way, in advance of, and apart from, simply making money. If merit is a property of individual human beings (including the investments in training allegedly lodged within them), it follows that it should behave in roughly the same way that other variable attributes of humans do. Human beings do in fact come in a variety of shapes and sizes and they possess very different qualities and accumulated skills. Some find joy in grinding out sixteen hours of work a day, some are ready to call it quits around lunchtime. Some run faster than others, some score higher on multiple-choice tests, and some perform much better than others in popularity contests, measures of emotional intelligence, and conversational skill. It would seem perfectly natural, and, setting aside questions of need, not in any obvious way unjust, that wealth and income might be unevenly distributed in the same way that all these other attributes are unevenly distributed. It would also seem a good thing to distribute rewards unevenly in regards to effort in particular (up to a point), insofar as this may tend to motivate individuals to maximize the use of their talents. So far, so boring.

Here is where the math gets interesting. Almost all such attributes of human beings, and arguably any that we might want to associate with merit, stay within certain ranges and fall to earth in what mathematicians call a "normal" or Gaussian distribution, also known informally as the "bell curve." The pattern pops up throughout the biological and physical sciences, and it works for human height, weight, IQ scores, indices of emotional intelligence, tolerance for pain, sleeping time, and more. To skip the warmed-over high school math, the resulting curve looks like, well, a bell, of the old liberty type. It generally shows a large, rounded mound of observations concentrated around the mean with slopes flattening out at the ends in a predictable mathematical relation to distance from the mean.

But income and wealth are not distributed in this way at all—not even close. As the nineteenth-century Italian sociologist Vilfredo Pareto observed, money generally follows a power-law distribution. In a power-law distribution, the proportion of the population diminishes as an exponential function of distance from the origin. It might tell us, for example, that for every 1,000 people with $100,000 saved up, there will be 100 with $1,000,000, 10 with $10,000,000 and 1 with $100,000,000— which is actually pretty darn close to the distribution of wealth in the United States today, as it happens. The same curve shows up almost everywhere that money has existed, from ancient Sumer and Mycenae to modern Russia. The critical fact is that it doesn't look like a bell at all. It's more like a ski slope of the supersteep, double black-diamond variety. About 90 percent of the population is crammed into a cliff at the left, while a tiny number coast off on a line that goes on to infinity.[30]

The upshot of the math is that, even if we solved the "who wins?" problem and managed to assign the highest reward to the smartest individual and so on down the line—a rather preposterous "if" to begin with—there would still be no proportion in any known economy between individual merit and reward. At the far end of the ski slope, microscopic differences in merit would correspond to massive differences in reward, while on the crowded cliff significant differences in merit would produce negligible changes in reward. Now add a dose of reality about just who exactly does slither to the top of that greasy pyramid and there is no reason to think that the distribution of merit will map onto the distribution of wealth in anything but the crudest and most approximate terms.

This is pretty much what sociologists and economists in fact observe whenever they attempt to study links between measures of merit and money: a crude correlation notable mainly for what it doesn't explain. In a detailed analysis of what would happen if people were paid according to traits that ostensibly measure merit, including cognitive ability, years of experience and education, conscientiousness, emotional stability, and more, Jonathan Rothwell finds that the Gini coefficient, a statistical measure of inequality, would plummet from 0.44 (the approximate level in the United States now) to 0.19 (below the level in any modern country).[31] As regards the actual match between intelligence measures and the distribution of wealth and income, a typical study shows that having an IQ in the top 2 percent makes zero difference in levels of wealth, though it is worth an extra $18,000 in income.[32] Apart from suggesting that smart people are bad savers, this is sad. Having an income (as opposed to an intelligence) in the top 2 percent is worth on average closer to $500,000 per year. So where is the other $482,000, Mensa man?

Most interpreters use this math to underscore the fact that luck plays a huge role in life. That's true enough, but it tells only the least interesting part of the story. Peeking out from the math is a much more profound challenge to the preconceptions about the origins of wealth tucked away inside the crackly wrapper of the merit myth. If wealth were the creation of individuals alone—even if it were the result of their ability to cheat and steal from one another—it would fall to earth in the shape of a bell curve. It would not land in the form of an insane ski slope. It would only do that if money were subject to some other force, like some kind of magnetic attraction of money for money, so that clumps of it might stick together and accumulate into ever larger clumps while they are still up there in the sky, long before they come within reach of the grasping hands of individual human beings. There must be some force that has nothing in particular to do with any of us and yet makes us collectively richer and then scatters the riches with sublime indifference to individual distinctions. What could it be?

AT A VERY ABSTRACT LEVEL, the math reveals a simple philosophical truth. The creation of wealth does not answer to the merit of individuals because individuals don't create most wealth. Groups of individuals create wealth. They do so partly by making best use of the unique talents that individuals possess and partly by establishing forms of cooperation that have nothing to do with the unique attributes of any given individual. This is the force that is hidden in the strange math of the power-law distribution of economic rewards.

The same conclusion about the interpersonal origins of wealth, paradoxically, follows from the fact that so much of the wealth is clearly distributed according to criteria that have no plausible connection with personal merit. If individual merit considered in isolation were the source of wealth, then excluding more than half of the population from realizing their potential on account of their sex or skin color would be like sabotaging more than half of all factories or making more than half of all homes uninhabitable. And it is bad—but not that bad (speaking only of immediate economic consequences). The economy is surprisingly, perhaps shockingly, indifferent to merit because, in part, merit is seriously overrated as a factor of production in many occupations. A banker can get by with limited talent for poetry; a truck driver can only be so good at driving trucks. It is also indifferent to merit because, in part, where merit does matter, it generally exists in immense oversupply. That's why we can afford to waste so much of it on the beer test or other, worse forms of discrimination. Mostly, the economy doesn't care that much about merit because merit isn't a factor at all in much of wealth creation. To the extent that wealth comes from networks of cooperation that extend across all of society, any individual will do, as long as they are willing to join the team.

The practice of rewarding merit can still be a very good thing in the right context, to be clear. But it is not principally a means of realizing the value of individual assets, as the purveyors of human capital theories seem to think. It is one of many useful tools for advancing cooperation among individuals. It amounts to a promise that power will be exercised reasonably and that contributions will be judged fairly and according to standards open to public scrutiny. The universal embrace of that essentially democratic promise is the actual foundation for wealth creation. The merit myth promotes the falsehood that talent is the origin of wealth—but a genuine meritocracy rests on the truth that justice is the origin of all wealth. Call this the Golden Rule of Merit.

The Golden Rule of Merit, paradoxically, points in a general way to the source of trouble in a society that pretends to decide the distribution of rewards entirely on the basis of supposedly individual merit. The fundamental problem in such pseudo-meritocracies is not that those with "lucky" genes win out over the unlucky, or that the "strong" crush the "weak," or that the smart people act like meanies to the dummies, as the self-congratulatory chest-beatings of meritocracy's pseudo-critics would suggest. The problem is that such systems involve the radical overestimation of individual contributions to wealth, and thus they inevitably cheat the many to reward the few. More than that, they necessarily concoct false measures of merit and demerit, of strength and weakness, and of good and bad luck, and then they encourage everyone in society to organize their values and desires around these fictional measures of imaginary wealth. The root of the trouble, in short, is that societies in the grip of the merit myth become unreasonable.

WE CAN GET MORE PRECISE about the nature of this irrationality in meritocratic systems with a final, closer look at the innermost chamber of the mathematical delusions that are the twisted scaffolding of the mind of the 9.9 percent. The crux of the matter has to do with the impact of rising inequality on our two statistical curves—and on the way in which those curves are then misperceived by the people who live within them. (Yes, this is going to get just a little abstract—but that is because the root of our problems lies in our refusal to face the math.)

Start with the fact that, when an economy becomes more unequal, the Gaussian distribution of individual attributes is not likely to change its shape. People are still people, and so the bell remains a bell. The power-law curve that describes the distribution of rewards, on the other hand, does change. It gets steeper on the starting slope and longer in the run to glory. Eventually, it's just a cliff and interstellar space—a mass of uniformly poor people and a tiny handful of super-rich individuals. Thus, the two curves move ever farther apart; that is, the distribution of talent becomes ever more disconnected from the distribution of wealth. This is the first, critical fact to bear in mind in times of rising inequality: the more unequal a society becomes, the less that individual merit can actually explain differences in reward.

Now consider what happens to human beings' perceptions of merit as inequality rises. The humans I know are mostly wonderful people, but they often fail to distinguish clearly between what they worked for and the good things that came their way. They are also not so good at seeing the difference between the character flaws of other people and the bad things that happen to them. In general, they calibrate the range of individual merit, and gauge their own success within that range, in terms of range of outcomes they see in experience. If some people are ten times as rich as other people, they tend to infer, then some people must be ten times as smart or ten times as tall as other people. As inequality rises, moreover, the competition for prizes naturally intensifies, even as the number of winners goes down, and this only serves to amplify the perceived value of merit. Humans routinely conflate the amount of effort it takes to land a spot next to the gusher with the value of the green stuff collected there. "I got here first!" is what passes for moral reasoning among many members of the species. (There is plenty of psychological research to back up all of these familiar insights into the shortcomings of human cognitive faculties.)[33]

It's important to emphasize that this delusion about the rising value of merit affects even—and perhaps especially—the people who are on the losing end of the merit spectrum. As one study confirms, "lower-income individuals are less likely to reject the meritocratic ideal where economic inequality is greater."[34] This may be why suicide rates are higher in more unequal times and places, regardless of aggregate wealth:[35] because individuals confuse their relatively low price in the market with a measure of their actual worth.

It is also worth adding that the merit delusion is bound to be greater in times of rising inequality as opposed to times of high but constant inequality because human beings tend to base their perceptions of value on what they remember from high school. Anyone who has heard a baby boomer lecture a millennial about how all it takes to succeed is to get off the couch and show up early at work will know this to be true.

This overestimation of merit in times of rising inequality leaves its most consequential trace on those individuals and institutions that serve as the gatekeepers of merit. With rising inequality, as we already know, the administrators of the beer test suddenly find themselves beset with hordes of expert beer swillers. Do they then toss aside the pretense of merit and admit that their meritocracy is actually just a high-stakes drinking game? No, they do not. They invent new and ever more stringent tests of merit. They'll want to see you drink that beer while standing on your head and dictating tasting notes. The escalation of merit tests then sets up a further, positive feedback loop in the minds of the meritorious. As a rule, humans measure the social value of their own job in terms of the number of people they had to clear out of the way to get it. Of course I deserve the job/spot at Elite U., the winners will exclaim; it took me years to master the art of upside-down beer tasting!

Now, put this second, critical fact about the perceptions of merit in times of rising inequality together with the first fact about the decreasing explanatory value of merit in times of rising inequality, and you have the Iron Law of Merit:

The more that merit seems to matter, the less it actually explains.

This law is made of iron because its implications are cold and hard. It describes a process that moves in only one direction: from bad to worse. It represents a certain kind of unraveling of consciousness. It is the fundamental principle of the anthropology of the gusher and the key to the mind of the 9.9 percent.

The Iron Law, it is hoped, may help us understand some specific aspects of life among those who live by the Creed of the 9.9 percent today. The orchid-compost paradox, for example, undoubtedly reflects the fact that, in times of rising inequality, the definition of merit will inevitably rise to orchid-levels of sophistication, even as the work to which the orchids are entitled by virtue of their exquisite cultivation becomes increasingly extractive and exploitative.

The extreme work ethic of the 9.9 percent is also a consequence of the Iron Law. The thing that Jean-Paul Sartre, along with many well-meaning critics of the meritocracy, didn't get is that the waiterly robot syndrome is not a universal constant of the human condition any more than the postwar Parisian café is. Bad faith grows with the disparities in power and rising misperceptions of value described in the Iron Law.

Particularly worth bearing in mind is that the Iron Law operates at all levels of the inequality spectrum. Even those near the top begin to perceive immense heights of merit above and gloomy abysses of demerit below, and thus everyone develops some sense of inadequacy. Every trace of remaining consciousness, however subliminal, whispers in the other ear of these desperate creatures that whatever success they have achieved cannot actually be due to their own individual merit. So they double down on the one variable they can control in life, which is their sweat levels, and impersonate the person they see through the gaze of their superiors. The Iron Law stands at the beginning of the slave morality.

The Iron Law may also explain why the merit myth disproportionately afflicts the white-collar classes in times of rising inequality. When people produce useful physical objects, like a piece of furniture, or they provide a direct service to others, like cleaning a house or delivering a package, the nature and degree of merit involved is typically hard to fudge. In the more deskbound occupations, on the other hand, fudge is always in plentiful supply, and it accumulates fastest of all in those professions that get to judge their own merit. In times of rising inequality, those people who *are* what they *do* are also the most likely to suffer from delusions about the meritoriousness of their work.

Perhaps the most useful aspect of the Iron Law for future anthropologists is that it may help us understand why meritocracy—born of the highest ideals of liberal democracy—so often turns into the handmaiden of autocracy. There is a false impression—perhaps unintentionally encouraged in Michael Young's otherwise prescient critique of meritocracy and often seconded by both the critics and the champions of the merit class today—that the grim end state of meritocracy is a land where the cognitive elite have captured the levers of power and established a futuristic tyranny of the brainy. The scene often involves Harvard graduates torturing resentful essential workers for sport before roasting them for afternoon snacks. In fact, the grim end state is much tawdrier and more pedestrian than that, and it doesn't make for great sci-fi. From the Iron Law of Merit, it follows not just that the wealthy and powerful will be perceived as having merit, but that whatever the people at the top happen to desire will take on the character of merit. Thus, the greater the inequality, the more that merit becomes synonymous with "whatever the boss wants." The triumph of meritocracy arrives when kleptocratic thugs have captured all of the eggheads and turned them into an omelet to be consumed on the Silk Road, as it were. The process is underway today and easily visible, up there on the rim of that crater where McKinsey consecrated its union with the authoritarian governments of the world.

SURVEYING THE MERITOCRACY PHENOMENON and its role in the rise of the 9.9 percent from a distance, it isn't hard to see that it represents a more general truth about the way in which inequality impacts human societies. The Iron Law is really just one example of a breakdown in the human faculties of moral cognition under the condition of extreme inequality. Some other examples have been covered in the preceding chapters, and the worst is yet to come, but it's worth outlining the general point here, since it is the main point of this book.

Human beings are "moral animals"—that is, they may be said to have faculties of moral cognition—in this limited sense: they come with certain instincts or preconfigured heuristics that permit the easy and rapid identification of and response to morally relevant features of the human landscape. They know, or think they know, how to identify a cheater, to know a friend, to distinguish a good deed from a bad one, and what it means to work, and their moral emotions follow immediately upon these acts of (pseudo)cognition. They no sooner feel that they have spotted the cheater than they feel the urge to nail him; they no sooner perform a good service than they feel entitled to a pat and a paycheck. Our moral emotions are mostly shortcuts to human collaboration. They are in this sense generally reasonable. But—crucial proviso—they take for granted certain understandings of the world and answer to reason only so long as conditions in the world match those understandings.

Most of these natural heuristics of the moral imagination were formed under the condition of relative equality, and they can be counted upon to yield useful actions only under that condition. This is the great anthropological truth that underwrites the Iron Law of Merit. In the tens of thousands of generations before history began, the ancestral village had 150 members, or so the anthropological evidence indicates. Consequently, no individuals were in a position to amass "Pareto-level" power in a Gaussian curve population. Natural selection therefore had no basis to select for those individuals who could distinguish between the effects of a Pareto curve and the effects of a Gaussian curve. The moral heuristics that supply the inherited part of the human moral imagination generally follow a tit-for-tat logic because in the ancestral world, the tits and tats were all roughly equal in dimensions.

When these same heuristics are applied in contexts very different from that original condition, however, they become incoherent. So, for example, actions that, were they to have been performed among named individuals, would count as moral outrages, when conducted at the level of communities so large that they exist only in the imagination, are routinely considered blameless, if not exalted in the name of religion. If you rob one person, you are a criminal; if you rob a couple billion people you may find yourself hailed on the magazine covers as one of the gods of the free market in social media. If you build a nice restaurant on the corner, you are an upstanding member of the local business community; if you corner the global market in retail e-commerce platforms, you are Atlas, the mighty upholder of the heavens.

In brief, under extreme inequality, human beings can no longer make moral sense of the world, and so they deploy the extremely powerful emotions of morality in perverse and ultimately self-destructive ways. To sum it up in a simple thesis:

Human beings are not built to function in a radically unequal world.

The way to get human beings to treat one another as moral equals is to make them moral equals on the ground, just as the way to make them reasonable in their ways of thinking is to make them reasonable in the relations they have with one another.

THERE ARE A NUMBER OF PRACTICAL IMPLICATIONS, though they differ from the remedies proposed by many contemporary critics of meritocracy. Most of the critics today take for granted that the solution to the problems of the merit myth is to adjust reality to fit the demands of the myth. So they expend their rhetorical energy trying to make sure that everyone's merit is measured on exactly equal terms and no one gets an unfair advantage in the increasingly competitive race to the top. But all such well-meaning efforts amount to treating the symptoms, not the disease.

The very idea that society should be organized so as to allocate wealth in ever more exact proportion to individual attributes is itself one of the delusions that arises in times of inequality. The more equal and just a society is, on the other hand, the more that people understand how much they owe one another for their actual well-being. The best way to stop Harvard graduates from trying to eat essential workers for lunch is not to tell the first to be nicer to the second, nor to allow a trickle of lucky individuals to flow from the second to the first, but to ensure that both are compensated in ways that reflect the fact that in a just society every human being is essential. A good place to start would be to break up the professional guilds that have inflated white-collar salaries, and to restore the collective bargaining power that would allow blue- and pink-collar workers to negotiate a fair share of the wealth. In short, the problem with meritocracy is inequality, and the solution is equality.

But we do not need to wait for economic justice before taking steps to dispel the merit myth and restore something closer to a genuine meritocracy that serves as a check on unaccountable power. It may be useful in this context to think of the system for allocating prestige in society as a market in its own right. In times of rising inequality, the Iron Law tells us, this market for prestige becomes corrupt. It packages up false measures of merit and then trades them off for cold cash. Direct interventions in the prestige market may help to make it answer to the public good (even if they cannot in themselves correct for the economic injustices that are the root of the problem).

In the land of the 9.9 percent, to get more concrete, the principal factories of prestige are the elite universities, and they have contributed to the corruption of the prestige market in three fundamental ways. First, in service of their own institutional needs, they have artificially constrained the supply of merit and thus inflated its value. Second, they have colluded with oligopolists in the financial services and corporate world to convert the scholarly merit in which they rightly specialize into an alleged business or managerial merit that is made of pure baloney. Third, they have contributed through inaction to the false idea that a college education alone can provide citizens with a claim to the equal dignity to which all humans are entitled.

The answer to the first problem is straightforward. Universities should accept everyone who is qualified to make good use of their services according to public and transparent criteria. If they cannot bring themselves to expand to satisfy this requirement, they should offer places to the pool of qualified candidates by public lottery. The best way to bring the perceived value of a Harvard degree in line with its actual value—and to underscore the public responsibility that should come with it—would be to distinguish clearly and visibly between the many people who deserve a spot and the lucky few who get one.

The answer to the second problem is to kick the investment banks and other consumers of manufactured prestige out of the dormitories. If universities exist to promote the pursuit of truth for the public good—that is what the mottos always say, isn't it?—then they should be working to place their graduates in those careers that actually involve using knowledge for the public good. It's time to dismantle the elite-university-to-professional-services pipeline—that strange obverse of the school-to-prison pipeline at the other end of the inequality spectrum—and bring back the Wisconsin Idea.

The answer to the final problem falls less on the colleges themselves than on those who live by the idea of the 9.9 percent. Higher education is a wonderful thing for those who can make use of it, just as careers in financial services are not entirely without redeeming value for humanity. But we need to accept that there are and ought to be many other ways to contribute to the common good and thus to achieve the dignity that is due to all who perform essential services for society. It is a fact, not merely a moral wish or college motto, that the freedom of each depends on the mutual respect of all, and it rests on us to recognize this fact.

Why We Make So Much Money

My neighbor Marty is a believer. According to his religion, there is only one measure of truth, and it is the Dow Jones Industrial Average. The way to tell if the country is doing well is to look at the Dow. The way to tell if a president is doing his job is to look at the Dow. The way to prove that we live in a free market, that everybody is earning what they are worth, and that business is business—is to look at the Dow. As for inequality, Marty is generally in favor of it, since rich people have almost all been proved right by the Dow. Although he doesn't want to be mean about it, he's pretty sure that poor people have failed to follow the way of the Dow.

In a weird way, Marty reminds me of my grandfather, with whom he would otherwise have had almost nothing in common. Although I just can't picture Marty spending his afternoons playing bridge at the club while punting on stocks, I can see him joining Grandfather in his religious ceremonies. Grandfather, too, believed in the Dow. So would you, if your lifetime income consisted almost entirely of an inherited portfolio of stocks. It is Marty's commitment to this particular religion that is much harder to explain.

Marty didn't inherit any money. He works for a living—pretty hard as far as I can tell. His actual stake in the stock market, to judge from his complaints about his children's tuition bills, amounts to an upper-middle-class 401(k) and an upper-middle-management position at the back end of the transaction-processing division of a large financial institution. Broadly speaking, two types of people dominate the economic life of the 9.9 percent, and Marty has a bit of both in him. On one side of the street, there are the "white coats" (or "white shoes," as the case may be): the doctors, the lawyers, the accountants, and other professionals. On the other side there are the "white collars," that is, the people who play managerial roles that you never knew existed in businesses that you had never thought about before. Together, these two types are the spiritual core and cash machine of the 9.9 percent. Marty happens to be a tilted hybrid: a white collar who occasionally puts on the not-altogether-white coat of an MBA management professional. Like most of the people in this neighborhood, in short, Marty's economic life takes place at least one or maybe two steps away from anything that looks like the kind of market that the Dow-ists claim to worship.

A curious fact about Marty is that he lives even farther from anything that looks like a rugged-individualist-market than even the typical 9.9 percenter. He works for an institution that would not have survived the last financial crisis without a massive, publicly funded bailout. He apparently spends most of his working days ordering around a team of coworkers and jockeying for desk space in an office building where the only visible market is the food court in the lobby. And even he does not believe that the "management professional" thing is anything more than boilerplate for business school brochures. No doubt we all walk around with some vague theory about how money is made and divvied up in the world, and surely all of our theories are approximate and unsubstantiated. But in Marty's case the disconnect is conspicuous and disconcerting.

Nonetheless, Marty and his fellow worshippers can find plenty of support for their system of belief from the many defenders of the status quo. In late 2009, just as investment bankers were rewarding themselves with heroic bonuses out of taxpayer subsidies for their brave work in cleaning up the mess that they themselves had made in the financial crash of the previous year, an adviser to Goldman Sachs delivered a sermon of sorts on the subject in a panel discussion at St. Paul's Cathedral in London.[1] (Yes, someone must have thought this was a good idea.) "We have to tolerate inequality as a way of achieving greater prosperity and opportunity for all," he intoned. He went on to suggest that it all went back to Jesus, who was apparently very supportive of selfishness. Around the same time, Lloyd Blankfein, the chairman of Goldman Sachs, backed up the sentiment with the suggestion that, in keeping the financial markets flowing, investment bankers were really only "doing God's work."[2]

More recently, the economic historian Deirdre McCloskey has brushed aside concerns about inequality as an unhealthy obsession with "how many yachts the L'Oréal heiress Liliane Bettencourt has."[3] Besides, McCloskey adds, "taking from the rich and giving to the poor helps only a little—and anyway expropriation is a one-time trick." In general, according to this happy line of thought, inequality, far from being a problem, is a measure of the success of the free market. It's all part of Adam Smith's plan for universal justice.[4] The concern about inequality, these luminaries suggest, is a case of misguided pity. The only real problem is what to do with the lame people who just can't manage to contribute to the great enrichment of society and the advance of the almighty Dow.

The market myth, to give it a name, is one of the great opiates of the 9.9 percent. It sits in the medicine cabinet right next to the merit myth. Relatively few 9.9 percenters mainline the stuff as much as my friend Marty does, but many more derive some comfort just from knowing it's there. It's there to give us the warm feeling that this land of white coats, white collars, and whoever it is that rides the buses answers to a single, unifying, and beneficent principle. While the merit myth tells us that we earned it because we are so smart and hardworking, the market myth says that, hey, even if we aren't all that hot, we earned it anyway because in a market guided by the Dow on high, the money you make is an exact measure of your value to society. There are versions of this idea not just in the manifestos of libertarian ideologues like Friedrich Hayek but in standard economics textbooks by Greg Mankiw and others. The market myth runs so deep in modern thought that even many of those who style themselves as critics of inequality unconsciously embrace it. They assume that because inequality seems to be rising in economies that the wealthy and their backers describe as a "free market," it is rising on account of a free market, and so they direct their fire at the very idea of a market.

EVERY RELIGION CAPTURES a little piece of the truth on the road to superstition, of course, and therefore it is now necessary to say some good things about the religion of the Dow. For example, it is quite true that markets can be good and useful things. Where the right conditions obtain—specifically, where there is a high degree of competition, where information is perfect and freely available, where participants behave rationally, and where externalities (impacts on the rest of society) are fully accounted for—markets can promote efficiency, dynamism, and innovation in human cooperation. Insofar as they grant individuals a high degree of autonomy, markets may also create a space where human beings can realize themselves and achieve a certain kind of dignity. Even better—and strangely at odds with the mystifying suggestions of economists like McCloskey and spiritually obtuse investment bankers—markets are levelers as a matter of principle, not concentrators of wealth, for competition prevents the kind of sustained excess returns that are generally required to produce massive accumulations of wealth. (This is the conclusion at which Thomas Jefferson and Thomas Paine arrived, by the way, with an assist from Adam Smith; they took for granted that the immense fortunes of European aristocrats in their time should count as evidence of the absence of competitive markets, not of their presence.)

It should also go without saying that the "free market," like the "perfect vacation," is not the kind of thing that can actually exist. It is a hypothetical construct against which one may compare, test, and measure reality—not a description of any actual or even possible reality. "Market" is not the opposite of "regulation" or "government" any more than "swim meet" is the opposite of "swimming pool." Every market needs its rules, these rules necessarily come from outside the market itself, and they aren't always written down. If by the "free market" we mean to imagine a world where rules and norms, too, are sold to the highest bidder, then we are imagining what the philosophers would call a "chimera"—an entity that, from its very description, cannot exist. The only really "free market" in this absurd sense is the jungle (or maybe Trump Tower), where everybody has the right to eat everybody else for lunch and no deal is worth the paper it is printed on.

A final point that it would have been nice to be able to leave without saying is that the market is just a tool for the creation of wealth, not the actual source of wealth. Like any tool, it can be put to bad ends, and it isn't the right tool for every job. For example, markets for slaves have existed since antiquity. And few people would think that the exchange of services on an open market is the best way to organize cooperation among, say, members of a family with small children. In a modern economy, there are two areas in particular where the creation of viable markets requires a certain suspension of market principles, and these two areas are of particular concern here because they happen to be central to the life of the 9.9 percent.

In those white-coat occupations in which specialized expertise endows providers with a systematic edge over the public and thus makes it difficult for the public to set the rules for the market, the idea of a "profession" comes in handy. The public in effect relaxes the requirements of transparency and disinterested enforcement required of most markets and entrusts the professionals with the responsibility for policing their own market, in exchange for which the members of the profession issue heartfelt pledges to place their clients' interests ahead of their own in applying their know-how. Similarly, in the many complex, white-collar-run activities in a modern economy that require the coordination of teams of individuals to deliver a single product or service, the idea of "management" comes in handy. Once workers step inside an employment relation in its modern form, the market goes away and managers step in to coordinate activities according to principles of leadership and communication that have little to do with market mechanisms. In earlier, functioning versions of the modern economy, the white coats and white collars offer a soft, norm-based form of market regulation that is essential to keeping any actual market in the human world free and efficient.

Now, to return to my friend Marty, if the market myth were merely a restatement of these important yet heavily conditioned truths—that the market is a limited but potentially very useful device for coordinating human activity, fostering dignity, and leveling wealth inequalities, provided it is used correctly and subject to necessary formal and informal conditions—it would hardly invite meaningful objection. But it isn't. The market myth says that the free market exists now, in real time, and it explains the actual distribution of glory. The market myth in fact amounts to a set of inferences from economic dogma masquerading as a description of reality. It's like saying that in a world where human beings are perfectly spherical, every encounter will be frictionless; therefore, there is no friction in the world today.

The right thing to do, if you want to explain inequality today, of course, is to look at the world as it is, not as the religion of the Dow says it ought to be. The next step is to turn around and ask why it is that so many people would rather cling to ideological fictions than face the facts. The ultimate enigma of the market myth is not that it has holes—what hypothetical construct of the human imagination does not?—but that the most ardent proponents of the theory often seem to be the people who live in those very holes. This is the strange tie that connects Marty with my grandfather, at least in my mind. Why is it that the greatest beneficiaries of captured markets are usually the loudest champions of the free market?

THE STANDARD OIL STORY BEGAN with a three-month episode in 1872 that came to be known as the Cleveland Massacre. Cleveland at the time was the nascent refining capital of the nation and it was bubbling over with competitive energy. John D. Rockefeller felt the competition was getting out of hand. He approached each of his twenty-six rivals in town with a simple message: "Join with us and your families will never know want." He was usually tactful enough not to say: "or else." Standard swallowed up twenty-two of them.

The key to Standard's subsequent domination of the refining market was its domination of the railroads. Standard used its massive share of the oil trade to negotiate exclusive discounts from the railroads, and then it took the extra step of forcing the railroads to fork over additional cash when they shipped some other company's oil. Pretty soon, if you wanted to move quantities of toxic liquids from any refinery storage tank into any furnace or factory across the country, you had to pay Standard a toll for the privilege—or deal with the full might of the nation's police forces, militias, the army, and the best lawyers money could buy.

The Standard monopoly hit peak earnings power in the 1890s, when it accounted for 90 percent of the American oil market. Like most monopolies, it went on to stifle innovation, underinvest in production, gouge suppliers and consumers, pillage the environment, and commandeer national policy for its own purposes. It represented one of the largest private systems of taxation that the world had seen hitherto and among the most regressive. Some of the winnings spilled down to the next generation, and a few crumbs landed on the holiday dinner tables of my youth. Most of the people along the way, starting with my great-grandfather, were ardent believers in capitalism, the free market, and the American way.

Over the past several decades, the U.S. economy has been experiencing a replay of the Cleveland Massacre.[5] Only it's happening in slow motion, it looks more like a genocide, and it feels as peaceful as euthanasia. Since 2000, about half of the publicly listed firms in the United States have disappeared.[6] For the most part, they have vanished into the bellies of their former competitors. Three out of four industry sectors have seen an increase in concentration, and the firms in highly concentrated industry sectors have enjoyed extraordinary profit margins and abnormal stock returns. Capital markets in the United States are now measurably less competitive than European markets.[7]

You can track our progress down the road back to monopoly-land in your own home. Start with your umbilical connection to the external world. Americans typically pay $300 per month for sluggish cable and internet service, while customers in Seoul, Hong Kong, and Tokyo can get double the data speeds for about $40 per month. That's mainly because in 61 percent of local cable markets there is no competition, so American cable companies can pretty much charge what they want.[8]

Now pull out your friendly mobile device—and then reach back into your pocket for the $250 that isn't there.[9] That's how much more Americans pay per year than Germans for their phone service, thanks mainly to our vibrant telephone oligopolies. It's also one reason why Verizon and AT&T have been returning large piles of that excess cash to their shareholders. Who wants to waste money building a better service when customers have nowhere else to go?

If you peek into your bathroom medicine cabinet, you'll find plenty of missing cash there, too. Americans now pay $1,443 per capita for pharmaceuticals, or about double the average for ten other high-income countries.[10] The extra money doesn't buy better drugs or health. What it does buy is squadrons of lawyers to game the patent system in the drug companies' favor, lots of bribes to politicians to make sure prices can never be properly negotiated—oh sorry, it's called "lobbying"—and, as you'll see if you turn on cable news during unemployed afternoons, an unending stream of advertisements for drugs with horrifying side effects that you can't even buy without badgering your doctor for a prescription.

Head over to the kitchen and you'll find the leftovers from another process of extraction. The top four food processors control 60 percent of the pork market, 50 percent of poultry, 80 percent of beef, and 90 percent of grain. Oligopolies like these turn up in many other places where you'd least expect see them: four companies control 97 percent of the cat food market; three companies control 92 percent of tobacco; three companies do 75 percent of beer; oligopolies, cartels, or outright monopolies now dominate in candy, chocolates, funeral caskets, porn, baby formula, and—who knew?—cheerleading.[11]

But don't worry! Most of these oligopolies are not using their market power against you. They're mostly using it to crush small producers and workers. They are the reason employees at chicken processing plants sometimes wear diapers: no time for bathroom breaks.[12] They are the reason why pork processing plants hosted superspreader events during the pandemic. They are the reason repetitive stress and musculoskeletal injuries are rising among low-wage workers. They are also the reason why top managers at some of the food conglomerates now routinely crash the list of most highly paid CEOs.

Thinking that maybe you can just fly away from it all? That's going to cost you, too. After a chaotic period of deregulation, the airline industry has finally come to earth as an oligopoly that divvies up the airways and delivers suitcases full of your travel dollars to corporations that will beat you to a pulp if you fail to obey, as passenger David Dao learned in 2017, when he was infamously dragged down the aisle and off an over-booked flight. As the pandemic of 2020 revealed, the airline oligopoly was actually a terrific example of how the "private" profits of the "free market" would go nowhere without public underwriting at taxpayer expense. In the decade preceding the crisis, the industry decided that investing in the mitigation of future risks was foolish, since it could just as easily funnel its oligopoly rents back to shareholders. And if anything really bad did happen, like a pandemic, then the government would step in to make it all good.

At least your money is safe in the bank. Or not. The banks are too smart to steal money directly from you (well, mostly—Wells Fargo recently tried that angle, too). The way the plan works is this: You deposit money with them, and they run off to the casino. If it comes up heads, they keep the winnings; if it's tails, no sweat, you will get your money back, thanks to a government guarantee. The only losers in the deal are the members of the general public—who have to pay for the guarantee—and anybody who thinks it's a good idea to have a stable financial system. In the aftermath of the financial crisis of 2008, it was universally agreed that problem was, in part, that the banks had gotten too big to fail. The solution, apparently, was to let them get even bigger. The share of financial assets in the hands of the giant banks rose from 16 percent in 1994 to 47 percent in 2006 to 59 percent in 2018.[13]

Airlines and banks, however, smell a little bit of yesterday's oligopoly. Tomorrow belongs to the leviathans of the tech industry. The largest of them, Google, controls 90 percent of the internet search market—the same share that Standard Oil had of the refining market at its peak—which gives it effective monopoly control over a certain kind of twenty-first-century railroad, namely, the one that transports manipulative ideas directly into your head. Amazon, meanwhile, has cornered another kind of twenty-first-century railroad. It has established a universal online platform that allows it to compete directly with other retailers even as it controls their storefront and gathers more information on their businesses than they dreamt possible. Facebook, having been allowed to buy up its principal competitors, runs an effective monopoly in social media, and together with Google manages a duopoly in the business of weaponizing the information that the public supplies for use against the public. Apple and Google oversee a duopoly in smartphone operating systems, with 94 percent of the market between them. In this they are taking a page from Microsoft, which was born of a monopoly on that lucky day when Bill Gates bought a used operating system on the cheap and then persuaded IBM to make it the standard for 90 percent of the personal computers in the world. If someone figures out how to put a patent on the English language and collect a penny every time people pronounce a word correctly, they might become even richer than many a tech monopolist and equally invaluable to humankind.

Probably no one understands better how the modern American market works than Warren Buffett, one of the three richest individuals in the country. "In business, I look for economic castles protected by unbreachable 'moats,'" Buffett explains in a 1995 letter to his shareholders.[14] And indeed, his investment strategy has focused unerringly on those redoubts of feudalism that are safe from the menace of competition in the free market. At the end of 2018, his Berkshire Hathaway holding company owned 65 million shares of Delta Air Lines, 56 million shares of Southwest, 44 million shares of American, and 26 million shares of United, representing between 7 and 10 percent of each airline. At the time, the airlines were busy hauling planeloads of cash from their cartel back to shareholders in the form of share buybacks. (Shortly after the pandemic blasted the airline shares out of the sky, Berkshire Hathaway sold its stakes at a steep loss.) Berkshire Hathaway also had 40 percent of its portfolio invested in the big banks—not this or that bank, but all of the biggest banks that money can buy. Because nothing says "I believe in the free market" like owning huge stakes of every major player in a single, oligopolistic industry that latches on to the rest of the economy like a giant mutant tick and, with the backing of a free government insurance plan, sucks the money out.

Economists typically use words like "rent-seeking," "barriers to entry," "market power," or "market imperfections" to describe the various forms of robbery discussed here. By this they mean to suggest that such things represent small and regrettable deviations from the shining path of the market. The underlying idea is that the "market" is some natural phenomenon capable of spontaneously organizing itself, and that it will naturally sprout from the jungle floor, as long as government stays the hell away. This is a profoundly lunatic idea, but let's set the self-serving ideology to the side. The important thing to know now is that these so-called imperfections in the modern American capital markets aren't a detour or a side show. They are the main event. They are how people make big money in America.

The five tech quasi-monopolies account for almost 40 percent of the value of all stocks traded on NASDAQ—and much of the remainder consists of companies patiently waiting to be devoured by them. The banks have converted their taxpayer-funded insurance program into a market capitalization of $3.7 trillion, or about 10 percent of all publicly traded capital in the United States. Together with all other financial institutions, they have increased their share of GDP from around 3 percent in the 1950s to almost 8 percent today.[15] Think of it this way: $1 out of every $12 in the United States goes to the people whose job it is to decide which pocket gets to hold on to the other $11. Meanwhile, the pharmaceutical companies have surfed on their licenses to rip off sick people to $2.2 trillion of market value. To be sure, there are plenty of open, competitive, and socially productive markets in America; it's just that they are not where the big money is.

Perhaps the most frustrating and yet most obvious fact about the euthanasia of the American market is that it was not an act of nature. It was an act of money. The gains made from captured markets were invested in capturing government, which then asphyxiated the market under a pillow of supposedly pro-business policies. A significant share of the credit should go to conservative icon Robert Bork, who first achieved fame as President Richard Nixon's willing executioner in the Saturday Night Massacre.[16] (For younger viewers: this was in a time when a president firing those who were attempting to hold him accountable to law was not considered just another Friday night.) On the basis of some tendentiously economistic reasoning, Bork gratuitously narrowed the analysis of potential antitrust violations down to their immediate impact on consumer prices. If it didn't raise the price at the pump tomorrow, well then, it wasn't a monopoly. This putative defense of the free market made snapping up competitors as easy as slipping the regulators a spreadsheet promising a few cost savings from the combination.[17]

Who wins in this euthanasia of the American marketplace? Everybody loses in the end, of course, but some people do pick up hefty paychecks on the way down. Economists Lina Khan and Sandeep Vaheesan point to the answer in the context of an influential analysis of Amazon's new, platform-based method of dominating the online marketplace: "Monopoly pricing on goods and services turns the disposable income of the many into capital gains, dividends, and executive compensation for the few."[18] They perhaps forgot to add the few who serve the few. The biggest winners in the destruction of markets have been the 0.1 percent, but the 9.9 percent can claim the consolation prize.

The list of managerial occupations that dominate the 9.9 percent overlaps neatly with a list of sectors that enjoy the greatest freedom from the market. As a matter of fact, if your plan is to turn that elite college degree into management cash, then all you really need to do is follow the Buffett Rule:

> *Find out where Warren is investing his money,*
> *and apply for work there.*

The merit myth says that if you put a bunch of brains in a room, they will figure out how to make money. But the footprints on the ground tell us that if you put a pile of money in a room, the brains will figure out how to get in—and how to lock the door behind them.

The Buffett Rule, to be clear, is of value only to those entering the anointed sectors at the correct level. You want to be the guy managing the chicken meat monopoly, not the one wearing diapers on the disassembly line. Before considering how it all plays out in the mind of the 9.9 percent, it is important therefore to extend the examination of the existing economic system a little further. The kind of market "imperfections" with which we have been concerned to this point take place mostly within the confines of what are euphemistically called the capital markets. To put it in terms that ancient Mesopotamians might have understood, they have to do with battles among warlords over who will control the harvest. They do not quite cover the more profound conflict between the warlords and the peasants who actually are the harvest. These capital market imperfections, as egregious as they are, should take second place to the most distorted market of all, namely the one that trades in the kind of capital that pushes through the door every morning on the way to work.

ONE OF THE FIRST AND MOST ASTONISHING THINGS you discover upon taking a respectable job in the vicinity of any of the gushers in the modern economy is just how little freedom there is in the free market. The overwhelming majority of deals made, favors traded, and resources allocated in the so-called free market take place not on any open exchange but within the confines of corporate hierarchies that, as philosopher Elizabeth Anderson has pointed out, are run mostly on the model of totalitarian dictatorships.[19]

In America today, once you've settled into a firm, your boss has far more power over you than any elected government. He can read your email at will, inquire into your private life, and replace you if he doesn't like what he smells.[20] He can force you to undergo searches and physical exams without warrant or cause or compensating you for the time involved. He can prevent you not only from expressing your opinions but even from talking with your coworkers. He can monitor your trips to the bathroom and discipline you for taking too many. He can strip you of your right to sue him in court. He can stop you from saying mean things about him, even if he is a certifiable asshole. And he can hunt you down after you leave and stop you from doing any number of things of which he does not approve. Man is born in the free market, as it were, but everywhere she lives in chains to management.

Then comes another remarkable discovery. A few days into the job, you see that real power is not invested in the personage of your boss. There's a bigger boss and he—or rather "it"—evinces even less empathy for the human condition. Up on the throne at the apex of the pyramid sits a fictional individual called the corporation, and this imaginary being is far more powerful than any human being.[21] Like the entailed medieval estates from which it descended, a corporation is immortal. Even better, it has a special power called limited liability that allows it to contract debts and then run away from them. It has no emotional attachments, no family to feed tomorrow, and is legally prohibited from doing good deeds that might in any way interfere with its pursuit of economic self-interest. It can't get sick and it has no need for health insurance, but, unlike humans, it can buy health insurance at a discount, as a courtesy from human taxpayers. It shares few of the responsibilities of humans and yet it has acquired the right to assemble, speak freely, exercise religion, and guard its privacy. It often has few or no competitors for the services of prospective employees, and they rarely have fewer than a boatload of rivals for the positions it offers. Once it absorbs a fresh human into its payrolls, it immediately starts accumulating information on and control over the assets and conditions on which that individual's future depends—the professional relations, the specific knowledge, the personal commitments, and many other circumstances around which mortals build a life. It has the power to take all of that away in an instant, at its own pleasure, or for no reason at all. If a corporation ever did come to life, as legal theorist Joel Bakan has pointed out, it would probably be diagnosed as a sociopath.

Then comes yet another disturbing discovery. You listen to the opinion makers tell you about the facts of economic life, and you realize that the most elemental realities never enter into the discussion.[22] Economic discourse, at least insofar as it drives politics and policy in America, can't tell the difference between real people and fictional entities, or between exchanges made in perfect freedom and deals negotiated with your back to the wall and a medical bill pointed in your face. In this fantasy land of pseudo-economic theorizing, there are only individual economic "agents," human and inhuman alike, and every deal they make is by definition the best way to get exactly what they want. The whole cubicle-zoo of vice presidents, trainees, contractors, pseudo-contractors, hired head-cutters, and the other fauna of an actual economy has been relegated to a handful of unglamorous subfields that aren't likely to get you invited to anything more impactful than a faculty tea party. Among the free market ideologues who have actually shaped our reality, the level of willed cluelessness is hard to overstate. They will say things like: "the firm . . . has no power of fiat, no authority, no disciplinary action any different in the slightest degree from ordinary market contracting between any two people."[23] Sure! Because setting up an offshore LLC to employ subcontractors at poverty-level wages with minimal health benefits is *just like* selling lemonade.

When people try to explain these mysteries, whether to celebrate them or to excoriate them, they often turn to a single word: "capitalism." Unfortunately, this is one of those words that describes a thing that does not actually exist. More exactly, it is a way of defining the world in terms of what some people wish it would be, not what it is. In reality, the system we now call "capitalism" excludes from its capricious understanding of "capital" many of the most important things that would belong to any natural definition of that term. It excludes, for example, claims on future wealth production arising from the massive investments that individuals and societies make in the rearing, care, education, and socialization of human beings. "Labor" within so-called capitalism also always refers only a certain, artificial way of understanding a certain subset of productive human activities, and excludes a tremendous amount of anything that naturally deserves the name of "work."[24]

The distinctive feature and organizing idea of the existing system is neither the "market," nor the productive deployment of saved resources that we call "capital," nor the ceaseless wonder of "disruptive innovation"—all of which are good things in themselves and may be found in differing degrees in many regimes throughout history—but rather the employment relation. More specifically, it is the idea that the limited subset of human activity that fits in an artificial category of economic activity should be organized so that human individuals sell their economic product in increments of time to fictional entities endowed with a distinctive set of legal rights and a distinctive set of legally enforceable claims to very specific categories of future wealth production. Call it the wage-labor-corporate-ownership system, or WACO, for short.

WACO has some tremendous virtues. It is in some respects the most underappreciated achievement of the industrial revolution—far more consequential than the steam engine—and it can still be made to work for the good of most people. Looking on the bright side, it is a potentially very effective way of organizing the cooperation of large groups of people engaged in complex activities to produce goods and services of value to the public. But the most obvious and important thing to know about it is that it is not an artifact of nature. It does not emerge from the spontaneous activity of naturally contract-making individuals entering into mutually beneficial contracts in some primeval clearing in the forest. It had to be invented and constructed out of law, cultural norms, human instinct, and the accumulated accidents of history. It is constantly evolving under the pressure of new technologies and social change. Above all, it is not intrinsically balanced or self-balancing. On the contrary, in most places most of the time, it is transparently and intrinsically unbalanced, with a distinct tendency to tip over onto the side of big money, and from there into misery and chaos.

At least since the Progressive Era, rational governments have understood that one of their most important roles in the WACO world is to redress the inherent imbalance in the employment relation. Minimum wage laws, overtime laws, child labor laws, collective bargaining laws—these are not "infringements" on a supposedly free market. They are (often imperfect) efforts to liberate a market for productive human activity that is otherwise decidedly unbalanced and unfree. Such laws and policies played an essential role in the rise of the middle class, in the emergence of relatively free and efficient markets, and in the Great Compression of inequality that took place in the middle decades of the twentieth century.

Starting with the Reagan administration, however, the U.S. government began deploying its massive power not to liberate but to obliterate the market for human labor and place the economy back in the chains of corporate power. Even as the administration gutted the antitrust law vital to functioning capital markets, it inaugurated a decades-long assault on labor, starting with the firing of all eleven thousand members of the striking air traffic controllers' union in 1981. Under brazenly named "right to work" laws, individual states were soon competing with one another to strip workers of as many rights as possible.[25] The share of workers represented in unions fell into a steep decline, dropping from 27.0 percent in 1979 to 11.6 percent in 2019.[26] The minimum wage was allowed to drift lower and is now 29 percent below what it was in 1968 in constant dollar terms—notwithstanding the fact that the productivity of American workers has doubled in the interim.[27] At the same time, macro-economic policy consistently favored capital over labor by prioritizing the fight against inflation over the fight for full employment. And then the tax code was amended in favor of capital gains so that the government might directly assist in redistributing wealth from workers to owners. This taxpayer subsidy for capital is so gratuitous that it is almost as if it was enacted to satisfy the symbolic demands of plutocrat-funded think tank intellectuals to broadcast the message that income earned from capital is morally superior to income earned from working for a living.

The payoff for this carefully engineered destabilization of the WACO system under the falsely labeled "free market" or "capitalist" regime can be measured in the aggregate statistics. In the period preceding the "free market" counterrevolution, between 1948 to 1979, productivity climbed at a remarkable pace of 2.39 percent per year and median hourly compensation for workers kept up in near-lock-step, clocking in at 2.15 percent per year. Between 1979 and 2018, however, productivity growth slowed to 1.36 percent, while hourly compensation nearly flatlined, creeping upward at a meager 0.28 percent.[28] The labor income of the bottom 90 percent fell from 58 percent of total personal income in 1979 to less than 47 percent in 2015, even as corporate profits increased from 5 percent of GDP in 1970 to 10 percent today.[29]

If any doubts remained about the impact that this planned desta-bilization of WACO had on workers and on the economy in general, the Covid pandemic should (hopefully) have removed them. As if in a moment of sudden awakening, the 9.9 percent opened its empty cup-boards and discovered that certain kinds of underpaid workers are "essential." The answer was not to pay them more; it was to come up with ways of forcing them back to work. In the midst of the pandemic, the lobbying machine for corporations known as ALEC called for action to "bring the economy back to life through a free market approach that gets big government out of the way."[30] Translation: corporations preferred to kill off parts of the population rather than see a reduction in profits, and they wanted big government to help with the program by depriving workers of their rights to unemployment insurance and thereby driving them back to work.

Perhaps the most critical thing to understand about a destabilized WACO system, and also the hardest to see, is that it isn't merely one advantage among many that immortal corporations can deploy in their struggle with human workers. It is the very reason that many firms exist in their present form, and the reason why many are so unnaturally large. There is nothing in the nature of the work involved which says that nurses, truck drivers, and funeral home directors, for example, should be employees of huge corporations. They could just as easily employ themselves and entrust the coordination of their efforts and the management of their collective interests to associations and cooperatives. Likewise, there is nothing in the business of transporting passengers or food in cars which says that it should be in the hands of one or a few massive corporations dominating a flextime workforce of pseudo-contractors. Some of the largest formations of "capital" in the American economy are merely accumulations of the wealth extracted from labor through the imbalances of the WACO system.

When economists propose theories of the firm, they usually mean to offer some economic rationale for the emergence of this particular form of economic organization. They'll suggest that it exists to reduce transaction costs, to overcome collective action problems, or just to coordinate work at large scale.[31] Such theories undoubtedly capture a part of the truth, inasmuch as the firm can and does serve useful purposes in the organization and coordination of productive activity. But they are also mostly just-so stories that predict only what already exists and cast policy choices as the outcomes of laws of nature. They overlook the fact that firms can come into existence for many reasons, not all of them good or economically sensible. Firms may well be—as they now are in many instances—symptoms of an economic disease.

Firms today come into existence in significant measure because the employment relation, such as it is currently constructed in a destabilized WACO system, and especially in its grotesquely unbalanced American version, is a standing invitation for some people to harvest the wealth that others produce. It is a license to exploit. When a society issues such licenses for sale, it may expect a fierce competition to acquire them. This will create the illusion of a "free market" and induce great celebrations of the success of those who amass wealth within its terms. But it won't change the basic economic reality. Firms are farms and their crop is people.

Who wins in the destabilized WACO world of human agriculture? The big winners, of course, are the 0.1 percent. The public likes to shower its affections on the sliver of the 0.1 percent who got there with a blockbuster novel, a sports contract, or a handy invention, and the defenders of market ideology routinely trot out J. K. Rowling as all the proof we need that inequality is the work of a system that leaves everybody shivering with delight. But the bulk of the 0.1 percent are not the fabled wizards of "capitalism" or the buccaneers of the "free market." They are those entrepreneurs of the WACO bureaucracy that we call "senior managers." The midrange-performing CEO you've never heard of at a Fortune 500 company that makes stuff you didn't know the world needed earns enough that he can blow his life savings at the beginning of every year and still count on joining the top 0.1 percent of the *wealth* distribution by the end of the year. The delusions that accompany this state of being are well known and dangerous to other people. It is the delusions festering one step below the top of the pyramid that require some more attention here. The farmer, after all, can't get the job done all on his own. That's where the 9.9 percent come in.

ONE THING THAT YOU DISCOVER, usually a few months and several hundred thousand frequent flier miles into your first serious job on the white-collar team, is that your coworkers lead some highly developed fantasy lives. You can read about it in the books they buy at the airport.

First, Break All the Rules, the titles exhort them, which they will surely do, once they get into a position where they won't get fired for doing so. Which will definitely happen soon, after they adopt the *Seven Habits* of the lords of management and take their admiring subordinates on a ride from *Good to Great*. In the meantime, they're just going to *Lean In*, because they're pretty sure that if they raise their hands in a few more meetings they'll get called on at last. If Andy Warhol came back to life and saw this stuff, he'd probably propose that everyone should get fifteen minutes as a CEO.

There's nothing wrong with indulging in a little fantasy life, of course. It just shows that you're grounded enough to think about escaping. Every stalk of corn dreams of being a farmer. The thing that deserves attention here is the paradoxical subtext of these managerial dreamscapes. The ultimate source of all those troubled reveries in white-collar land is the unsettling bargain that necessarily sustains the economic life of a big part of the 9.9 percent in times of escalating monopoly power. Here's the deal: You sign up to operate the machinery of an unbalanced WACO system, and in exchange you receive an extra helping of the crop. The complication is that, all things considered, you're still part of the crop. But at least you get to dream of one day standing on the other end of the plow. The 0.1 percent, after all, is just the 1 percent of the 9.9 percent. The people who agree to the deal constitute what was once called "middle management." But in the new age of firm-based human agriculture, the very idea of management has changed in character.

In the beginning, management was leadership. Insofar as it involved technical and logistical challenges, it was grubby, too. It mostly happened on the shop floor, the railroad depot, or at army headquarters, where it was left in the hands of stewards and sergeants. Not very many people distinguished it from the actual work being accomplished. Management in this sense was—and remains—an extremely useful activity. Organizing large groups of people to operate a railroad, build a bridge, and in general get something done is how humans prosper.

But management in this sense may now be considered pre-agricultural, as it were. Human beings can benefit from organization and leadership, but crops just need to face the sickle. Leaders and consensus builders necessarily give way to technicians and reapers, the better to increase the yield. Thus, the modern idea of shareholder-management is born, and with it a new kind of management-industrial complex. The exclusive focus on shareholder value in the new managerialism is at bottom an attempt to define the very rules that make for a stabilized WACO system out of existence. It is a way of turning the market against itself for the benefit of the powerful. It is sociopathy dressed up as a theory about free markets.

Instrumental in the rise of the new, pathological form of managerialism were the management consulting, investment banking, and the other similarly mysterious professions that over the past four decades have come to occupy the vanguard of the 9.9 percent. The immortal, WACO-empowered corporation discovered by accident—in the way that fictional creatures often do—that nothing is so useful to its purposes as a cadre of mercenaries who will wage war on its behalf without suffering from any of the complicating social or organizational ties that might weaken their resolve. These free agents of corporate power proved very successful in imposing greater burdens on workers, eviscerating middle management, and funneling ever more of the wealth into the pockets of corporations and their top managers.

No analysis of the new white-collar consciousness would be complete without some consideration of the other pillar of the management-industrial complex, namely, the business schools. Perhaps the most representative discipline in the business school, as I have explained elsewhere,[32] is the largely fictitious discipline of "strategy." Michael Porter wrote the book on the subject, and he borrowed most of it from a pre-existing subfield in economics that was intended to ferret out the monopolistic behavior responsible for excess returns in certain sectors of industry. Only, Porter copied the ideas out backwards because his mission was to turn the field upside down. The point of business school in times of inequality is to teach people how to generate excess returns by operating monopolies—because if they succeed in business, that is what they will be doing.

THERE IS ANOTHER WAY. The alternative to the white-collar lifestyle, for aspiring members of the 9.9 percent, is to put on a white coat (or white shoes, as the case may be). The deal here is to seek shelter from an unbalanced WACO system in those specialized activities that we used to call "professions." This was once thought to be the safer option. But that turns out to be another one of the delusions of rising inequality. As the WACO world unravels, the very idea of a profession changes in character. In fact, it turns into an empty husk of its former self. And then things get even worse. One fine day, the white collars take the white coats out to lunch and they eat them.

There are still some professionals, don't get me wrong. It's just that there is new way of being, and it involves looking like a professional rather than being one. Let's call it "professionism." Professionists are actually just a category of workers, but they do everything they can to distinguish themselves from other workers. In general, it is much better to be a professionist than a worker, as professionists have used their proximity to actual power to run a bright yellow highlighter pen over everything that might set them apart.

When workers get together to advance their interests through collective bargaining, for example, that's called a union. Union people, we have been told, are thuggish, violent, and corrupt. They wear baggy sweatshirts and are frequently tossed into rivers with cement on their feet. When professionists get together to advance their interests, on the other hand, that's called an association. They wear white shoes or white coats, and you have to listen to them because they know what they are talking about.

When workers attempt to exclude other workers from competing for their jobs, that's called an abuse of market power and an infringement of the right to work. Call in the antitrust police! Open the doors to free trade! But when professionists strangle their potential competitors in the crib by choking off the supply of internships or immigrants, for example, it's about maintaining standards and protecting the public.

When workers contribute to political campaigns through their unions, they are buying favors and trying to mooch off the system. Maybe they are even infringing on the constitutional rights of those union members who oppose mooching (at least, that's what the plutocratic wing of the Supreme Court says). When associations lobby politicians to gut health care reform, or when bankers write the rules for bankers, on the other hand, that is called expert testimony. No problem with free speech there!

One of the best ways for professionists to add value is to destroy it first. The way this is accomplished is by making problems so complicated that only fellow professionists can solve them. For example, professionists in the "private sector" work with professionists in "government" to come up with rules that only very large organizations employing lots of fellow professionists can begin to understand or follow.

Evidence for the success of professionism in securing a safe shelter in the WACO world is plentiful. Consider the case of doctors. To be fair, there can be no doubt that physicians and other health care professionals are indeed genuine professionals to some degree, in the old-fashioned sense, and they perform many valuable services on honorable terms. But that doesn't explain their compensation. American physicians are on roughly double pay compared with other advanced countries, after adjusting for general economic differences. So are dentists. This is not because they are twice as educated or twice as good at saving lives or pulling teeth as their global peers. It's because they are much better at the professionist game of organizing cartels that limit competition. That explains not just why it is expensive to call your doctor, but why you may not be able to call your doctor in the first place. Professional associations have figured out that the key to high salaries is engineered scarcity, which is why the United States has fewer physicians per capita than most peer nations. The Hippocratic Oath really needs to be amended. The "do no harm" clause may still apply to individual patients, but it clearly does not apply when those patients are reduced to statistics in a business plan designed to advance the economic interests of the medical profession.

If that makes you want to call your lawyer—don't. Americans spend $1.66 for every $100 of GDP on lawyers, while Europeans get by with $0.66, in large part because the American Bar Association operates a cartel.[33] Florists, real estate agents, auctioneers, interior decorators, and a number of other professions of recent provenance have learned to play the same game of restricting competition through licensing.[34] About a quarter of American workers now need a license to show up to work—and that doesn't count the de facto license known as a college degree, now required for many jobs that were once happily performed by high school graduates.

Over the past five decades, professionism has become so profitable that many writers hold it accountable for rising inequality. But this view is mistaken. Very few of these pros make it into the top 0.1 percent, where the real wealth has accumulated over the past forty years. The professionist game is strictly for the 9.9 percent. It is a way of beating down, not climbing up to the very top. It is, in the final analysis, a symptom, not the disease.

Professionism is at bottom a corruption of professionalism and a betrayal of the trust on which any genuine profession must be grounded. But that does not mean it is a constant in the long history of human vice. On the contrary, it is what some categories of workers will do to save themselves under the condition of rising inequality in the context of a destabilized WACO system.

One piece of evidence on this crucial point comes from cross-country comparisons of the premia that professionals earn. The assumption that undergirds the self-esteem of any profession is that the premium it earns is a direct function of the specific knowledge and skills it possesses. But the data show that the professional bonus varies much less by occupation than by the degree of general inequality in the country in which it is practiced. If doctors are paid well in your country, for example, then so are the lawyers, dentists, architects, psychotherapists, and, above all, managers of every type. And if they are all paid well, this is associated with high income inequality across the board. This can happen only because rising inequality itself, not profession-specific factors, is driving the gravy train.

How exactly does inequality spread through professions that in theory have nothing in common? Why should there be any correlation at all between the salaries of corporate lawyers, thoracic surgeons, and management consultants to the financial services industry? A first principle is that, when you work for people who make a lot of money, you can charge a lot of money. Thus, if you plan to be a professionist, please pay attention to the Buffett Rule and be sure to direct your services to people who live on the right side of the moat. In management consulting (I know this from personal experience), the most profitable clients are the ones in financial services, telecommunications, and similarly monopolistic industries. The second principle is that the "merit" on which the professionists rely for their "human capital" comes mostly from the same small pool—not because human talent is scarce, but because, as discussed previously, the corruption of the prestige market has turned merit into a fungible commodity. As any campus recruiter can confirm, the prices of a fresh doctor, a lawyer, and an MBA from Harvard tend to converge—not because the knowledge in each field is miraculously equalized but because each field is looking for the same, generic quantum of prestige, not specific skills.

Many professionists still like to think that it is their specific knowledge, rather than their market power, that sets the price. So they rest easy in the feeling that they control their own destiny. But this serves only to prove that self-delusion is one of the occupational hazards of professionism. To guard against this hazardous misperception, aspiring professionists may wish to remember what has happened to those workers who sadly still call themselves "professors."

There may have been a time when the people who taught in colleges and universities might have been considered members of the professional class. Indeed, if knowledge were the criterion for becoming a professionist, then who but a "professor" could be more professorial? But it isn't. Today, 75 percent of college faculty are "contingent" or non-tenure-track, and 50 percent of these are part-time or "adjuncts."[35] Adjuncts are paid by the course, have zero job security, may cherish no prospects for advancement, enjoy minimal or no health or retirement benefits, and average about $30,000 in income per year—which leaves a fair number of them below the poverty line and on public assistance programs. They sometimes make the news when they are discovered to be living in their cars, or die from cancer that they can't afford to treat, or take up sex work to cover the bills. In short, professionists of this sort are what we call "workers." In this respect, they have followed in the footsteps of schoolteachers, who were once on the happier side of that divide, too. (The kiss of downward mobility, in their case, happened precisely when women entered the profession in force: a point that physicians, now also tilting female, may wish to bear in mind.)

If you want to locate the real winners in the modern university, just as in the health care system, you need to look at the top of the food chain, where now is feasting time. The future of education belongs to the white-collar team, not to those defrocked knowledge workers in the faculty lounge. As of 2016, sixty-one college presidents collected more than $1 million in compensation, and another 145 cracked the half million mark.[36] Topping the list was Ken Starr of Baylor University, who received severance pay of nearly $5 million—a sweet kiss-off indeed for the man who brought us the news about Monica Lewinsky and then sailed to the defense of Donald Trump in his first impeachment trial. Starr resigned, by the way, in the aftermath of mishandling a rampant sexual assault scandal on campus.

THE MARKET MYTH IS SIMILAR to its cousin the merit myth in this respect: the less it explains, the more it seems to matter. Even as the actual economy moves ever farther from anything that may count as a genuine market, paradoxically, the myth tightens its grip on the office-bound imagination. Indeed, one of the great mysteries of the modern economic age is how the useful, limited, and inherently leveling idea of the market—which really ought to point in the direction of equality—has evolved into the ideological justification for its opposite: a regime of escalating inequality and unfreedom. This is the contradiction that shapes the religious life of my friend Marty, not to mention that of my grandfather. It is also, perhaps not coincidentally, something that their religion has in common with the political ideology of the American slaveholders of the nineteenth century. Back then, too, the loudest champions of freedom were the greatest beneficiaries of unfree labor.

To a significant degree, it should be clear by now, the rise and rise of the market myth is a matter of naked self-interest. When all the marbles roll across the table in one direction, the people with all the marbles are liable to insist that the table is just as flat and as even as can be. Those whom the existing laws of property favor will ever favor the existing laws of property. The seemingly unstoppable spread of the market myth is also quite obviously a consequence of successful propaganda. All of those investments in free-market think tanks and economics faculties have paid off. And yet there is something more to the story. If you have spent time with people like Marty or my grandfather, you will know that they aren't faking it. When it comes to acknowledging the many unfreedoms on which their own freedom relies, they're more like the proverbial fish who have no idea what water is. Something happens in times of rising inequality that makes it almost impossible for people to see what is keeping them afloat.

At the core of this strange phenomenon lies a certain cognitive failure, or so I would suggest. Let's call it the property delusion. We humans are sometimes prone to thinking that we "own" our cars and houses in exactly the same way that we "own" our arms and legs. But the truth is more complicated. Our property in things never amounts to more than promissory notes from other people, most of whom also have arms and legs, involving what should happen in the event that anyone else should run away with "my" car or invade "my" house. These promissory notes, moreover, come with many stipulations and debatable provisions about what exactly will count as "mine," and they aren't always worth the paper they are printed on. In a healthy society, where the equality and interdependence of human beings is recognized, this distinction between self and property is easier to see, and the delusional belief that we have some direct relation to our toys and cars, unmediated by other people, is less common. Some hunter-gatherer societies make a point of passing along all of their useful gadgets and possessions to others after a time, in recognition of the fact that the real thing of value is not property itself but the network of mutual cooperation that makes the provisional ownership of things possible in the first place.

As inequality escalates, however, individuals find it ever harder to separate themselves from their titles to exchangeable objects. Even those who are nowhere near the top of the economic hierarchy find it difficult to tell the difference between the actual sources of their well-being and the hoard of stuff that distinguishes them from the people down below. They start to think that their home is an extension of their innermost being, and they become convinced paying the taxes and supporting the community that makes it possible to own a home amounts to an infringement on their freedom. They throw themselves into projects of accumulation that are bound to leave them inexplicably unsatisfied. They take for granted that every operation in the market is an act of perfect freedom, where individuals exchange a car, a house, an arm, or a leg, and there is no other human being to be seen for miles around apart from the parties to the transaction. Thus, the market myth blends in with the water, until it becomes indistinguishable from reality itself in the minds of those suffering from this delusion.

Curing ourselves of the property delusion is definitely a project worth pursuing. In fact, it is the reason for having long books like this one. At the end of the day, however, the more reliable path to justice is to remove the causes that produce the delusion in the first place. If an unequal economy is the source of trouble, then a more equal economy is the answer.

The best way to return the 9.9 percent to the professional and managerial ideals that it once embodied is to reestablish American markets on their proper foundations. We need an antitrust policy, not a pro-trust policy in disguise. As Zephyr Teachout and Tim Wu have argued, we need to break up the tech monopolies, break up the banks, break up the airlines, and keep on breaking up whatever new monsters arise to threaten free and productive exchange among humans.[37] We also need to empower workers so that they can bargain effectively with employers rather than simply choose how to get screwed. That means raising the minimum wage, bringing back collective bargaining, making health care a right rather than a perk of employment, and stripping corporations of their obscene power to interfere in the labor market with anticompetitive contracts. We need to vaporize the insane doctrine that corporations owe nothing to anyone but shareholders. We should demand instead that they reciprocate on the licenses and privileges that the public grants them with transparency in all operations (and not merely for publicly listed corporations), and governance that reflects the interests of all stakeholders. Most of the solutions to the present crisis of inequality, it is worth reiterating, call not for the abandonment of markets but for a better understanding of what markets actually are and what they can and cannot do.

Why We Are So Fit

G race lives with her husband and two camera-friendly children in an impressively suburban house in Boston. Last year, her husband bought her an in-home exercise bike from the fitness company Peloton, and she has produced a thank-you video-selfie tracking her arduous journey to fitness. When she first got the bike at the beginning of the year, she was slim and gorgeous, and, after anxiously panting her way through spinning routines while the seasons change outside her charming garden window, she remains slim and gorgeous at the end. Out in reality-world, tweety fingers twitched into action, angrily accusing her sexist husband of imposing a grueling exercise regime on his needy and visibly oppressed wife. Exactly how much offense may be taken from the behavior of characters in a thirty-second advertisement is open to debate. Still, what does come across in the Peloton ad that got the internet outrage-machine worked up in the 2019 holiday season is the desperate quality of Grace's quest for fitness. A limerick-tweeter caught the mood well: "The Peloton wife/ Has a beautiful life/ And a general aura of fear."[1]

On a typical summer Saturday in the best coastal enclaves, you can see versions of Grace everywhere. Stroll past the juice bar and you'll find a group of women hikers in colorful athletic wear relaxing over avocado toast. A trim fifty-something man in jeans and a T-shirt glides past them on a motorized skateboard. A toddler totters around in a helmet, with a nanny close behind but no tricycle in sight. Must be protection against the sidewalk. Down the street there is a fitness club with spiritually uplifting messages on the door. At the new studio a couple of doors farther down, they stretch your muscles for you. Inside a father and his teenage daughter are buying what sounds like a family package—twelve sessions times two at $90 a stretch. Good deal! The family that stretches together stays together. Or is it the family that gets stretched together? Everyone here is checking everyone else out. The vibe is competitive in a side-eye way. Like Grace, they sometimes seem almost anxious in their pursuit of physical perfection. It's as if they were determined to use their bodies to prove some other point about themselves.

In the land of the 9.9 percent, fitness is a luxury good. The richer you are, the more you have of it; and the more you have of it, the richer you look. The fitness industry has been growing at a brisk 3–4 percent clip over the past decade, and the number of personal trainers has been rising even faster.[2] At the top of the pyramid, the pharaohs of the new economy sometimes appear to be the fittest of all. The old stereotype of the fat plutocrat with a top hat and cigar is only for aging game boards. The new billionaires have well-toned deltoids and flattened abs. Sometimes they look like personal trainers themselves. Witness the transfiguration of Jeff Bezos from schlubby engineer to cool-sunglasses action hero. Their helpers in the 9.9 percent, like Grace, are more likely than not to be fit even before they get on their bikes.

If you get on your bike—the kind with wheels, I mean—and ride it around other parts of town, however, you will be exposed to some very different sights. As you leave behind the land of the titanium jogging-strollers and vegan-Peruvian cafés, pedal past the bus stops that bring in the help, and enter the zone of the increasingly widely spaced convenience stores, the human landscape begins to change, too. In Washington, D.C., you can glide along the river path, mostly downhill, from a neighborhood where the life expectancy is nearly ninety-four years to another one where it's sixty-three years.[3] In the San Francisco Bay Area, you can cycle across the bridge in about an hour from neighborhoods where the life expectancy is ninety-one years to zones where it's sixty-four. In New York City, thirty minutes will take you from the best of the

Upper East Side, where they live to ninety, to the heart of the Bronx, where they die at seventy. Along the way, you will see a number of people who, with all due respect for their humanity, are not likely to be regular Peloton riders. It is as if some giant invisible hand had descended on the population, reached inside every living human, reshaped the bones, modulated blood sugar, fiddled the vascular compression, reconfigured neurons, pummeled faces from behind the skin, so that every human body might bear the physical trace of its point of origin.

When you cycle back to the happy world of avocado toast and middle-aged hoverboarders, the paradox sparkles with all the luster of a rack of mountain bikes in the California sun. I love my people, don't get me wrong. They are healthy and beautiful. They will survive. Nothing wrong with that. And I would definitely rather be ruled by Greek gods and goddesses than overweight men with bad tobacco habits. Yet something about the interpretation that this calcifying social class lays on top of its own good health gives pause.

In the mind of the 9.9 percent, nothing is more *you* than your body. Your physical fitness is a test of your moral character, just as *their* lack of fitness says everything you need to know about them. It's a tenacious system of belief, no doubt rooted in the same primal instincts that drive us to preserve our bodies. Yet it lives in visible contradiction with the evidence that can be gathered on a short bike ride around town. How it has survived the experience of a pandemic that selected its targets with a degree of socioeconomic precision that sociologists might envy is an enigma well worth exploring.

The most curious fact about this body delusion of the 9.9 percent, and the point to which I draw attention in this chapter, is how nearly timeless it is. Most conversations about inequality take place close to the present, and most therefore also take for granted that the sources of the trouble are shiny and new, like a suite of smartphone apps or some edgy, fictionalized state of being such as "late-stage capitalism." But the kind of inequality that matters most is that which leaves its trace on the human body, and there is no surer sign that inequality today is reviving some very old dynamics than the reemerging physiological division of the species. The pattern of life distinctly visible across the modern

American landscape is about as old as civilization itself. A useful way to untangle the twisted perceptions to which this dynamic gives rise in the mind of the 9.9 percent is to go back to somewhere near the beginning of recorded time.

AMONG THE HUNDREDS OF HUMAN REMAINS found in the 4,600-year-old ruins of the ancient Sumerian capital of Ur, archaeologists had little difficulty identifying Queen Puabi.[4] She was the one with an elaborate headdress made of gold leaves, lapis lazuli, and carnelian beans. Surrounding her corpse lay a glittery stash of Bronze Age luxury goods: a carriage encrusted with precious stones and mother-of-pearl, a collection of musical instruments made of gold and other valuable material, caches of military-grade weapons, a giant chest of clothing, and a gaming table. She also came with an ID card in the form of a stone cylinder that shows her reclining in comfort while receiving services from some of her many attendants. In the archaeological remains of the first large-scale human civilizations on earth, in Mycenae, Egypt, Mesoamerica, Central Asia, and elsewhere, the outlines of the story are the same. The most reliable signs of civilization are the tombs, and in those tombs the bones of the rich are as easily distinguishable by their possessions in death as they presumably were in life. But the more startling differences are to be found in the bones themselves.

When paleoanthropologists first examined the 3,500-year-old human remains from Bronze Age Mycenae—the supposed home of the heroes of Homer's *Iliad*—they found that the bones of the aristocrats were so unlike those of the common people that they had to be treated as a separate sample, almost as if they belonged to a distinct species.[5] The femurs and the fibulas were thicker and more rounded. The teeth scored five times better on an index of dental health. The skull base heights were 30 percent larger, and the pelvic bones were fully arched and properly formed. Later tests would confirm that the gene pool was the same across the classes. Yet mighty Achilles and his fellow nobles towered 6.4 cm on average over the common man, and the princesses had 6.6 cm on the common woman.

In the graves of ancient Mesopotamia, Mesoamerica, and pretty much every other early, large-scale civilization, the same pattern of pseudo-speciation emerges; and the pattern persists in varying degrees for most of recorded history. In the cemeteries of medieval Poland, fourteenth-century Japan, and seventeenth-century Germany, the rich bones are almost always appreciably nicer than the poor bones.[6] Perhaps the most extreme example comes from a study of military cadets in nineteenth-century England, where young men of the upper class towered an astonishing eight inches over their working-class cousins.

The literary remains of ancient culture seem to agree with the archaeological evidence on the great physiological divide. The hero of the cuneiform *Epic of Gilgamesh*, whose name matches that of a Sumerian king roughly contemporary with Puabi, is "lordly in appearance," "the handsomest of men," "perfect in strength," and a full head taller than his fellow humans.[7] No one seems surprised to learn that he is one-third human and two-thirds god. Homer's heroes, too, enjoy physical endowments so excellent that their status appears to be rooted in the order of nature itself. This is how Thetis, the half-god sea nymph, describes the well-nourished childhood of her noble son Achilles:[8]

> *Like some fair plant beneath my careful hand*
> *He grew, he flourished, and he graced the land*

Achilles has a physical opposite, and his name is Thersites. A commoner and democratic radical who stands up for the people in protest at King Agamemnon's needless war of aggression against Troy, Thersites has a lame foot, bowed legs, hunched shoulders, pointy head, bad hair, and an irritatingly squeaky voice. Homer calls him "the ugliest man who came to Troy."[9] When Thersites tries to speak truth to power, mighty Odysseus promptly thrashes him with the king's scepter, to the general merriment of the crowd, and warns him not to "lift up your mouth to argue with princes."

This division of the human species seems at first so universal as to be a fixed part of the human condition. But a little more digging in those archaeological pits reveals a further startling fact. Bones dating from the paleolithic period indicate that the common man in the period preceding the emergence of the Bronze Age super-states era enjoyed excellent nutritional health. The femurs are well rounded, the skull base heights are respectably large, and the pelvic bones are fully arched. The average Stone Age Joe was taller not just than the average Bronze Age Joe but than the typical Bronze Age Achilles. In between a high mark ten thousand years ago and a low four thousand years ago—that is, precisely during those millennia that culminated in the civilizations of Puabi, Gilgamesh, and Achilles—the average height in the eastern Mediterranean plummeted 16 cm for males and 12 cm for females. Not until 1955 did the average male in the eastern Mediterranean attain the stature of a Mycenean king, and only more recently have Europeans matched their paleolithic precursors.

Some cultural memory of this surprising fact about humanity's Stone Age health survives in the literature of the ancient world. Gilgamesh, for example, does have one rival in beauty and strength, but the competition does not come from within the city walls. Enkidu is a "wild man," "innocent of man-kind," who knows nothing of "cultivated land." He enjoys a hunter-gatherer lifestyle and has the physique to show for it. It takes the services of a "harlot" to lure him out of his health-spa lifestyle and into the squalor of the city. When he strides into the city market, the stunted throngs gather around and say, "This is the one who was reared on the milk of wild beasts. His is the greatest of strength."

Yet Gilgamesh and his chroniclers, no less than Achilles and his bards, glide without comment past the implications of the evidence they record in their own words. No one at the taller end of the ancient world indicates much awareness that their enviable physiques might be attributable to human causes rather than natural causes. On the contrary, the moral vocabulary of early civilization consistently reverses the palpable sequence of cause and effect. The aristocrats dominate the narratives because they are the fairest, the mightiest, "the best"—literally, in ancient Greek, the *aristoi*—even though, as a matter of fact, they are the fairest of them all because they dominate. The language of the time routinely describes political power in metaphors of bodily strength, and yet their bodies are best understood as physical metaphors for political power.

SOMETHING THAT GRACE ISN'T TELLING YOU is that she probably works in biotech. Or in some occupation connected with health. Or her husband does. Or maybe they both co. At least, that's what a decent reading of the odds will say about people who live in mansions in central Boston with well-fluffed outdoor furniture and who buy premium exercise bikes as surprise holiday gifts for their superfit spouses. About 10 to 15 percent of the national biotech research sector resides within a two-mile radius of Cambridge's Kendall Square,[10] and the average wage at Boston's 430 biotech companies in 2018 was $161,281.[11] It's also possible that Grace and husband are a doctor-doctor couple. With so many research hospitals, Boston has 8.7 times as many physicians per capita as the rest of the country—and all but the younger, more idealistic, and more female (who earn less on average) among them are fully paid-up members of the 9.9 percent.[12]

To be more precise, Grace probably works in the health care sector, not in health itself. Stroll around the office districts where she likely spends the day and it's easy to spot the difference. Where you see a glistening fusion of stone, glass, and high-concept architecture, there you can be sure lies a pharmaceutical company, a prestigious medical school, or some other flagship of the health care sector. Where you see a funky cement block of a building, or what looks like an outlet for a private-equity-owned payday lender, there you will find a school of public health, a community clinic, or some other institution focused on issues affecting human health (like, you know, pandemics—which are surprisingly unprofitable to treat).[13]

Broadly speaking, the health care sector is really a disease management business. It deals with the effects of ill health, not the causes. It is organized around the idea of making money, not saving lives. In theory—and especially in the salvific eschatology of the "free market"—the two purposes are not necessarily exclusive: the health care sector makes money by saving lives. In practice, in recent years, the American health care sector and American health have been moving in opposite directions. The money pours in, and the people die faster. In the three

years from 2015 to 2017, the United States experienced the longest sustained decline in aggregate life expectancy since the Spanish flu pandemic of 1918.[14] It's quite the mystery.

Let's talk about the money first, because that's more fun. Overall, as
indicated in the previous chapter, it is a great time to be in the health
care business. The sector employs about 11 percent of the working population but it represents 18 percent of U.S. GDP and accounts for an
even larger share of the top earners. Physicians alone fill up 16 percent
of the top 1 percent.[15] Toss in the upper-middle managers at insurance
companies, hospitals, pharmaceutical companies, and the professionals at legal, consulting, marketing and other service firms that gather
around the honeypot, along with the most highly compensated dentists
in the history of the modern world, and there can be no doubt that the
health care sector is one of the cornerstones of the 9.9 percent.[16] To live
by the idea of the 9.9 percent in America is, at least a quarter of the
time, to aspire to be a health care professional like Grace. At the elite
universities that spawn the 9.9 percent, as many as 15 percent of the
nation's best and brightest are on the "pre-med" track.

The health care sector is also radically overrepresented in the 0.1
percent—but with a twist. Apart from a few celebrity doctors, the health
care 0.1 percenters are almost entirely on the business end of the business.
Between 2012 and 2018, while nurses saw their pay creep upward a total
of 3 percent, hospital CEOs saw their median annual compensation jump
from $1.6 million to more than $3 million per year.[17] That still left them
a digit short of the sixty-two health care CEOs who collected almost
$20 million apiece in 2018, or $1.1 billion in total—which is more than
the CDC spends on all chronic disease prevention, as it happens.[18] The
biggest winners in the health care game, however, are not these jockeys
of the health-industrial bureaucracy but the health care hedge-funders,
who typically have more money than a private jet stuffed with health
care CEOs.

Now, about the die-off. The health care sector didn't kill them, of
course; at least, not in any direct way. The rising harvest of death in
America has resulted not from an absence of cures but from a plethora of
causes. As economists Anne Case and Angus Deaton show, the decline

of life expectancy in the United States in the years that preceded Covid is mainly attributable to an increase in "deaths of despair" among white, middle-aged Americans of low educational attainment.[19] The opioid crisis was the biggest part of the problem, but alcohol abuse and suicide were not far behind. According to a 2019 congressional study, you have to go back to the Great Depression to find suicide rates as high as they are now, and back to the eve of Prohibition for comparable levels of alcohol-related deaths.[20] As more recent research by the American Communities Project confirms, the deaths of despair are concentrated in "middle suburbs"—that is, predominantly white, middle-income suburbs in economically challenged regions in the Midwest that fell to Trump by a 13-point margin in 2016.[21]

Almost every statistical measure available confirms what one may gather from a glance at Grace: the best way to increase your odds of leading a healthy life is to become a paid-up member of the 9.9 percent. The longest life expectancies are concentrated in the best zip codes; higher income is correlated with lower rates of almost every form of chronic disease; and more time in college and graduate school is correlated with greater physical fitness.[22] While 70 percent of college-educated Americans report good or fair health, only 42 percent of the high-school-educated population do. About 40 percent of U.S. adults over twenty are now obese, up from 23 percent in 1988, and that condition, too, is concentrated heavily in the lower-income, lower-education groups. According to the Department of Health and Human Services, only 5 percent of adults get thirty minutes of exercise every day and only one in three reach minimum weekly targets for physical activity. Not coincidentally, signs of mental health distress, psychosomatic disorders, and depression have increased measurably between 1980 and 2010.[23] And—here's a weird fact—after a long and illustrious history in the annals of human stature, when they routinely stood taller than members of other nations, Americans alone in the developed world have been getting measurably shorter on average, not taller (though that trend may be explained by immigration patterns).[24]

When the pandemic hit in 2020, many opinion makers were quick to imagine that the world would never be the same. It was 9/11 all over again, only this time with a lifeless strand of RNA as the enemy. In reality, the pandemic was more like an accelerated version of what had been happening in American society for some time. Covid-19, the data soon revealed, is particularly deadly for individuals suffering from pre-existing conditions, and the pre-existing condition that mattered most was the same one that mattered in the slow-burning pandemic that preceded the arrival of the coronavirus, namely, living at the wrong end of America's racial and economic inequality spectrum. Even the feel of the pandemic was different in the wealthier neighborhoods. Though it claimed some casualties among the 9.9 percent, the crisis was less a matter of survival than of adaptation and existential exploration. The 9.9 percent wiped down their grocery deliveries, zoomed from virtual office gatherings to virtual dinner parties, discovered what it means to clean one's own home, fled to the country home, and finally understood the true meaning of the Peloton experience.

As far as Grace is concerned, of course, all of these health gaps are very unfortunate. If you ask her why she is so fit and the people packing up her deliveries at the warehouse are not, she will probably say that, sadly, they do not have Peloton bikes. If you were to suggest to her that her good health has something to do with their bad health, she would likely give you a funny look, and return to her workout routine. They are the ones popping pills and drinking themselves to death, after all, while she is the one on the fitness bike working toward the cures. Everyone starts off in life without a Peloton bike, as Grace might put it, and the fact that a few people get them should count as a point in their favor, not against them.

Behind Grace's line of thought lies a certain theory about the human condition. This theory has received ample aid and support from a number of distinguished defenders of the status quo today, and it is a vital tenet in the Creed of the 9.9 percent.[25] The premise is that misery is the default condition of humankind. Why, all we need to do is look at the burial grounds of ancient Mesopotamians to see that life has never been a piece of cake. Inequality in itself, it follows, is part of the solution, not part of the problem. It is the way we drag ourselves up from the cave to the Age of Peloton. Popular Harvard professor Steven Pinker sums the idea up well: "Inequality is not a fundamental component of well-being," he declares, but it may well be "a harbinger of opportunity."[26] Princeton philosopher Harry Frankfurt further assures us that poverty and inequality are two very different things, analytically speaking, and the one has nothing to do with the other. Who cares if someone has more than others, he asks; we should be happy as long as everyone at long last has enough.[27] Grace would surely find this theory comforting.

THE REFRESHING THING ABOUT THE RULERS of the ancient world, for us, is that they speak with a certain clarity about the origins of poverty and inequality in human society. Indeed, if you set aside the self-congratulatory poetry of the ancients and take a second, closer look at the bones, you will see that they had a very clear perspective on the matter.

Puabi's gold-encrusted, mother-of-pearl carriage was undoubtedly the product of many thousands of hours of fine, human craftsmanship, but she was not about to waste it on the living. Nor did she imagine that it would drive itself into the underworld. She was counting on the services of the three dead oxen and four groomsmen whose corpses were buried alongside the vehicle. The bejeweled musical instruments meant to ease her way into the afterlife were very fine, too, but they weren't going to play themselves. They were found in the bony clutches of a band of dead musicians. A squadron of cadavers dressed as soldiers stood guard near the door, and a banquette of female bodies, adorned with fine jewels and blue-gold headdresses, sat ready to serve their mistress. All told, fifty-two human beings accompanied Puabi in death. Some appear to have been murdered with a pointed hammer to the skull; others may have had their throats cut; and others, for all we know, eagerly drank the Mesopotamian version of Kool-Aid. Yet it seems that Puabi may not have been the greatest ruler of Ur. Next to her tomb lies another, dubbed by archaeologists "The Great Death Pit." It holds the remains of seventy-four human beings.

In the early civilizations of the Americas, Hawaii, China, Israel, Egypt, Southeast Asia, Greece, and Rome, the story is mostly the same.[28]

Independently of one another, for the most part, wherever societies stratified, the rulers of the ancient world accumulated great treasures that would have had much value for the living; yet what they could not keep for themselves in this life, they buried underground, because the living had no value except in service. And then, to prove the general point, they harvested some additional humans and included them among the buried treasure. In shards of folk songs and verses remaining from the popular cultures of these regimes, as Peter Turchin points out, the common people can be heard comparing their masters with "sharks" and referring to them as those who "devour" human beings.[29] In some cases, notably in Mesoamerica, the beautiful people literally did eat their human subordinates.

A cuneiform inscription from the Near East dating about 3,100 years ago gives voice to the reigning idea of early human civilization.[30] In the space of several thousand words, an Assyrian ruler named Tiglath Pileser—"King of all Kings, Lord of Lords: the supreme" by his own reckoning—catalogues the extraordinary pain he inflicted on those people who had been "disobedient" and who had withheld "the tribute and offerings due." "I plundered their wealth," says mighty Tiglath. "Their cities I burnt with fire. . . . Their carcasses covered the valleys and the tops of mountains. . . . I cut off their heads. . . . I have imposed on them the bond of servitude." He repeats this charming message with minor variations about forty-two times—once for each of the neighboring chiefdoms that his armies crushed into submission. Particularly telling are the metaphors with which Tiglath celebrates this harvest of death. He routinely cuts down his enemies "like grass" or "like weeds"; he scatters their corpses "like chaff"; and then he shackles the survivors under "the heavy yoke of my empire." On some of this human herd, following the custom that was at that point already older than any of the world's major religions are today, he imposes a fate worse than enslavement: "I led away their young ones, like tame goats. These little wild animals, the delight of their parents' hearts, in the fulness of my own heart, together with my own victims, I sacrificed to my Lord Ashur."

This is the actual story of the origins of human inequality. Sometime after human beings domesticated plants and animals, they discovered—step by step, most likely without much conscious awareness of the destination—how to reap a far more valuable harvest. Corn and cows were good to have, but human beings proved to be the richest crop of all. The invention of conventional, nonhuman agriculture mattered, to be sure, but mainly because it had the effect of crowding humans into small spaces, cutting off the escape routes, and leaving them dependent on an insecure food supply. Once rendered vulnerable in this way, humans could be pushed to the hard edge of subsistence and compelled to labor on behalf of those who tamed them. Civilization did not begin with the invention of the plow. It began with the domestication of humans.[31]

The global human population expanded as much as a hundredfold in the several thousand years following the invention of civilization, but this giant leap for humankind was not in every respect a triumph for human beings. Humans multiplied across the planet in part for the same reason that sheep and wheat proliferated. The vast majority of those born after the advent of civilization—which is to say, the majority of human beings that have ever lived—were hurried into life to labor on behalf of others, their bodies stripped like living carcasses for whatever had value, and sustained just long enough so that they might invest their hopes in children who would carry their burdens into the next generation. The human being had stepped for a moment into sunny abundance; then she stepped back into a shadow much darker than anything that came before.[32]

Violence is nothing new in nature, of course, but the domestication of humans involved the invention of a new, nearly invisible, uniquely human, notionally victimless form of violence that remains central to any understanding of inequality even today. No direct violence is necessarily exchanged *between* humans when a warlord exacts a tribute from other humans in order to protect them from himself and his band of health care providers. The violence in effect disappears from the interpersonal statistics. (This is one reason why histories of violence that purport to reduce the subject to an index of interpersonal statistics are so shallow.) It shows up, to the extent that evidence can be collected, only in what people do to their own bodies in order to survive—and perhaps also in what they do to their own minds on account of the artificially lowered estimation of their own value that follows from their subjugation. The genius of human sacrifice, in this context, is that it reenacts in a viscerally symbolic way the real crime of ancient civilization: in order to exploit humans, it is necessary to kill them first, metaphorically speaking.

Poverty is the name we give to this new, distinctively human form of intrapersonal violence. It is the collateral damage of a war continued by other means. The impoverishment of humans, to be sure, is not itself the warlord's goal any more than clipping a vine or whipping an ox is the purpose of agriculture. It is merely the necessary consequence of disempowering others just enough to rise above them. Philosophers like Harry Frankfurt and Steven Pinker have the luxury of making fine logical distinctions between poverty and inequality, but for the longest part of human history separating the two would have made little more sense than distinguishing thunderclouds from rain.

Possibly this is the story recorded in between the lines of the first book of the Bible. Though it seems incredibly ancient to us, the Bible in fact arrived well past the chronological midpoint of human history to date (and it also, by the way, borrows a few items from the older story of Gilgamesh and includes possible references to the prior practice of human sacrifice). When life in the Garden of Eden comes to an unhappy end, thanks to an unintelligible crime on the part of a loose woman, the common man is told that his sustenance may now be obtained only "from the sweat of your brow." He accepts that his life is not his own to lead but belongs to another. Dominion, we learn, is the basis of all order: the dominion of God over men, kings over people, master over slave, man over woman, one race over another race, humans over animals, and of written words in general over any stray thoughts and suspicions. Most of human culture is the culture of the crop. If corn could speak, it would probably write a Bible, too.

IN EXPLORING THE CAUSES of the recent setbacks that trouble the health care landscape outside Grace's condo, it's easy to get lost in the weeds of distress. The effects of globalization and other economic dislocations, the pro-death rejection of gun safety regulation, the rancid culture of white grievance in the heartland, and the criminally greedy pharmaceutical companies—all of these and other factors would have to be part of any complete story about the die-off in middle America. Stagnant incomes are undoubtedly central to the explanation, but, as Anne Case and Angus Deaton point out, the income trends don't line up perfectly with the mortality rates. Likewise, although studies across countries and across American states routinely show that income inequality correlates with falling health indicators, there, too, the year-to-year and place-to-place relationships are always partial and imperfect.[33]

Case and Deaton sensibly hypothesize that the root source of the trouble is the "cumulative disadvantage" that certain groups in society have faced over a long period of time. The varieties of disadvantage, they suggest, include: the decline of marriage and marital prospects, the loss of power in the labor markets, the breakdown of local communities, and some negative cultural developments, such as a decline in the perceived value of industriousness. These burdens generate stress in a hundred shades of gray, and the stress in turn delivers death and disease.[34]

On closer inspection, however, it is clear that "cumulative disadvantage" is mostly a euphemism for a new kind of poverty. It's the kind of category that economists invent to describe a form of impoverishment that does not fit within the narrow categories they use to frame human experience. To be clear, the official poverty rate has held more or less constant over the past four decades of escalating inequality, as defenders of inequality today are often eager to point out. But that proves only that we have succeeded in deluding ourselves about the nature of wealth and poverty. Being poor in marriage prospects and community, poor in nutritional options and exercise opportunities, poor in time and in control over one's life—these aren't simply effects of poverty. They *are* poverty, whether or not they are accompanied with just enough spare change to buy macaroni at the grocery store or a plateful of junk food. The way to tell if you are poor is if you are dying unnecessarily.

Economists have trouble seeing this because they measure wealth in terms of money. A very large part of material inequality today, however, shows up not as differences in income or even financial wealth but as differences in levels of risk and power over one's own life.[35] In a fast-changing, high-tech economy, life is unstable and nerve-racking, or so the comfortably ensconced champions of disruption at the business schools keep reminding us. The United States tops the league for employee churn, with one in five employees losing or leaving a job every year, but it ranks second-to-last in spending on active measures to help the unemployed.[36] The CEOs get this. That's why they are careful to negotiate severance packages for themselves that can take them safely back to earth in golden parachutes. They believe in "creative destruction"; they just don't want it in their lives. That's the game plan for the 9.9 percent, too. The point of the professional associations, the well-funded retirement plans, and the generous health insurance packages that pad the walls of the 9.9 percent way of life is to protect its members from the stomach-burning churn that afflicts everybody else in the economy that they run.

Meanwhile, back in flatland, ordinary families suffer adverse income shocks—when a household loses 50 percent or more of its annual income—at a rate achieved in the 1960s and 1970s only during the worst recessions. While 9.9 percenters ponder their energy rhythms and "work-life balance," the 90 percent ponder how they will balance their checkbooks in the event of a dental crisis or any other emergency. While 9.9 percenters see nontraditional schedules as a form of liberation—I can pick the kids up from school myself!—most other workers find that off-hour schedules come at the expense of their ability to manage family responsibilities and community life.

One of the most stressful aspects of life in America for those who haven't yet made it into the happy land of the paid-up 9.9 percenters is interacting with the system that is ostensibly there to deal with the consequences of stress. Through a paradoxical and yet necessary logic, the inequities of the health care systems are themselves a major cause of health problems. Three in ten Americans report not taking medicines as prescribed in the past year on account of cost—far more than citizens in other developed nations.[37] Insulin in America is now so expensive that those who can't smuggle it in turn to cheaper alternatives—even if, as in the case of twenty-seven-year-old diabetic Josh Wilkerson of northern Virginia, it kills them.[38] It comes down to the simple fact that, at roughly $11,000 per person per year, Americans are asked to pay about twice as much for health care relative to income as the citizens of other OECD countries. It's "like a tribute to a foreign power, but we're doing it to ourselves," Anne Case said at a 2020 conference. "A few people are getting very rich at the expense of the rest of us." She and Angus Deaton expressed surprise that "Americans aren't revolting against these taxes."[39]

It gets worse when you realize that much of that tribute paid to the health care sector is reinvested into efforts to stop you from getting the treatment you need. The United States spends more on health insurance administration as a percent of GDP than it does on the entire business of agriculture, and then it doubles down with even greater spending on hospital administration.[40] If the lack of coverage doesn't kill you, maybe the paperwork will.

The negative impacts of dysfunctions in the health care system on health came into grim relief with the Covid pandemic. America's health care professionals undoubtedly saved a great many lives during the crisis, but they were fighting a system that takes away many lives at the same time. The United States appears to be the only major country to have collectively decided that in a pandemic, when many people lose their jobs, they should also lose their health insurance. The lack of access to care, combined with the economic motivation on the part of workers to risk spreading the disease, multiplied the impacts. As Arthur Caplan, the director of NYU's medical ethics program, told Bloomberg News, "the coronavirus loves the inequitable health care system we've got."[41]

At first glance, from Grace's window, this panorama of distress and the resulting, new form of poverty—some of it caused by the health care system, some by operations of the economic system from which the health care system emerges—might seem perfectly gratuitous. Why can't we have the same economy without the life-challenging job churn, or a health care system without the ulcer-inducing paperwork and the wallet-emptying tribute? But if you turn the camera back on Grace, it becomes clear that there is nothing gratuitous at all about this extra measure of misery. Take away the overpriced medication that the pharmaceutical clients of her boss's advertising agency are pushing through the daytime television ads that she helps produce, for example, and she won't be able to afford that Peloton bike.

The impoverishment of the many is not an incidental effect of a system that redistributes resources upward; it is a necessary feature of the system. The way to keep the 0.1 percent happy is to keep wages low, and the way to keep wages low is to keep workers desperate. The operating principle in times of extreme inequality is to provide employment under conditions bad enough that workers will be glad just to have it, just as the operating principle of the health care system in times of inequality is to sell the cures at prices that make people sick enough to need them. Essential jobs are easy to fill if they are essential for survival. The task of the 9.9 percent is to lubricate the machinery that administers the pain—and then to suggest by example that the 90 percent have a shot at the joining them in a life of ease, if only they would work just a little harder.

ALL THINGS CONSIDERED, of course, it is much better to be an aspiring member of the 9.9 percent than one of those people that Tiglath Pileser referred to as "goats." Human sacrifice is no longer a thing. We're proud of that. It took a long time for humanity to arrive at the American health care system, one could argue, and we're just a few medications and maybe a handful of life-saving apps away from ensuring a healthy future for all of humankind. Steven Pinker is there, as ever, to encourage us in the belief that the system is delivering the goods, and that the thing to do is to keep pressing ahead.

Progress is indeed real, and nothing could be more important than to understand its sources. The extraordinary improvement in basic human living conditions over the past two centuries or so—amply embodied in the recent increases in human height and health indicators mentioned above—is indeed the single most important fact in human history. Unfortunately, the 9.9 percent routinely misunderstand the actual source of human progress. To be more precise, as inequality rises, the 9.9 percent make their living out of misrepresenting the nature of progress.

According to the view favored by the 0.1 percent today and promoted by the intellectual vanguard of the 9.9 percent, all progress is technological progress. It advances from the beginning of time to the present along railroad tracks laid down in the fabric of the universe. Like a silver bullet train, it always aims for the improvement of the human condition. All we have to do is step on the train and let money drive it toward its destination.

In light of the extraordinary and extraordinarily recent developments of the past couple of centuries, however, two facts about the preceding eighty centuries or so of recorded history are worth more attention than all the others put together. The first is that there was no progress. (To put the matter more delicately: relative to what we now know to be possible, such improvements in the human conditions as were attained were small and tenuous enough that they may be safely rounded to zero in light of subsequent developments.) Aristotle, Polybius, Confucius, the authors of the Upanishads, Machiavelli, Edward Gibbon, and countless other thinkers and historians who lived during the Great Stagnation took for granted that the proper metaphor for history is not an ascending line but a circle: human affairs improve and degenerate as the wheel of history turns. They believed this not out of religious prejudice or willful ignorance, but because the alternative had no basis in experience. Economic historian Angus Maddison estimates that the global per capita economic growth rate between 1 CE and 1500 CE was 0.01 percent per year.[42] At that rate, a generation of workers on, say, a dollar a day, might know that, after one hundred years of hard labor, their great-great-grandchildren would be hauling in $1.01. There is little reason to think that things were meaningfully different in the preceding 1,500 years—or the 1,500 years before that.

The second fact, which we have already met, is that inequality during the Great Stagnation was stupendous, even by twenty-first-century standards. The Egyptian pharaoh Khufu (circa 2589 BCE) expended about 400,000 man-years of labor on his second-life home—out of a population that numbered about 2 million.[43] Qin Shi Huangdi (259–210 BCE), the first emperor of a unified China, had 700,000 men—out of perhaps 10 million—working for three decades on an immense necropolis in which he was eventually buried with 8,000 terra-cotta soldiers and a number of live human sacrifices (including the artisans responsible for building the place).[44]

These two fundamental facts of history—persistent stagnation and extreme inequality—are hardly unconnected. Indeed, the second explains the first. The domestication of humans is a costly business—for humans. Scholars often artificially limit their analysis of the topic to times and places when the data are friendly, and so they study the relation between narrowly economistic ideas of inequality and growth only within the exotic microcosm of the past hundred years or so. This is a little like trying to gauge the effect of diet on mortality by asking people what they ate in the morning and checking to see who dies by the end of the day. Even so, the traces of the ancient predicament of human civilization are distinctly visible in the modern statistics. The United States and the developed world achieved their highest growth rates in the period of lowest inequality, from 1945 to 1975. The return to higher inequality over the past four decades, conversely, has coincided with a decrease in growth rates. In an extensive 2014 study across countries, IMF economist Jonathan Ostry concludes that "lower net inequality is robustly correlated with faster and more durable growth." Reviewing the evidence in 2018, he underscores the "tentative consensus" that inequality "tends to reduce the pace and durability of growth."[45]

The ways in which inequality caused the Great Stagnation are many, but the one that deserves more attention than it typically gets passes through the human mind. Inequality disrupts progress because inequality distorts consciousness. A case in point would be Queen Puabi. She believed in a certain kind of progress, too. One can hardly view the objects she took with her to the underworld—some of them on display now at the British Museum—and not come away with the impression that she really imagined her body was going to live on forever. The 9.9 percenters who dutifully applied hammers to skulls in order to supply her with servicepeople in the death-life were on board with the program, too. (Or at least they faked it well enough to get on with the job—career security had to have been a concern for them.) Emperor Qin was a believer, too. He ingested mercury because the researchers told him it would preserve him; then, with impeccable logic, he surrounded his necropolis with rivers of mercury to kill off would-be grave robbers. He used so much of the stuff that the ground in the area is still considered a health hazard. After burying huge chunks of GDP in this way, he went on to torpedo all succession plans. Who needs a successor when you're going to rule the universe forever? The 9.9 percenters who sculpted his toy army probably thought it was worth a shot, too, until they got buried alive. Gilgamesh was another fan of the afterlife plan, and so was Khufu.

This, apparently, is something that the rulers of the ancient world had in common with Peter Thiel, Larry Ellison, Sergey Brin, Jeff Bezos, and Elon Musk. All of these modern moguls, too, have invested in what is now called "life extension." Some of them (Bezos and Musk) appear to be interested in carrying on these extended lives in outer space. Thiel, who seems to be vying for a title as the creepiest of the bunch, sometimes says things like: "I'm looking into parabiosis stuff."[46] Parabiosis: that's where you siphon blood from healthy young teens and pump it into horny old billionaires in hopes that they can squeeze a few more years of joy out of life. In the early twentieth century, they tried the same thing with juices squeezed out of monkey glands.

If you put yourself in the mind of an ancient agricultural-hedge-funder, it might just make sense. From a young age, you learn that you can bring forth artificial mountains and pearl-encrusted luxury devices by simply making the right clicks. The world encourages you to believe that your body houses a god. Why wouldn't you want your body to go on forever? Weirdly, you feel subordinate to some higher power that seems to have the final word over your body, even as you rise far above other mortals. You find yourself feeling insecure in the competition with a small number of others who also seem to possess vaguely superhuman powers and might just want to claim your throne. So you start to think that the only safe path is make the transition complete.

The reality, of course, is that you have lost the ability to distinguish between the powers you derive from your position within a social network that entitles you to appropriate other people's labor and the rather more modest powers of your actual body. This "you" that you wish to preserve, this image of yourself as the billionaire venture capitalist or ancient pyramid builder, or whatever it is, is a tenuous fiction, constructed out of the temporary confluence of certain trends and events, altogether too dependent on the merely human side of your existence. The result is that even as you pretend to organize the labor of a vast society toward some higher good for humanity, you actually divert their collective energy into an incoherent project that involves sucking the blood of teenagers or pickling human flesh in vinegar and stuffing it under a pile of rocks.

The syndrome is common enough that today even the not-so-famous 0.1 percenters seem to be afflicted. The media theorist Douglas Rushkoff reports that he was recently invited to dine with a handful of hedge-funders who ostensibly wanted to know how to "survive environmental collapse."[47] They were apparently staying up nights worrying about questions like: How do I keep my security forces from rebelling against me after "the event"? Upon further discussion with these flaming butt-heads, it became clear to Rushkoff that "what they really wanted to know was how to transcend the human world they look down upon." That's the thing about the winners today and in any age. They really have no idea where their wealth comes from or what the end will look like. Their vision of heaven is just a place where they are bigger dicks than they already are. So long as they remain in charge of progress, humanity progresses nowhere.

But the pharaohs aren't the only ones who participate in the delusions of inequality. Amid the ruins of the camps that housed the pyramid construction crews in ancient Egypt, for example, archaeologists discovered evidence that the top tier of pyramid-craftsmen were regularly feasting on the finest cuts of meat available on the Nile delta at the time.[48] The elite overseers were paid as much as a hundred loaves of bread a day. Imagine what you could do with all that bread! Naturally, they chose to establish miniature pyramid schemes of their own, with themselves at the apex and the busloads coming in from the agricultural hinterland filling up the base.

The economic logic of the 9.9 percent has always been pretty much the same: it is the form of life that flourishes one step down in a cascading system of bribery that flows earthward from heaven. The psychology, though immensely varied in the detail of history, is therefore always the same in a fundamental way, too. In times of inequality, everyone dreams of having a pyramid of their own and maybe a little bit of that pharaoh attitude, too. In a society organized around the salvation of the rich, it is the madness and the nihilism, not the wealth, that trickles down.

There is no silver bullet train to the future because inequality always throws progress off the rails. It reliably induces delusions about the nature of the human condition and the origins of human wealth, and then it places power in the hands of precisely those individuals most likely to suffer from these delusions. Real progress is not, for the most part, a story about what humans have done with their gadgets. It is mostly a story about what they have been able to do in collaboration with one another. The measure of progress is not to be found in the domination of human beings over nature but in the relations of human beings to other human beings. The beginning of all progress lies in the recognition of human equality, and its practical foundation is justice.

HERE'S THE THING ABOUT GRACE. She really has it good. She's got a happy family, a great house in central Boston, lots of toys for Christmas, and a first-class body that makes you wonder if those children really are hers. And her in-home bike probably is a good idea, under the circumstances. Working out online with shout-outs from a trainer in Tampa is definitely better than yelling at the screen from the couch with popcorn in hand. But if you ask Grace why she has it so good, she won't tell you that she works as a marketing consultant for the pharmaceutical industry (or whatever it is) and that she has a great employer-sponsored health insurance plan. She won't tell you that the key to her success is actually pleasing her boss, or her husband, or whoever it is that's making her so frantic. She also won't tell you that the price of in-home fitness is $2,474, and another $468 a year in annual membership fees, which means that the real point is to save you time, not money, so that you can spend more hours at work and cling to your iffy plan of moving up to an apartment that looks at least a little like her all-neutral-tones life-pad but maybe without the second floor and the outdoor furniture. She won't tell you that all of that spinning will leave your body fit, if not somewhat overworked, but won't change a damn thing about the system that is the source of that stress. No, she is going to point her smartphone camera at herself, as she is sweating through her routine, and tell you that it all comes down to taking care of yourself. She's going to suggest that you can have your little slice of the pyramid, too, if you'll just get with the program and pedal like a bunny popping uppers. No wonder the internet got upset.

But let's get practical. There really are no good excuses for the American health care system. There are only bad ones. "If you like your insurance, you can keep it" is just a way of saying that if you're happy with the fact that the senseless tribute you pay to the pharaohs is less than that of your fellow citizens, then you can keep on paying that senseless tribute. "Don't let the government stand between you and your doctor" is actually a pretty sick joke in a sector that uses all of its influence on government to ensure that you may not have a doctor and that if you do you will pay far more than citizens of every other country for her attention. Making health coverage dependent on employment is not an example of the free market in action; it is just another layer of coercion in the labor system that locks many people into unrewarding jobs, deprives many others of coverage, floods emergency rooms with people who lost bets against their own health, and creates vectors for diseases and conditions that affect even those who are happy with their place on the pyramid. Granting licenses to drug companies to profit off technologies made possible through publicly funded research also has nothing to do with the free market; it's just a publicly organized form of hostage-taking. The question is not whether the United States should move toward a system of universal health care that makes health care a right and not merely a privilege. The question is why it has not done so.

The answer obviously begins with the entrenched interests that benefit from the current regime. But it necessarily passes through the mind of the 9.9 percent. Decades of marketing have confirmed us in the belief that we make our own worlds and shape our own bodies through our individual purchasing choices and lifestyle decisions. We have come to take for granted that health is something you accomplish in perfect privacy, on your in-home bike, and not something that humans achieve by working together. All of this makes us heroic as consumers and compliant as citizens. We are a people well suited to continue with the mission of building pyramids for the pharaohs.

Why Other People Are So Racist

Jeffrey, as I will call him, really does care about racial justice. So does his neighbor Billy. You are unlikely to meet any two people more sensitive than these two highly educated, white, middle-age rivals for the title of most-community-conscious resident of one of those highly-educated southwestern zip codes that 9.9 percenters aspire to join. During the pandemic month of June 2020, neither left their home-bound laptop lives except to participate briefly and safely in a local Black Lives Matter protest. It therefore came as something of a shock when Jeffrey accused Billy of committing the moral equivalent of racially motivated murder.

The alleged offense took place in cyberspace, in the course of about a half dozen email exchanges between members of a committee planning a neighborhood association meeting. It started when a third commit-tee member drafted an invitation to fellow residents in which passing, favorable mention was made of the fact that some committee members were busy at the time joining the protests that erupted upon the death of George Floyd at the hands of Minneapolis police on May 25, 2020.

Jeffrey wanted something bolder. He circulated a revised announce-ment, and in his version, committee members would declare that they were united as a group rallying in the streets and would urge all invitees to join with them immediately. Billy objected to the edits, noting that, while he himself had joined the protests, not all of the other members had done so. He added that invitees might have other, legitimate ideas on how to advance racial justice, and, besides, none of this had much to do with the subject of their conference. The discussion blossomed into a flurry of long, historically informed analyses of the American crisis.

Among the dozen or so on-again off-again members of the somewhat lackadaisical committee, only one was a person of color. Demographically speaking, this was not surprising. Only 3 percent of the zip code's population is Black, even if 97 percent of residents are vocally committed to racial justice. By contrast, the zip codes immediately to the south and east, where aspiring 9.9 percenters generally do not wish to live, are 90 percent nonwhite. In the course of the committee's erudite but increasingly tense exchanges over the protest-solidarity issue, the lone person of color on the committee, who had not been actively participating in the discussions, announced that he had "too much going on" to serve and, without further comment, resigned.

As far as Jeffrey was concerned, this silent disappearance could only be interpreted in one way. The lone nonwhite committee member must have been so distraught over the committee's blatant indifference to racial justice that he could no longer even speak. His voice had been strangled, metaphorically speaking, just as surely as if the committee had kneeled on his neck. "Guys, we've just had our own 'I can't breathe' moment," Jeffrey announced to the group. He went on to offer a recommended reading list for Billy and fellow committee members, which included some popular titles on white fragility and the history of racism. Unable or unwilling to muster a comeback to the imputed charge of perpetrating a hate crime of the highest symbolic order, Billy resigned from the committee and tacitly ceded the title of most-community-conscious resident to Jeffrey.

EVEN AS THIS MOMENT OF SIMULATED ANGUISH was playing out in a neighborhood blessed with both extraordinarily high real estate values and an exquisite awareness of its own racial insensitivities, a Trump 2020 ad (the sponsor is not known) offered a window into the consciousness of people from even whiter but less prized neighborhoods.[1] The ad starts with a jumpy phone video showing a white, MAGA-hatted man yelling

"Go!" while chasing an Uber car driven by a Black man. The individual recording the video, a young person in a hipster beanie who is clearly not MAGA, is then shown posting the video alongside a snide comment slamming her "racist neighbor." The clip attracts the approving clicks of a series of transparently non-MAGA people, and soon it's a virus. Next, the ad shows CNN blaming Trump for yet another racist incident.

But then the ad goes back in time and switches to a reconstruction of the original scene. We gather that the Black Uber driver was stuck in the snow. We see the white MAGA man patiently explaining to the helpless driver how to get his car out of the snow. Then the kind MAGA man pushes the car from behind while helpfully yelling "Go!" The lesson, delivered about three weeks after the murder of George Floyd, is that all of this talk about racist Trump supporters is a fabrication of "cancel culture" and the "fake media." The real victims here are the good white folk of America, who are only trying to teach Black people how to drive in the snow. The comments section indicates that the ad hit its mark. "This is reality!" says a Trump 2020 fan. Trump himself repeated the message in the final presidential debate of 2020, when he described himself (once again) as "the least racist person I know."

It would seem that even the racists today do not want to be seen as racists (setting aside a few very fine people in Charlottesville and some of the individuals who stormed the U.S. Capitol on January 6, 2021). Meanwhile, the anti-racists in the 9.9 percent who sit at the top of the socioeconomic hierarchy are policing one another's thoughts with a vigor that would do a religious inquisitor proud. All of that must count for something. Presumably it is better than having crowds of people marching around with tiki-torches and confederate flags and shouting out racist slogans. But it does raise a question for the curious. If there are (almost) no racists left in America, then how did we end up with a racist country?

CONSIDER SOME OF THE MOST BASIC, well-known facts about the racial distribution of wealth in America. The median Black household has about 3 pennies for every dollar in wealth of the median white family, and the median Latino household has about 4 pennies (estimates vary; the exact number depends on profound methodological questions like whether or not the car counts as wealth).[2] There is a top 1 percent of Black households in wealth, and to make the cut a Black family needs to have approximately $1.2 million in net assets as of 2016. But that same level of wealth will only land you just inside the bottom of the top 10 percent of all households. The best guess (the data are surprisingly rough) is that Black households represent something less than 2 percent of the 9.9 percent, even while they represent more than 13 percent of the total U.S. population. Latinos come in somewhere over 2 percent of the 9.9 percent, even while they account for about 17 percent of the population. Asian Americans, on the other hand, appear to have proportional representation, with about 5 percent of both the 9.9 percent and the total population. The net of all these differences is that the top decile of wealth in the American economy is the whitest of them all. The American Dream remains, as it ever was, much whiter than the American reality.

The data on income distributions might at first glance seem less stark than that on wealth distribution. Black households earn about 60 pennies, and Latino households earn 72 pennies, for every dollar of white household income.[3] But it only takes a second glance to see that the underlying story is the same. For one thing, the disconnect between the income distribution and the wealth distribution is itself evidence that there is a substantial racial disparity in the mechanisms that convert income into wealth (much of which has to do with housing, as discussed previously). More startling is the trend—or rather, the absence of a trend—in the racial income gap. Properly adjusted to account for the extraordinary rate of incarceration of Black men, as economists Patrick Bayer and Kerwin Kofi Charles have documented,[4] the difference between the median wages for Black men and white men remains about where it was in the 1950s.

The same racial disparities show up in health data, as discussed in the previous chapter, which make abundantly clear that Black and brown children in America have shorter life expectancy, higher incidence of chronic disease, higher infant mortality, and a greater chance of dying in a pandemic than their white peers. The same disparities show up again in the statistical aftermath of the criminal justice system, which show that having black or brown skin substantially increases the probability of getting arrested, getting shot at by police, getting convicted, and getting imprisoned.

These basic facts about the racial divide in America are well known enough not to belabor. The remarkable thing—or at any rate the point of interest here—is how we manage to live with this reality. More than that, the issue is how we absolve ourselves from any involvement in producing it. In order to understand how we dissolved the problem of racism in our own minds, it is important to know something about how we defined it—and defined it away. The idea of the 9.9 percent comes with a certain idea about the nature of racism, and this underlying theory of racism is the thing that requires some attention here.

The 9.9 percent theory of racism goes something like this. Racism, it says, is a state of mind that afflicts individual consumers. The harm of racism occurs through individual acts of discrimination, and it falls entirely on members of the target race. The benefit, such as it is, is shared equally among all members of the preferred race in the form of a privilege. The solution, and the ultimate aim of all anti-racist effort, is to achieve purity in thought. This desired state of mind, some analysts go on to suggest, is as rare and difficult to achieve as the highest stage of enlightenment is for the most advanced gurus. This 9.9 percent theory of racism, it is important to add, comes wrapped in a narrative of inevitable historical progress that takes us on a march up from slavery through the civil rights movement and Black Lives Matter. It says that, inasmuch as racism is a bad state of mind, it is mainly a legacy of the past that will fade as the last of the old-timers die off.

The 9.9 percent theory of racism is not entirely without truth. In some respects, it is hopeful, inspiring, and even necessary. But it is just wrong enough to distract us from the actual problem and its real solutions. Racism is not in fact an individual state of mind but a system of organizing political and economic power. Individual acts of discrimination, though necessarily an aspect or consequence of racist systems, are far from the only means of their operation. The harm that racism inflicts on the target population is great and inexcusable, but it is not the only nor even the principal harm of racist systems. The benefits of racist practice, such as they are, are not divided evenly among members of the privileged race. On the contrary, it is more useful to think of those benefits in terms of what I will call a "race dividend" that is distributed very unevenly and decidedly in favor of the 9.9 percent, without regard to the purity of individual opinions or even necessarily individual racial identity. The solutions to racism have less to do with the purity of our souls than with economic justice, because racial injustice is ultimately inseparable from the economic injustice from which it arises.

The 9.9 percent theory of racism is ultimately a way of framing the problem that leaves our contribution out of the picture. It grows in appeal in nearly exact proportion with rising inequality. Sometimes, even worse, it is a way of turning anti-racist rhetoric into the means of consolidating the power of a new, multiracial, economic elite. It is a good example of how, in order to betray justice, inequality invites us to redefine it first. It is also a good example of how, in order to supply a more pleasing explanation for the present, inequality leads us to make up stories about the past. In fact, one of the best ways to understand the dangerous limitations of the 9.9 percent theory of racism is to contrast its misrepresentations of the history with the actual history of racism in America. It is useful therefore to begin a critique of this 9.9 percent theory of racism with some observations about the generally unremarked historical errors on which it rests.

"SLAVERY . . . HAS BEEN CALLED by a great many names, and it will call itself by yet another name; and you and I and all of us had better wait and see what new form this old monster will assume, in what skin this old snake will come forth next," Frederick Douglass said at the meeting of the American Anti-Slavery Society on May 9, 1865.[5] The Civil War was over, Congress had passed the Thirteenth Amendment prohibiting slavery, and some of the leaders of the Anti-Slavery Society had put forward a motion to disband their society permanently. This was their "mission accomplished" moment. But Douglass objected. He harbored hopes for a multiracial republican future, to be sure, but he thought it unwise to take for granted that the struggle for justice was over. Douglass and his allies defeated the motion to disband, and subsequent events soon proved their judgment prescient.

In retrospect, the twelve years of Reconstruction that followed Douglass's speech validated both the opportunity and the danger he identified. When the system of chattel slavery ended, astonishingly, the racism that sustained it fell back just long enough for some Americans to glimpse a very different future in a world free from the old monster of slavery. In the same unsettling spring of 1865, while Douglass was meeting with his antislavery comrades, for example, a white newspaper editor and erstwhile pro-slavery pastor named James W. Hunnicutt returned to Richmond from his refuge in Philadelphia and formed an alliance with Albert Royal Brooks, a Black Richmond businessman who had bought his own freedom during the war by working side jobs.[6] At a gathering in the First African Baptist Church, the two men were elected to the executive committee of the state Republican Party. Together with other local activists, Black and white, they campaigned through the streets of Richmond before large crowds of workers, mostly Black but some white, and advocated a revolutionary program for the state of Virginia. They called for the establishment of public schools, the support of manufacturing, and the redistribution of land to help "the poor and humble" of every color. Hunnicutt in particular was adamant in demanding not only political rights but "full social equality for the Negroes."

When Douglass's erstwhile coeditor Martin Delany, often called "the father of black nationalism," toured South Carolina after the war and spoke about the importance of Black identity, the freed people there told him to change the subject.[7] "We don't want to hear that; we are all one color now," they said. Around the same time, an upcountry white farmer wrote to the new governor of the state to say, in broken grammar, that he prayed that the new leadership would work "to protect the humble poor without distinction to race or color." In Austin, Texas, a visitor reported having a wonderful stay in "a cosmopolitan city, albeit on a small scale" where there was a "free intermingling of colors." In 1871, the state of Texas ordered that all railroad carriages be open to people of all colors. Across the South, six hundred Black people, many of them former slaves, took elected office in federal, state, and local governments in the eleven years following the war over slavery.

Of course, as we know, it didn't last. Hunnicutt and Brooks's alliance was crushed, a counterrevolution swept the South, and in 1877 the Republican Party traded away civil rights and the South for the presidency and unfettered freedom for the emerging class of Gilded Age monopolists. By 1888, when he toured South Carolina and Georgia, Douglass knew very well that the old monster of slavery had slithered back in a new skin. "I denounce the so-called emancipation as a stupendous fraud," he declared upon his return.[8]

In the prevailing narratives favored by the 9.9 percent, the return of a racist regime in the aftermath of the counterrevolution is represented as a continuation of racism from the past. Slavery was the original cause of racism in the past, it says; slavery in the past must therefore be the cause of racism in the present. According to Douglass's analysis, however, this is inaccurate in a subtle but crucial way. The fundamental cause of racism in the Jim Crow period was not slavery in the past but a new form of slavery in the present. Racism is and always has been a creature of the present. This point could be seen clearly by distinguishing what was genuinely new in the new regime from what was old.

What was new were the specific mechanisms of the new slavery and, to a surprising extent, the specific forms of the racism it called forth. The new slavery involved convict-leasing schemes, the manipulation of property law to keep Black farmers down, and the active suppression of Black political power. The new racism did not emerge from the hills unchanged; on the contrary, it was the work of conscious, active, and vigorous investment on the part of a new set of masters working in this new economic regime. In the antebellum period, as Douglass notes, racism traded on the slander that Black people were "only fit for slavery." The prevailing stereotypes therefore represented Blacks as docile, inferior, and in need of a white, paternal hand. In the face of Black political power, so vividly illustrated during Reconstruction, racism suddenly fixated on the alleged power lust of Blacks, who were represented as assertive and aggressive. Although racism had always gravitated around sexual anxieties, the new racism was different in this respect, too. In the slave period, concern often centered on the sexuality of enslaved women, who in reality often served as sexual victims for white enslavers. In the postwar period, as lynching became the most reliable tool in the arsenal of racial terror, the paranoia about Black male sexuality, though present earlier, reached a hitherto unparalleled degree of intensity.

The most significant change, however, was in the relative balance of physical and psychological forms of enforcing the racial division. Although the new form of coerced labor that took shape in the postwar American South was in some respects less physically violent than the old form of slavery—here one has to weigh the several thousand lynchings of the postwar period along with other terrorist incidents, such as the massacre in 1873 of 153 or so men at Colfax, Louisiana, against the uncounted instances of whipping, deprivation, rape and indiscriminate murder that were the everyday business of the slave system—the new form of racism was in some ways more psychologically intense, or at least more deeply implanted in the white part of the southern psyche. Under the slave system, perhaps surprisingly, the races often lived in close physical proximity. They went to church together (in segregated pews, of course), and, in some cases they played together as children, as Douglass himself did with the family of his white enslavers. In the new system, the mingling of colors in itself increasingly counted as an offense. The churches were rigorously divided by color and the children kept far apart. The performative aspects of racism— that is, the need not merely to oppress the target race, but to make public display out of its humiliation for the benefit of the preferred race—rose in prominence. In effect, the new American system of apartheid asked the individual mind, under intense social pressure, to carry out and enforce that part of the process of subordination that could no longer be encoded in the law of the land.

Yet certain aspects of the pre- and postwar racist regimes remained constant. As Douglass could see, the structural linchpin of both chattel slavery and the new American system of apartheid was located not in those individuals who supplied the coerced labor but in those whose labor is required to sustain the coercion. That is, the real key to the power of both the old masters and the new was not the subservience of the Black population but the subservience of the non-slaveholding and non-landowning part of the white population. These were the people who manned the militias, chased down fugitives, supervised the plantations, filled the pews, monitored the Black Codes, carried out the lynchings, and in general supplied the votes and the manpower that made these systems of racist oppression viable. And yet—here lay the mystery of the system—these indispensable enforcers of the system were not at all the beneficiaries of the racism in any material sense.

The antebellum American South produced some of the largest fortunes in the world at the time, but the wealth was at least as concentrated then as it is now, and the aggregate wealth was far lower than in the North. Less than 10 percent of the white population of the slave states actually owned slaves (though a larger number were members of households that did). Among this subpopulation of enslavers, the differences were vast. A few thousand families, representing less than 1 percent of the southern population, claimed ownership of a plurality of the enslaved population and lorded it over plantations that enslaved five hundred or more individuals at a time. The rest of the enslavers typically had only one or two human beings to call their own. As contemporary observers such as Frederick Law Olmsted, Theodore Parker, Hinton Rowan Helper, and Douglass himself repeatedly confirm, the white underclass suffered an astonishing toll under the system that it enforced.[9] On almost every metric available at the time—in rates of disease, indexes of dental health, mental health, and substance abuse, median income and median wealth, rates of literacy, educational attainment, and access to services—the mass of whites in the South endured miserable conditions when compared with their peers in nonslave states. Hinton Rowan Helper drew the logical conclusion in a bestseller that made the rounds among Republicans on the eve of the Civil War: "There is but one way for the oligarchy to perpetuate slavery in the Southern states, and that is by perpetuating absolute ignorance among the non-slaveholding whites."[10]

In the Jim Crow period, even as the social, legal, political, and economic arrangements all changed, it was this basic structure of grotesque inequality that remained the same and was the fundamental cause of the new form of racism. "The interests of the poor whites and the colored people are identical," Douglass explains. "Both are ignorant, and both are the tools of designing educated white men; and the poor whites are more particularly used to further schemes opposed to their own best interests." The strategy, as Douglass sees it, could hardly have been simpler: "the poor white man is taught that he is better than the black man." The elites thus "command the poor white man to murder the black man, to burn down his school-houses, and to in every conceivable manner maltreat him, and the command is obeyed. This tends to make the ex-slaveholder more powerful, and is of no good to the poor white."[11]

Racism in the sense that Douglass identifies here clearly does not reduce to individual attitudes on race, even if it makes use of them; it is first and foremost a system of organizing political and economic power. The lynch mobs "are not alone responsible" for their crimes, Douglass writes. "They simply obey the public sentiment of the South, the sentiment created by wealth and respectability, by the press and pulpit." Racism in this sense also has nothing to do with any putative attributes of the targets of race hate. There is no "negro problem," Douglass explains; the Black person "has as little to do with the cause of the Southern trouble as he has with its cure. There is no reason, therefore, in the world why his name should be given to the problem."[12]

W. E. B. Du Bois, who differs from Douglass on many other matters, agrees with him on this point: "So long as the southern white laborers could be induced to prefer poverty to equality with the Negro, just so long was a labor movement in the South made impossible." The leaders and ideologues behind the white supremacist Confederate regime offer essentially the same theory, only they represent it as a good thing. The beauty of racism, according to Jefferson Davis, the president of the Confederacy, is "that it dignifies and exalts every white man by the presence of a lower race" and is therefore "essential to the preservation of the higher orders of republican civilization."[13]

To put the matter in formal terms, Douglass and Du Bois in effect make clear that there are at least three elements of society involved in a racist system. The first group, which we may identify as the "target," is the despised minority, and it clearly takes on the most immediate and brutal blows of racism. This second group, which may be called the "mark," is the disempowered majority that, having been inculcated with racist beliefs, performs the race labor, and suffers a distinct, less acute, more chronic set of harms. Above these two groups sits the "beneficiary" group, or all of those who have a material interest in promoting the racist system. This last group could be further subdivided into the "big winners"—the major slave- or landholders—and their "enablers"—or what Douglass identifies in his time as "the press and pulpit." Today we know them as the 0.1 percent and the 9.9 percent respectively.

These insights that Douglass (and Du Bois) offer about racism, and the history of war and Reconstruction on which they draw, are fairly widely understood today, and perhaps do not require further attention here. But they are worth remembering for the light they shed on the contradictions of the 9.9 percent theory of racism. We'll explore some of those contradictions next, but the general picture that emerges from the history should be clear. At the heart of Douglass's narrative lies a helpful corrective to the triumphalism embedded in the 9.9 percent theory of racism. The favored view today typically represents the key moments of American racial history—notably emancipation and the civil rights movement—as revolutionary victories that solved certain problems in perpetuity. The history that lives in Douglass's writings, on the other hand, shows that those revolutionary moments mark the end points of certain processes of liberation more than the beginnings. Emancipation was the consequence, not the cause, of the growing power and productive value of the enslaved population itself—a power that expressed itself first in insurrections, then in organized escapes, and finally in the force that Black soldiers brought to the Union Army. The civil rights movement, too, is best seen as the culmination of a long period of Black advance in America. Indeed, as current research confirms, the largest gains in Black economic and social power occurred in the decades preceding the civil rights acts of the 1960s, not those that followed.[14] The triumphs are worth celebrating, to be sure, but they are always only temporary victories over the past; the future has to be met on its own terms.

JEFFREY LIVES IN A NICE HOUSE, which he owns. It's got a couple of thousand square feet of space and is worth well over $1 million. Billy, too, lives in a nice house, of roughly the same proportions. This being America, you can drive ten minutes to the neighborhood next door, where paid-up members of the 9.9 percent are few and far between, and discover houses that have the same physical dimensions but are worth about half as much. This being America, none of this seems to be worthy of much comment, because the market is thought to explain and justify everything. The funny thing is that it very obviously does not. In fact, a good place to start on the question of where the material benefits of racial oppression come from and how they are divvied up is to examine more closely that part of the racial economic gap that economics fails to explain.

From an economistic perspective, it is perhaps not surprising that Black households in America own proportionally fewer homes than white people, and that these homes are of lower value and represent substantially lower net equity. This is simply what it means to have lower average incomes and lower average wealth, or so one might think, and people of every color can share the experience. But it is surprising, or at least more interesting to know, that Black home values are lower in part for no other reason than the fact that the owners are Black. In a study that confirms what one can gather from a drive through the various color-coded suburbs of Washington, D.C., or Atlanta, Georgia, researchers found, even after controlling for the quality of local amenities, schools, locational advantages, size of the home, quality of construction, and whatever other characteristics might factor into the value of a home, that homes in majority-Black neighborhoods are worth $48,000 less than homes in comparable white neighborhoods.[15]

Looking at the number from the other side of the tracks, this $48,000 discount for Black-neighborhood homes is simply the premium that Americans will pay for the privilege of living in a white neighborhood. We'll get to the details of those transactions in a moment, but the important point for now is that this premium is paid out in real cash. It is not a merely psychic wage for being white of the kind that W. E. B. Du Bois identified (though that fake currency is a part of the modern economy of racism, as we'll see). This white premium pays for utility bills and a piece of the mortgage. It adds to college savings and retirement savings. It puts teachers in schools and keeps the roads in good shape. Let's call it the "race dividend."

The race dividend can be collected in the office, too. It is (sadly) not surprising at this point that the median Black household earns $29,000 less than the median white household. But a closer look at the wage gap data shows that the main reason that whites earn more than Black people on average is not that they get paid more for doing the same job (though that does happen), but that they work in different kinds of jobs. Black people are notably underrepresented in both the professional jobs that are the apple pie of the 9.9 percent (notably banking, technology, and medicine) and in traditionally unionized jobs (electricians, steelworkers, and heroes of Bruce Springsteen songs in general). Conversely, they are overrepresented in relatively low-wage, unprotected occupations (home health aides, security guards, and anything that women predominantly do).

Now, on the reigning economistic assumption that the job market is another marvel of market efficiency, there is nothing surprising about the fact that groups of people identifiable by different wage-earning capabilities (for whatever reason, fair or foul) should end up in occupations with different wage levels. But the thing about the predominantly white jobs is not just that they are highly paid, but that they are overpaid when considered along any number of metrics, such as relative to other countries, to other jobs with similar educational and skill requirements, and to effort demanded. And there is no good reason not to suppose that they are overpaid precisely because they are perceived to be white occupations. The distinguishing feature about the predominantly Black occupations is not just that they are low-paid, but that they are underpaid by many of the same measures. And they are underpaid precisely because they are perceived to be Black occupations. This difference—not in wage levels per se but in wages relative to all other factors of value—is the race dividend. It is how much more the "market" (meaning people, who are not necessarily as rational as the market expects them to be) will pay for the services of those who work in white economic spaces than those who do not. The occupational version of the race dividend is the direct analog of the residential slice of the dividend, only it trades in the virtual real estate of the job market.

The race dividend is far from the only factor determining home values and wage levels, of course, and it may be small enough to get lost in the shuffle of everyday lives. But it appears to settle at levels that materially alter the risk-reward profile of individual lives in the American economy. For the purposes of the system, this is a feature, not a bug, since it reproduces the economic disparities that then serve as the psychological foundation for the race dividend in the first place. In the case of homeownership, the Great Recession proved the point with as much clarity as statistics ever allow. In the aftermath of the collapse, the homeownership rate among whites fell by 1 percent, but among Black people it dropped by a punishing 5 percent. The mythology says that buying a home is the safest path to the American Dream, but it usually leaves out the clause that says you have to pick up the householder's version of the race dividend along the way if you want to avoid the potholes. The mythology likewise assures us that the first step toward that Dream home is a college education, but it forgets to mention that, for those unable to collect on the occupational side of the race dividend, a college education is more likely to be the first step toward bankruptcy.

Where exactly does the money that funds the dividend come from? The simple answer, favored by the prevailing 9.9 percent theory of racism, says that it represents a transfer from Black to white—but this is a case where the simple answer actively blocks a clear view of the whole truth. The race dividend is undoubtedly the product of racial prejudice in the population at large. It is the monetization of hate. Viewed in the aggregate, it is the sum of countless small decisions and an even greater number of inactions—a mortgage denied over here, a door closed over there, daily insults to one's sense of self, an inexplicable preference for this kind of neighborhood over that, and so on in the miserable catalogue of human cruelty and indifference. But that is not at all the same thing as saying that the wealth that the dividend appropriates comes entirely or even mostly from the targets of racial discrimination—or that the payoff ends up in the hands of the immediate perpetrators. Some of the wealth transfer does flow in that way, to be sure, but the real story of the race dividend takes place precisely where it does not.

Here is an easily overlooked but obvious fact about the race dividend. You don't have to be a racist to collect it. You can rely on the racism of other people to deliver your piece of the action. You also don't have to commit any act of discrimination against any individual person. It is highly unlikely that the person who *didn't* buy your house or *didn't* take your job can ever be named. You don't even have to be white. You just have to buy a home in a (mostly) white neighborhood, or take up a job in a (mostly) white occupation. The catch is, if too many Black people try to claim the dividend, it evaporates. When racism becomes monetized, oddly enough, it becomes color-blind at the individual level even as it reliably delivers on the odds in the aggregate.

Some of this insight is reflected in the widely used term "systemic racism," which accurately captures the possibility that individuals without any racist belief may nonetheless contribute in essential ways to a system that produces racist outcomes. Unfortunately, that term, too, often replicates other misrepresentations characteristic of the 9.9 percent theory of racism. The idea of systemic racism is often taken to mean that the system as a whole operates more or less like a racist individual writ large. That is, it conjures up the image of a system that harbors animus toward one race and seeks to exploit that race for the benefit of another race. But, as Frederick Douglass would have known, this is not how racist systems work at all.

Consider another easily overlooked fact about the race dividend. You can't claim it just because you are white. You need to have something to invest in the first place. This is not a universal "white privilege" afforded to all white people. The fact that white homes appreciate faster than Black homes doesn't help the white person who can't afford a home; the fact that white college degrees pay more than Black ones does little for the white person who doesn't get past high school. The race dividend is for those who already have something, and the more you have, the more you get. The bigger the house—and the bigger the job—the bigger the dividend. This is the one thing that the resentful white MAGA Uber-helper in the Trump 2020 ad gets right, in a sort of twisted way. MAGA man does not like to be called a racist, not necessarily because he isn't one, but because he isn't the one who is cashing in on the racism. What really pisses him off is that the dividend keeps showing up in some other guy's pocket, some beanie-wearing hipster with a professional job who has the luxury of pretending not to be racist.

Which brings us back to the actual source of the wealth that gets transferred through the race dividend. Here is how we know that this wealth does not come entirely or even mostly from the exploitation of the target race, as the 9.9 percent theory (along with most of its "systemic racism" variants) supposes. The race dividend can generate substantial returns even in contexts where there are relatively few members of the target group to exploit. Indeed, sometimes the target group is so small in numbers that it could not possibly account for all the wealth that trades hands as a race dividend. It is even possible to imagine a society in which the target group exists only as a fictional construct—and yet the race dividend continues to pay off. That's because the source of most of the wealth that is transferred through the race dividend is the people who are actually paying it—that is, the people overpaying for those white homes and overpaying for their white service. For the most part—at the risk of some oversimplification—the race dividend is a means of transferring wealth from one white pocket to another white pocket by destroying it in a Black pocket.

A further essential fact about the race dividend is that, like any investment product, it can be managed for growth. To some degree, in a general way, the race dividend reinvests in its own growth as a matter of course. By systematically impoverishing the target group of racial discrimination, as already noted, it lays the grim foundation in experience for the racial contempt and animus that generates the dividend in the first place. But the race dividend can also be the object of a conscious investment strategy. Race labor can be actively encouraged with the promise of still greater psychic rewards, and the existing pool of race labor can be coordinated to produce "better" results, that is, a higher dividend rate. No principle stops a savvy "race entrepreneur" from organizing this race labor, supplying it with the race wages that it craves, and extracting from this a still greater race dividend to be shared among society's lucky beneficiaries. This was the entrepreneurial formula that George Wallace, for example, pursued in his grim sequel to the Jim Crow era.

A final, critical fact about the race dividend, especially relevant in the age of the 9.9 percent, has to do with its profound connection with economic inequality. As Douglass could see, grotesque economic inequality necessarily invites race entrepreneurs to step forth and consolidate their economic power by stoking racial prejudice. The critical additional insight is that economic inequality and racial inequality grow in tandem even without further increase in the underlying racial prejudice. That is because the race dividend rises with inequality, independent of any change in people's opinions. Higher inequality translates into a higher premium paid for living in the best neighborhoods, as we know, and the best neighborhoods—speaking only statistically and financially—are the white neighborhoods. The same holds for all of those occupations that put dinner on the table of the 9.9 percent. In a racialized economy, the more unequal the economy, the more unequal the races.

The data on income gaps from the past seventy years confirm this critical connection between general inequality and racial inequality in a rough but telling way. Between 1950 and the mid-1970s, while inequality across the economy was falling, the Black-white earnings gap among males narrowed—even before the formal rights secured by the civil rights movement were fully in place. During the counter-revolutionary period, from the late 1970s to the present, when general inequality rose, the Black-white male earnings gap increased (adjusting for incarceration), notwithstanding the gains in formal rights and (arguably) in cultural reconciliation secured by the civil rights movement. In short, economic inequality, given enough time, reliably produces racial economic inequality. Whole armies of scribblers have fired off countless narratives to explain the ebb and flow of racism in American culture during the post–civil rights era, but they could have saved a lot of ammunition if they had consulted the fundamental changes in the wealth and income distribution first.

The big winners of the racist system today, just as in the slave period and in Jim Crow, are the 0.1 percent. Racism is one of the essential tools for producing a large pool of disempowered labor, of all races, and this pool of undervalued human exertion is the real source of the great piles of wealth celebrated today as triumphs of the free market. But the people on the next step down the pyramid do pretty well in the bargain, too. To the paid-up members of the 9.9 percent, the race dividend is worth much more than the paltry $48,000 premium on the merely median white home, or the $29,000 difference in median wages. The more unequal the economy, one may add, the harder it is for the 9.9 percent *not* to claim some part of the race dividend. If you are in the 9.9 percent today and you do not buy a house that earns the race dividend and do not clean it with workers who do not earn the race dividend and you fail to send your children to a school that counts on proceeds from the race dividend, then you may not stay in the 9.9 percent for long.

It is more or less a law of economics (to the extent that there are such laws at all) that whoever benefits in a material way from a particular process, however distasteful, is likely to find a way to support the perpetuation of that process. The 9.9 percent is no exception to this rule. Notwithstanding its loud and (I think) sincere avowals of its anti-racist mindset, the 9.9 percent has come to play a vital role in sustaining the American system of the race dividend. In order to see how this part of the system works, it is helpful to draw out one more aspect of Frederick Douglass's analysis of racism.

AT THE PLANTATION OF COLONEL LLOYD on the Eastern Shore of the Chesapeake Bay, Frederick played frequently in a group that included Daniel Lloyd, his enslaver's youngest son. The two boys bonded in the usual ways: over games, jokes, and cake purloined from the manor house. "In Mas' Daniel I had a friend at court, from whom I learned many things which my eager curiosity was excited to know," Douglass recalls.[16] "Are you a child with wants, tastes and pursuits common to children, not put on, but natural? Then, were you black

as ebony you would be welcome to the child of alabaster whiteness,"
Douglass writes. "*Color* makes no difference with a child." And again:
"colors alone can have nothing against one another."[17] Coming from
a man who spent a lifetime getting assaulted in railway carriages and
fending off rotten eggs and brickbats on account of the color of his
skin, this is a formidable conclusion. But he was right: the color line
does not exist in nature. Someone, somewhere, has to draw that line,
and then perform it for all to see.

In the land of the 9.9 percent, the separation of people by color begins
before birth, and is in any event accomplished in a thousand baby steps
by the time school starts. The cradle of racism in America today is the
residential neighborhood.[18] As is by now well known, the archipelago
of mostly white suburbs that still dominates the American landscape
emerged when racist housing policy collided like a tectonic plate with
the interests of big business. Richard Rothstein[19] ably catalogues the
many racist devices deployed in the process: redlining certain neighborhoods as ineligible for mortgage finance; zoning bans on rentals and
apartment complexes; "steering" of nonwhite buyers (as well as members
of targeted ethnic minorities, such as, notably, Jews); and various other
schemes. The division of the races extends to renters, too. In Boston,
a recent study that involved sending Black and white applicants with
equal financial and other qualifications demonstrates beyond question
that discrimination in the rental market is real and huge.[20]

Sticking to aggregate measures, it is possible to tell a happy-ish story
that racial segregation in neighborhoods is down modestly from the
historic highs achieved in the middle decades the twentieth century.[21]
But that does not mean the system has disappeared. About 40 percent
of African Americans live in majority-Black neighborhoods, while the
overwhelming majority of whites live in neighborhoods where at least
nine out of ten neighbors are white. In the subset of the population
comprising young families with children, there is some evidence that
the trend is actually moving toward greater segregation. This is because,
to be more precise, the cradle of racism is not the suburb but the local
school—which increasingly colludes with the outsourced prison to
keep the color line in place. Schools are more racially segregated now

than they were at the dawn of the civil rights era.[22] In 1970, the typical Black student attended a school that was 32 percent white. In 1980, after a heated decade of integration efforts in the face of intense white backlash, that number rose to 36 percent. By 2010, it was down to 29 percent.[23] In 1998, Latino students on average attended schools that were 40 percent white; by 2010, it was down to 30 percent.[24]

Many factors have gone into this resegregation of local education, but they mostly come back to the race dividend. The driving force is of the process is the choices that white parents make—even as most deny actually making them. Although people of all racial identities routinely tell pollsters that they prefer mixed neighborhoods, research by sociologist Maria Krysan finds that while whites express preference for neighborhoods that are 46 percent white on average, they actually search for homes in neighborhoods that are 68 percent white, and they end up living in neighborhoods that are 74 percent white. The numbers for people of color are markedly different: they, too, prefer mixed neighborhoods; they actually look in mixed neighborhoods; but they end up in neighborhoods that are 66 percent nonwhite.[25]

When asked why they look in particular areas, white families with children almost always list schools as a top concern. When asked what they like about schools, studies show, white families frequently use the words "urban" and "suburban" as synonyms for "bad" and "good."[26] Then they turn around and use the same words as proxies for "Black" and "white."[27] Even after controlling for other criteria of school quality, as research from USC sociologist Ann Owens indicates, white parents prefer whiter schools.[28] To be more precise, they prefer some amount of diversity, but not too much. The evidence makes clear that there are "tipping points" of minority presence beyond which neighborhoods become undesirable. The numbers vary from 5 percent in the more nervous suburbs to 20 percent in more tolerant urban centers; but once the threshold is crossed, neighborhoods tend to slide swiftly to the other side.[29]

Not everyone in the business of home-seeking thinks the same way, to be sure, and even fewer articulate the basis of the underlying calculus. But enough do speak out that we may be confident that the mechanisms of the race dividend are working as intended. At the time of this writing, for example, a resident of a 9.9 percent-ish neighborhood in Wake Forest, North Carolina, laid out the math quite plainly.[30] When an interracial family moved in, this individual sent over a neighborly note warning the newcomers not to put up BLM signs. "Please remember that the rest of us live in an upscale neighborhood and have spent the extra money to stay out of mixed neighborhoods and/or the ghetto," they wrote. "No one wants trouble or any circumstance arising which could turn our neighborhood into a 'semi-ghetto.'"

There is likewise no shortage of evidence that the separation of the races is sufficient to provoke the fear and loathing of the other upon which the race dividend relies. At around the time of this writing, over in St. Louis, Missouri, when white personal injury lawyer Mark McCloskey and his wife saw a multicolored group of peaceful protesters walking down their gated street, they perceived that they were victims of "the very definition of terrorism." Naturally, they rushed outside of their monumental, Tuscan-style, 9.9 percent-dream-palazzo fully armed in self-defense. He waved around his AR-15 machine gun, and she pointed a small, silver-colored, but very real pistol at the street people. In recognition of their bravery, President Trump invited these anti-terrorist heroes to speak at the 2020 Republican National Convention, where they warned wealthy white suburbanites that their neighborhoods, too, would soon be overrun with people of many frightening complexions.

As a supplement to the residential system of producing division and dread, the incarceration system has had few equals in the history of American racism. As long as Black men are six times as likely to be in prison as white men, and as long as the United States remains by far the world champion in total rates of incarceration, there will be impoverishment, there will be fear, and there will be "law and order" politics and many other features of life that turn the collection of the race dividend into a golden business opportunity for some.

In recent years, the criminal justice system has established partnerships with schools to make the process of division that much more effective and efficient. An extensive study in Texas reveals that even after controlling for eighty-three other variables describing social and economic status, Black students are far more likely to receive suspensions and ultimately get handed over to the criminal justice system.[31] Children with disabilities also receive disproportionate discipline, and Black children with disabilities are the least favored group of all. The school-to-prison pipeline is just one aspect of the "tough-on-crime" politics that has proven both extraordinarily popular with many voters and extremely effective in reproducing racial segregation and disadvantage.[32]

THE ARTICLE OF THE 9.9 percent theory of racism that ultimately matters most is the one that says racism must necessarily fade away with the passage of time. Before one can say whether racism is on the upswing or downswing, however, one must answer a simple question. How is racism to be quantified? The 9.9 percent theory of racism, as we know, has a simple way of answering the question: the sum total of racism is the sum total of bad thoughts in people's heads. This turns out to be a convenient way of framing the question for the 9.9 percent, because it turns out that racism in this sense happens to be on a clear downward slope.

Here is the good news about racism in America today—and it is genuinely good news, taken on its own. Google searches on racist terms are down. Unconscious racism, as measured in responses to flashing images of people of various ethnicities, is declining, say Harvard psychologists, in particular among younger people,[33] and researchers at the University of Pennsylvania agree.[34] Interracial marriage, banned in many states as recently as sixty years ago, is increasingly common. Surveys today regularly find both a growing awareness that racial discrimination exists and a growing belief that the problem should be addressed. In the aftermath of George Floyd's death, support for Black Lives Matter soared to a majority of the American population—at least, for a time.

But to end the story of racism in America today with this batch of good news is to willfully misrepresent the way in which racist systems work and the nature of the harms they engender. Racism is not just a collection of personal opinions. It is a system of power. This is the core of the message that Frederick Douglass reads out of American history.

The harm racism inflicts on a target group is a means of perpetuating the system, not the end. The actual purpose of a racist system is to enrich the few, and its real effect is to impoverish all of human society. Measured in relation to this purpose and effect, racism in America today is not in fact on a downward slope, as aspiring members of the 9.9 percent like to tell themselves. On the contrary, it is indisputably on the rise. The American political system is substantially and measurably more racialized now than it was fifty years ago, and this racialization is the principal reason why the American public remains unable to defend itself from the rapacious forces of inequality. Racism now, more than ever, is the kryptonite of the American political system.

It was easy to see the point before the rise of Trump and inexcusable not to see it in the aftermath. Immediately following the 2016 election, there was some unedifying debate about whether economic anxiety or racism drove voters to deliver an electoral college victory to Trump. If the question about race and class is artificially limited to the motivations of individual voters in this way, then the answer in the data is unambiguous. It was not the economy, stupid; it was racism. But this fact reveals more about the premises of the question than it does about any underlying reality. It ignores the ways in which the economy, through the reinvestment of the race dividend, reproduces racism without going to the trouble of explaining to racists the economic roots of their racism.

In *Identity Crisis*, political scientists John Sides, Michael Tesler, and Lynn Vavreck provide all of the necessary evidence on the matter of individual voter motivations in 2016 that wasn't already made plain in the winning candidate's words.[35] Party identification apart, the best predictors of support for Trump were not simply being white but identifying with being "white" and expressing resentment against people who are not white. As Michael Tesler elaborates, one of the best ways to spot a Trump voter is find out whether they agree with the astounding proposition that "discrimination against whites is as big a problem as discrimination against minorities."[36] Political scientist Philip Klinkner adds that it is also helpful to ask, "Is Obama a Muslim?"[37] It is also worth noting that Trump's victory was followed with an increase in hate crimes. Indeed, hate crimes tripled specifically in counties that hosted

Trump rallies.[38] Also significant, as Tesler and colleagues point out, is that measures of personal economic financial distress or anxiety are only weakly associated with support for Trump.[39] The median income of Trump voters was actually a pip above the median national income (though not above the median white income).

The data, to be clear, do not indicate that racial resentment was the only factor driving support for Trump. As we saw in previous chapters, both gender difference and gender-based resentments also mattered. It would also be inaccurate to assume that either racial resentment or gender resentment are unique to white Americans. The significant support for Trump from Latinos, and especially from Latino men (36 percent according to a 2020 exit poll), and the nonnegligible support from African American men (18 percent), are evidence that the racial dynamics play out in a space that is much more complex than the Black-white divide of traditional race narratives.

The data also make clear that it isn't just about one president. Studies consistently show that "racial attitudes strongly explain the two-party vote choice among white voters;"[40] and that "racial animus among voters helped Republicans at multiple levels."[41] Among the best predictors of membership in the Republican Party at present is agreement with the statement: "It's really a matter of some people not trying hard enough; if blacks would only try harder, they could be just as well off as whites."[42] Even where Republicans and Trump supporters in particular express economic or cultural concerns, moreover, they consistently do so in highly racialized language. The economic problems the nation faces, as many of them see it, boil down to too many moochers mooching off "hardworking" people, and there is very little doubt about the presumed racial identities of the two sides. As Tesler puts it, "economic anxiety isn't driving racial resentment; rather, racial resentment is driving economic anxiety."[43] Alleged cultural issues such as abortion are often inseparable from highly racialized descriptions of just what kind of people need to have their sexuality put under control.

Faced with this blatant and well-known sorting of politics by racial attitudes, the traditional narratives fall back on the belief that it is all the continuation of legacies from the American past. But this is to miss the actual plot of the story. The racialization did not happen spontaneously. It did not shoot up fully formed from the grass roots. It has been the conscious political strategy of the post–civil rights Republican Party. And the party embraced and promoted it with particular efficacy precisely on account of rising economic inequality. Really, it's all about the race dividend. The race dividend, as Frederick Douglass anticipated, can be the object of conscious investment, and the amount invested along with the returns generated increase in direct proportion with rising inequality.

In 1992, Thomas Edsall published a book pointing out what Republican operatives such as Lee Atwater explicitly stated: that the Republican Party was using racist appeals to drive working- and middle-class white voters to the side of the anti-tax, anti-regulation agenda that its corporate and plutocratic sponsors wanted. In 2019, Edsall was able to write, "The situation hasn't changed much."[44] Except that it has changed in that the strategy has become significantly more effective in achieving its aims. This is the single most important story in American politics over the past half century.[45]

Significantly, the Republican strategy has succeeded less by increasing the absolute amount of racial prejudice in the population than by harnessing it more tightly to a political agenda. Research from political scientists Adam Enders and Jamil Scott confirms this critical point concerning the changing effectiveness of political mobilization in converting racist sentiment into a racist system of political power.[46] In 1988, their data show, there was no correlation between racial resentment and views on health care, just as there was no correlation between racial resentment and party identification. By 2018, there were very strong correlations of 0.4 (out of 1) and 0.5 between racial resentment and health care views and party identification respectively. "White racial resentment has remained remarkably stable over time," the authors conclude, "but that racial resentment has become much more highly correlated with particular political attitudes, behaviors, and orientations." In brief: Republican operatives weaponized racism—and in the process, they made the rich richer, and distributed some of the crumbs to their helpers in the 9.9 percent.

The expressions of racial resentment that play such a central role in Republican politics, it is critical to add, only sometimes involve explicit expressions of racist belief. That is, they are more typically articulated not as noxious claims of supposed white superiority but rather as preposterous claims of white victimhood. This may not seem much of a difference, and yet recognizing the distinction between these two manifestations of racism is critical to understanding the unhappy role of the 9.9 percent in perpetuating the dynamics of racialized politics.

The hottest rage of those grieving their whiteness is reserved not for the members of another race but for the members of another social class. And the fundamental complaint against this other, higher class is that it wields its anti-racist rhetoric as a shield to protect its own wealth and privilege. This is the small grain of truth that gets stuck in the craw of the Uber-sympathizing MAGA man in that Trump 2020 ad. And every time that one of those educated, urban elites claims moral superiority over him in virtue of the purity of their own racial consciousness, it only makes the resentment directed at their privilege that much hotter. None of which amounts to a justification for the malignant politics of white grievance. Nor should it be taken as evidence that the good work of anti-racism in raising consciousness of racial injustice is in itself a bad thing. But it does serve to illustrate that the 9.9 percent's self-serving theory of racism comes at a price. Construing the pursuit of racial justice as a matter of personal virtue may come at the cost of ignoring the economic injustice from which racism arises. It can be a way of absolving oneself of the crime while perpetuating the cause. Anti-racist practice, to the extent that it serves to obscure class divisions, is not a cure for white grievance but a contributing condition.

From a distance, the effort to consolidate economic privilege through the politics of racism may look like a wealth-preservation strategy for the 0.1 percent and the 9.9 percent. But it isn't. To be sure, it may pad a few bank accounts at the top with extra tax cuts for a time. But in the long run, racist systems inevitably serve to diminish the aggregate wealth of a society, and this fact is evident in the paradoxical economic status of Trump nation. The individuals who voted for Trump may have been at or slightly above the median income, but the counties that voted for Trump were not. In 2016, according to a Brookings estimate, the counties that voted for Trump represented a mere 36 percent of GDP.[47] In 2020, the Trump-county share was down to an abysmal 29 percent of GDP. The same grim economic divide characterizes Republican and Democratic congressional districts.[48] Between 2008 and 2018, according to Brookings data, Democratic districts saw a 39 percent increase in GDP, while Republican districts lost 2 percent. In 2018, Democrats held seats representing 64 percent of GDP, and Republicans made do with the remainder. It's worth adding that the white people in Trump country also score poorly on measures of physical and mental health relative to whites in the other counties. Indeed, their scores are low enough that being white in the United States is a predictor of poor health.[49]

The same impoverishing impact of racism can be read out of the national accounts. If you want to know why, relative to every other developed country, the United States is unable to manage a coherent response to a pandemic; why it chronically underinvests in education, child care, housing, infrastructure, and most of the other things that make for a better and more productive future; or why it celebrates public subsidies for private oligopolies as the epitome of the "free market"—the best single-word answer is racism.[50] When white people die from drug overdoses and gun violence, they are to some degree victims of racism.[51] When commuters of whatever racial identity suffer through miserable journeys across widely scattered neighborhoods over dilapidated bridges and on underfunded public transportation, they are victims of racism. When families struggle to find child care and a decent education for the children while juggling multiple jobs, they are victims of racism. This of course takes us to the core of the paradox about racism in the age of the 9.9 percent. Even as the damage from racism piles up, we have managed to convince ourselves that it is just a few spiritual exercises short of disappearing.

As POLITICAL SCIENTIST Eitan Hersh aptly points out, many college-educated progressives are "political hobbyists."[52] Like Jeffrey and Billy, they enjoy the sport of national politics, they follow the news closely, and they cheer when the good guys win. Apart from waving signs around in all the right places, however, they don't actually do much political organizing on the ground. That's because politics for much the 9.9 percent has become a symbolic or cultural field. It is a place where one goes for spiritual reward, not to secure real change through political action. The reason for this spiritualization of politics isn't hard to see. The whole game plan of the 9.9 percent is to secure a spot in the cherished neighborhoods that secure a spot in the right educational institutions that guarantee a spot in a high-status and materially rewarding profession somewhere just below the top of the economic pyramid. Why would anyone expect that they are going to be agents of change?

But we should not be too hard on Jeffrey and Billy. Even if they have fetishized racial identity and turned their anti-racism into a weird kind of status competition in its own right, that is better than the alternative. At least they are not waving machine guns at peaceful citizens in front of their palazzos or trying to violently overturn democratic elections. When you see them with their placards out there in the streets, or making efforts to bridge the racial divides on their committees and in their communities, or volunteering for service in other parts of town, it is impossible not to feel hopeful that the multiracial democracy we've been promising ourselves is not too far in the distance. When you meet their children, you might feel even better.

Still, they do remind me of a certain subset of the abolitionists—not the subset to which Frederick Douglass belonged, but the other one, the high-minded faction revolving around William Lloyd Garrison that devoted itself entirely to taking moral stands and that hoped to move society in its direction by the force of its own moral purity. Today we like to think that those abolitionists were on the right side of history and that they therefore succeeded. The reality is that they failed. That's why there was a civil war: because moral suasion did not stand a chance against the extraordinary economic interests at stake in the slave system. Douglass understood the point. He spent the war mobilizing Black soldiers to claim with arms a freedom that they had already earned through their labor.

It follows from the logic of the race dividend that no lasting progress on racial justice is ever sustainable without economic justice. Inequality in the material conditions of life will always amplify racial difference because power always makes use of all available tools. In an earlier time, forty acres and a mule would have changed almost everything. The fundamental answer to racism is not different now.

The best way to make sure that the overpaid jobs do not end up mostly in the hands of a privileged race and that the unprotected jobs do not end up mostly in the hands of a target race is not to have overpaid and unprotected jobs in the first place. The best way to separate the value of homeownership from the color of the neighborhood is not to have wealth-coded neighborhoods. A higher minimum wage, adequate collective representation in those underpaid occupations that had to be deemed "essential" during a pandemic in order to compel workers to perform them, the removal of barriers that shield the premium occupations from fair competition, the return of zoning control to the entire people, and real taxation of the massive, unearned fortunes at the top of the economy—these and other seemingly race-neutral economic policies will decide the course of American racism in the future. The rest is mostly posturing and evasion, which has become something of a fine art in the age of the 9.9 percent.

— 10 —

Why Everyone Is
So Unreasonable

Whatever happened to Amy Chua? The tiger mother business was intense, but it was never particularly ideological, except maybe in the fanaticism with which it evangelized for a plain-vanilla version of the meritocracy. Chua has described herself as a "socially liberal independent,"[1] and there is little reason to suppose that she strays far from the centrist, anti-Trumpist politics characteristic of the larger part of the faculty at the Yale Law School. She does not appear to be a member of the Federalist Society, for example, which is where the right fringe of the legal world typically gathers in preparation for ascending to the federal judiciary. And yet, in a July 2018 op-ed for the *Wall Street Journal*, Chua went to bat for the very not-socially-liberal, not-exactly-nonpartisan, Trump-anointed, card-carrying Federalist Supreme Court nominee Brett Kavanaugh.

Not content merely to vouch for Kavanaugh's legal expertise as a Yalie and fellow meritocrat, Chua went out of her way to laud him as above all a "mentor to women."[2] What she did not mention was that, according to some of Kavanaugh's prospective mentees, Chua herself had previously warned her female students that the great "mentor to women" had a less-than-ideal history with respect to his female assistants. It was "not an accident," she allegedly warned her advisees, that Kavanaugh's clerks all "looked like models." She apparently hinted that female candidates interviewing with him might wish to dress in accordance with his tastes.[3]

Then Christine Blasey Ford's credible sexual assault allegations hit the news, and the public discovered something about Kavanaugh—something more interesting than his sexual history. This man was angry—and he was angry in a way that seemed to transcend whatever gender issues were in play, or even whatever emotional response one might expect from someone who takes himself to be falsely accused. At the climax of his spittle-flecked testimony before the Senate, the prospective Justice unexpectedly revealed that in his mind the last-minute accusations of sexual assault were part of an orchestrated plot for "revenge on behalf of the Clintons"—the two most famous graduates of the Yale Law School. This was the same rage, with the same general target, that Justice Clarence Thomas, another Yale Law graduate, displayed when he ranted that he would not retire until 2034. "The liberals made my life miserable for forty-three years," he explained, "and I am going to make their lives miserable for forty-three years." It was the same rage that Justice Samuel Alito, also of Yale Law, exposed when he visibly mouthed "not true" during the State of the Union address of President Obama (Harvard Law). It was a partisan rage, for sure, an aggrieved-male rage, possibly, but also, more interestingly, it was a species of insider rage. It was Yale-on-Yale, or elite-versus-elite. It surged out from one wing of a highly pedigreed world and aimed for another wing that, if one were to put a face to it, would have to look a lot like Amy Chua.

And yet, through it all, Chua stood by her man. Kavanaugh was just another upstanding member of legal academia, she seemed to suggest. As for her prior knowledge of the prospective Justice's behavior toward women—Chua claimed that the allegation that she had warned female students about Kavanaugh's behavior was "100 percent false." A number of her students disagreed. "I personally heard her" say that Kavanaugh's clerks all looked like models, said one. "So I personally know that for her to say the allegations are 100 percent false is a lie."[4]

Then it got even weirder. Even while Chua was sticking up for her antihero, her own daughter—a tiger cub who happened to be a law student at Yale herself—was interning for none other than Judge

Kavanaugh. As journalist Elie Mystal soon pointed out, Chua failed to mention that, should Kavanaugh be confirmed, her daughter would stand first in line to receive a clerkship at the Supreme Court. A position of that sort is just the kind of plum that sweetens the most extravagant of meritocratic fantasies.

When news of this unexpected connection emerged, Chua's daughter rushed to mom's defense. It was all fake news, she tweeted in from the sidelines. She would not be in a position to take up a clerkship at the Supreme Court, she claimed, because she would be too busy serving her country as an officer in the army.

Eleven months and many hundreds of news cycles later, Chua's daughter quietly took up her clerkship at the side of Supreme Court Justice Kavanaugh.[5] The triumph of the meritocracy surely tasted sweet. But it did not last long in the Chua household. In a final twist in the tale—technically irrelevant and yet somehow morally or perhaps psychologically pertinent—Chua's husband, Jed Rubenfeld, who was also on the faculty at Yale Law, was suspended in 2020 from his position following investigations into allegations that he had sexually harassed students.[6]

It's a rather sordid little story, hardly representative of the entirety of life among the intellectual vanguard of the 9.9 percent. Except in one or two small ways. Like in what it says about what remains of the life of the mind in the current age of political unreason. The strange embrace of Amy Chua and Brett Kavanaugh is really a story about how, in a period of escalating inequality, the two sides in the mind of the 9.9 percent, though superficially opposed to one another, find common ground in their betrayal of the public trust. As it happens, Amy Chua herself can serve as a guide to these useful insights into the present crisis. Well before this small saga of sexualized striving in the land of the meritocrats, Chua took the trouble to publish some comments about the state of political reason in these unusual times. Those comments, too, are as interesting for what they omit as what they include.

THE TRIUMPH OF UNREASON is the crisis of American politics today. Lies have become more powerful than truth. Facts are whatever the loudest voice says they are. Evidence counts for little; passion proves everything. The people fight for their servitude as if for salvation. This triumph of unreason, as the philosopher Hannah Arendt observed in 1951, is the essential prequel to a collapse of democracy: "The ideal subject for totalitarian rule is not the convinced Nazi or the convinced Communist, but people for whom the distinction between fact and fiction . . . and the distinction between true and false . . . no longer exist."[7] What is to be done?

In her 2018 book *Political Tribes*, Amy Chua delivers her answer to the crisis of the age. "Humans are tribal," she announces, and the tribes are not communicating well right now. They make use of unreasoned instincts (tribe good!) to pursue goals that better-informed people can accept as reasonable (cooperation good!). That's why things are getting out of hand. "Elites in the United States have either not cared about or been remarkably oblivious to the group identities that matter most to large segments of ordinary Americans, including people they are supposedly trying to help," Chua writes.[8] The larger point—and who would object?—is that we just need to have a sit-down and talk.

For example: One of America's tribes achieved viral success in 2016, observes Chua, with a meme that reads: "European Christians built this nation. They didn't come to bitch, collect welfare, wage jihad, and replace the American Constitution with Sharia Law." According to Chua, these fine people were expressing, perhaps in an instinctive and unreasoned way, the reasonable desire for membership in a tribe that shares certain values and a common identity. They differed little in this respect, says Chua, from mean-spirited progressives who put out headlines like: " 'White working-class narrative' is a racist dog whistle."[9]

Another example: When prosperity gospel preachers (who teach that Jesus was as deservedly cash-rich as they themselves are) collect on their teaching even as they manipulate voters to support demagogues in hopes of extending their own political influence, according to Chua, they, too, are offering their flock a valid expression of certain inarticulate yet reasonable longings. Joel Osteen, whose gospel business scrapes $55 million every year from his followers' wallets, "preaches that his congregants are not 'victims' but 'victors.' " And Creflo Dollar, a prosperity gospel entrepreneur whose congregation recently replaced his private jet after the first one skidded off the runway, "teaches that even the poor control their own destinies."[10]

In taking on the burden of assisting fellow meritocrats in their task of understanding and aiding the tribal (or identitarian) masses, Chua was joining a crowded field.[11] Jonathan Haidt, to cite perhaps the most prominent figure in the genre, has long taken it as his mission to explain to secular liberals that their conservative political opponents operate with a different set of "moral taste buds." One taste bud is as good as another, we may presume, and anyway all taste buds have been validated by evolution. Thus, when white conservatives shut down public assistance programs out of concern that the money might end up in the hands of undeserving people of a different color, for example, they are appealing to values of proportionality, loyalty, and purity that liberals seem unable to taste in their food. "Trump is bringing in emotions and concerns that were not well-represented on the traditional left-right scale before," Haidt says.[12]

The political philosopher Francis Fukuyama has recently come back from the end of history to offer a darker twist on the same basic analysis.[13] Packaging the identitarian longings of the masses in the ancient Greek word *thymos*, a cognate of "breath" signifying "spiritedness," (which is really not helpful), he suggests that these gut-level instincts for recognition and community, understandable as they are, make it hard for humans to establish reasonable forms of self-government. This passionate side of human nature, we are given to understand, is why liberal democracy is so hard to maintain.

The politics of unreason, according to the line of thought favored by Chua and her many fellow travelers, boils down to the politics of misunderstood reasons. It amounts to a battle of misread symbols and gestures. It represents a timeless dysfunction in human culture, perhaps attributable to natural defects in human psychology. The solutions, therefore, lie mostly in the realm of translation. The joyful news at the end of this line of thought is that peace is (almost) at hand. All we need in order to reestablish the politics of consensus is a version of the talking cure. A group called More in Common, for example, provides a catalogue of America's "hidden tribes" and then offers to mediate among their different, but equally valid, vocabularies of belief.

It is very touching, this effort to reconcile the liberal remnant of the meritocracy with its "other." It's also very sad. As any sane observer knows at this point, the people that, according to Amy Chua, we "are supposedly trying to help" will not be reciprocating these earnest attempts to split the difference with unreason. They will not be responding with matching efforts to articulate the semi-rational instincts of the meritocracy in hopes of reestablishing the consensus on which we may base a civil dialogue. They are much more likely to pick up another book from Ann Coulter, who has compared liberals with cancer cells and has said that Timothy McVeigh made a mistake in not parking his explosive van in front of the *New York Times* building.[14]

If the plan is to win over the angry men of the Federalist Society, it looks even sadder. Consider the moral taste buds of Senator Josh Hawley—the Yale Law graduate, Federalist Society darling, and vocal anti-elitist who famously raised a clenched-fist salute to the people we are supposedly trying to help just before attempting to overturn the democratic election of President Biden.[15] By Hawley's own reckoning, the disease of liberalism goes all the way back to the fourth-century monk Pelagius, who taught the scandalous doctrine that human beings are born free to think for themselves and choose the best path in life on their own. Stamping out this odious liberal heresy, says Hawley, is the great challenge of the age. What part of that message is going to dissolve with translation?

Maybe the most disturbing part of the plan for universal peace-through-tribal-reconciliation has to do with the individuals who keep conjuring up the politics of consensus as an apology for the politics of unreason. Intellectuals like Amy Chua and Jonathan Haidt occupy the most meritorious perches in the American hierarchy of learning. Why do they have so much trouble calling a con job a con job? If they are not standing up for reason, then who is? The vanguard of the 9.9 percent are supposed to be a forefront of knowledge in our society, and yet they come within spitting distance of the wreckage of reason that is the defining crisis of our time only to trot right past it with a vacuous smile. What exactly is going on with *their* tribe?

The answer I will give in a moment is simple enough to telegraph up front, and it reflects a fundamental fact about the 9.9 percent that extends beyond the handful of squabbling professors who stand for its intellectual vanguard. Inequality distorts human rationality. It turns the life of the mind inward, away from the actual problems of the world, and focuses it instead on a destructive competition. Some of the competitors, nurturing grievances, turn their rage on the same machinery of reason that they are charged with protecting. Others seek shelter in relativisms that allow them to pass as champions of reason even as they seek favor from an unreasonable system. Both sides frame the crisis of unreason in a way that leaves their own contribution out of the picture. Both commit a kind of treason of the intellectuals. If we are to make sense out of the present crisis of American democracy, we need to step back from the cramped and self-involved perspective of the 9.9 percent and consider the evolution of reason in human politics from a world-historical point of view.

IT HAS TO BE SAID that human beings can be quite unreasonable, even before they get political. They think fast when they should think slow. They come to their conclusions first and then hunt around for the reasons later. They weigh recent and familiar evidence more than the strange and remote. They judge what is true based on what other people are saying, and they often confuse authority with truth.

Today, whole careers in the social sciences are made of such insights, and the results supply much of the background for the politics of consensus that Amy Chua favors.[16] Those who wish to reduce politics to psychology may point to recent studies that show, for example, that individuals who identify as liberals and conservatives have measurably different personality types: Liberals and conservatives react very differently to pictures of dirty toilets, people with sores, and mutilated animals; they differ about the merits of broccoli; they have different theories about how to keep a room tidy.[17] The underlying premise of the research is that the findings represent some new discoveries about human nature or the human condition, and that these discoveries may explain the current politics of unreason.[18] But this premise is quite obviously false. The rational shortcomings of human beings were well known to every major philosopher on record from the time of the ancient Greeks up through Benjamin Franklin; at best they might contribute to an explanation of why politics have always been unreasonable, not why they are unreasonable now. The interesting thing about the modern perspective on the issue is what has been forgotten.

"Happy is the state which is ruled neither by the very rich who are reared in luxury, nor by the poor who are too degraded, but by the middle class who are equal and similar," Aristotle observes. [19] Unhappy is the state divided between rich and poor, conversely, and it is unhappy specifically because inequality renders its members unreasonable. "He who greatly excels in beauty, strength, birth, or wealth, or on the other hand who is very poor, or very weak, or very much disgraced, finds it difficult to follow reason," Aristotle explains. "The rich know not how to obey, nor the poor how to rule, and thus arises a city of masters and slaves."

Aristotle's underlying insight—overlooked today and yet so widely shared among ancient philosophers that it rarely needed to be stated—is that the state of reason in society is a political and historical achievement. While unreason in individuals has natural causes and thus changes little over time, unreason in politics has political causes, and therefore varies according to political conditions. Crucially, the condition that matters most is the degree of equality of mutual regard that Aristotle associates with a middle-class state.

The Greek historian Polybius takes for granted the same collection of insights in his explanation of the rise of the Roman republic.[20] As the first Romans learned to expect reciprocity in their dealings with one another, he says, they achieved a certain mutual recognition of their equality. From this they developed a notion of duty to one another, "which is the beginning and end of justice." When the political order began to distribute rewards and punishments according to the requirements of justice, the old forms of tyrannical kingship gave way to a republic, and "ferocity and force" yielded to "the supremacy of reason."

The radical philosophers of the early modern world, such as Spinoza, absorbed this understanding of the politics of reason and then their successors, some of whom played prominent roles in the American Revolution, inserted it, if imperfectly, in the founding documents of the American republic.[21] At the root of their analysis lies a modern update on the ancient distinction between genuine democracy and demagoguery.

Genuine democracy, according to Spinoza and his American successors, is the most natural form of government, inasmuch as it involves the recognition of the natural equality of human beings. (In this the moderns differ from the ancients, for whom democracy—as they defined it—is generally a bad idea and demagoguery the proof.) Democracy, according to this line of thought, is self-government, and self-government is another word for freedom. But freedom, in both the ancient and the early modern understanding, means nothing without reason. Democracy is not the rule of the people but the rule of reason, for it is only through reason that the people can rule themselves. The distinguishing features of the democratic republics established in the early modern period—the reliance on systems of representation, the insistence on the public and universal character of all laws, the guarantees of individual rights, the separation of powers, the formal constitutions—all follow from this principle that the sovereign power of the people can be realized only to the extent that it is held accountable to reason. Their purpose is not to establish by fiat some collection of putatively eternal truths but to establish a machinery capable of testing all claims to truth against reason. The point of that machinery is not to congeal the pre-existing preferences of the people but to allow the people to change its mind in accordance with reason. This rule of reason, however, is possible among humans only under certain fundamental conditions of society, and the most important of these is the condition of relative material equality—which was Aristotle's main point.

Demagoguery, on the other hand, is what happens when the people rule according to the passions, not reason. Demagoguery comes to power by telling people what they want to hear, not what they need to hear. It looks like freedom on the surface, but it is actually the opposite. It may have a shorter road to power in the form of government that the ancients identified as democracy, but it can just as easily surface in the context of other forms, since the mass of people have many ways to throw their weight around outside of formal institutions. The defining condition of demagoguery is not in fact the formal political equality of a democracy, but the extreme inequality in material conditions among the population that makes an appeal to the passions possible.

Sustained material inequality, according to both the ancient and the early modern philosophers, produces citizens who believe that the world answers not to common purposes but to unthinking power, that the way to thrive in life is not to work with other people but to screw them before they screw you, and that the distinction between friend and enemy matters far more than that between truth and error. It favors essentially passive citizens, who believe implicitly that politics is mainly a spectator sport, that it doesn't produce real change, and that its only use is to offer the symbolic satisfaction that comes with the ritual humiliation of enemies. In short, inequality reliably creates a population distinguished by its resentment, distrust, ignorance, and nihilism, and this population is an easy mark for appeals to unreason.

The message that appeals best to such a population is typically that their troubles are all the work of an alien group. The leader that appeals best to such a population is typically one who embodies the unreason the people see in the world, a leader unconstrained by the scruples of political correctness and capable of inflicting great pain on the alien sources of their distress. The leader, in turn, understands at least intuitively that his power depends not on the reasonability of the people but their unreason. Soon he starts to wage war on truth itself, and the people passionately embrace him on the path to mutual destruction. Extreme inequality, in brief, brings forth a politics of unreason.

Sound familiar? To the early modern philosophers who shaped the foundations of the American republic, it certainly did, and the common reference points were to be found mostly in the history of Rome. The trajectory of Rome in the centuries after Polybius chronicled its peak in fact offers a stark illustration of how inequality begets the politics of unreason.

Already in the second century BCE, leaders such as Tiberius Gracchus could see that rising inequality had rendered Rome nearly ungovernable. At the time, the largest fortunes in Rome totaled about 4 million sesterces (equivalent to roughly 8 million loaves of bread) even while about a third of the population was enslaved and the overwhelming majority of the rest were so impoverished that many stopped having children.[22] But the rapacious oligarchy blocked the necessary changes, and the surly masses were easily manipulated into sabotaging the reform efforts, too. Gracchus was the first of many would-be change agents to be murdered at the hands of a mob. A string of dictators and civil wars followed, all arising fundamentally out of the extraordinary inequalities of the time, the resentments to which they gave rise, and the opportunities they afforded to the ambitious.

Yet, even as one demagogue after another harnessed the tremendous power of the dispossessed population, the political process delivered ever greater inequalities. Two decades after the murder of Gracchus, the largest fortunes in Rome quadrupled in size, even while the masses subsisted in unchanging misery. In the next four decades, those fortunes quadrupled again. By the time Caesar arrived on the scene, they had doubled again. They peaked at around 400 million sesterces in the first century CE—falling just short of producing the first billionaires in bread—at which point the Roman kleptocracy achieved a state of perfection and began to consume itself from the inside.

As the relentless consistency in the direction of Roman politics indicates, the politics of unreason is not a random walk through history. On the contrary, those political agendas with the least foundation in reason will be the most likely to turn to unreason, and those psychological dispositions among humans that are most prone to manipulation will be the first to be targeted. The politics of unreason is not an equal opportunity employer. It always favors injustice over justice and it always targets those who are most vulnerable, psychologically speaking. It does not infect everyone alike with the same quantity of unreason, but rather leaves a large number of individuals to watch in dismay as their fellow citizens march off to their own destruction.

These long-established insights from history and philosophy are worth bearing in mind when considering the psychological research into humanity's rational shortcomings on which theorists like Amy Chua rely to advance their politics of consensus. The research is interesting, but not for the reason supposed. There is nothing natural in the fact that your response to pictures of dead cats is today expected to line up with your policy preferences on the matter of tax cuts; or that your taste in broccoli dictates your position on gun safety regulation; or that your vote in the next election might be predicted with a glance at how you organize your bedroom. The reduction of politics to psychology reveals something about the condition of our politics, not about the human condition. It shows that human shortcomings have been weaponized and placed in the service of political agendas. It is some of the best evidence we have that inequality has already taken us far down the road to the politics of unreason.

SETTING ASIDE TRIBAL EUPHEMISMS, the people whom Amy Chua has in mind as the ones we "are supposedly trying to help" are for the most part the people who voted for Trump in 2016 and 2020. (There are presumably many other tribes in our world, but we only seem to care about the ones that turn nihilistic.) The first and most obvious thing to know about the members of this particular "tribe" is that, taken on the whole, and considered in spiritual terms, as it were, they are what the 9.9 percent is not. As noted in previous chapters, Trump won white voters without a college degree by 37 percent in 2016 and 29 percent in 2020, according to exit polls, even while his margin among white college graduates dropped from 3 percent to zero.[23] The part of the economy represented by Trump counties, as we also know, plummeted from 36 percent of GDP in 2016 to 29 percent of GDP in 2020, even while those counties represented 43 percent of the population in 2020.[24] Of the eighty-two counties with the highest opioid death rates, seventy-seven went for Trump in 2016.[25] Trump won white voters with "no social ties" by a margin of 32 percent in 2020, while he was up only a point among those white voters who actually have some friends.[26] As a statistical rule, and allowing for all the necessary variations among individuals, Trumpism did not emerge from the shiny land of the meritocratic future.

Conversely, one could also say, in the same spiritual-statistical vein: the 9.9 percent is what Trumpism is not. To be clear, a substantial share of voters in the 9.9 percent of the wealth distribution are Trump supporters. According to an analysis by Thomas Piketty,[27] Trump won just over 40 percent of the top decile of the income distribution in 2016, while Clinton carried just under 60 percent. The Democratic ticket won the bottom two deciles of the income distribution in 2016 by roughly the same margin—no doubt in large measure due to the higher proportion of younger, nonwhite voters in that group—leaving Trump with majorities in all the deciles in between. This represents a dramatic shift from the postwar norm, where the top decile leaned Republican by margins of 12 percent and more, and the lower deciles got more Democratic as they got poorer. The new alignment is even more pronounced with respect to the distribution of education. In 2016, 76 percent of PhDs, 70 percent of people with master's degrees, and 51 percent of BAs supported the Democratic ticket, leaving Trump with a commanding majority of all those who are not on the favored life plan of the 9.9 percent.

The influx into the Democratic Party of a large contingent of white, educated, and affluent 9.9 percenters has had a significant impact on its political agenda. Most importantly, the Democratic Party has slowly backed away from grappling with the economic inequalities that are the bread and butter of its new contingent of supporters. In the battle of the zip codes, as we saw in Chapter 5, to cite the most glaring example, the party has quietly sided with the wealthy homeowners of the 9.9 percent. There is little surprising about this development: political parties generally succeed by reflecting the economic interests of their supporters. The surprise is that the same is not true of the Republican Party. Its success has come to depend precisely on betraying the interests of its base. In order to explain this divergence, it is vital to recognize the other, obvious fact about the people we are supposedly trying to help.

The Trumpist population, taken on the statistical whole, are profoundly unreasonable in their politics. To be clear, they are not unreasonable in some universal sense. The safest assumption is that they are not any worse or better than the typical human being in the degree of rationality with which they approach the challenges of everyday life: they succeed in getting out of bed in the morning, locating some sustenance in the refrigerator, and finding their way to the train station without causing too much unnecessary harm to themselves or others. But that assumption is not at all safe with respect to their political rationality.

Here are the facts. In 2016, 46 percent of Trump supporters knew or suspected that Hillary Clinton was involved in a child sex ring that operated in the back of a pizza restaurant; 43 percent maintained that human beings did not evolve from any other species; 39 percent said that the stock market went down under Obama; 27 percent accepted as fact that vaccines cause autism; and 25 percent thought Ted Cruz just might be the Zodiac Killer.[28] By 2020, the comparable numbers were, if anything, higher. When asked whether "top Democrats are involved in elite child-sex trafficking rings," 50 percent of Trump supporters said yes, and another 33 percent were unsure. One week after Joe Biden won the 2020 election, 86 percent of Trump voters surveyed maintained that Biden had not won the election.[29] On January 6, 2021, thousands of Trumpists stormed the Capitol, confident in the belief that the election had been stolen, and in the aftermath of that insurrection, majorities of Republicans continued to tell pollsters that they, too, believed in the same transparent lie of a stolen election.

When reporters file the obligatory reports from Trump rallies and diners in the Midwest stocked with an endless supply of allegedly "forgotten" Americans, representative comments go something like this: "[Obama] was breaking the law left and right and nobody was paying attention to it. With Trump you don't have to worry about it. He's the most vetted president in our country's history."[30]

On the issue of climate change, too, the survey evidence suggests that Trump supporters might as well be living on a planet where facts don't matter and logic is for other people. A 2018 study shows that 74 percent of conservative Republicans deny that human activities are causing climate change—make that 88 percent for regular Fox News viewers—as against 31 percent of all other registered voters.[31] A fascinating but disturbing additional finding is that, although higher education levels are generally associated with lower levels of climate science denialism—no surprise there—the correlation points in the opposite direction among conservatives.[32] The more educated conservatives get, the more likely they are to call the whole thing a hoax.

Sometimes it is offered, by way of apology, that the manifest unreason of America's Trumpist population is merely a shorthand way of signaling a commitment to a certain suite of rational public policy preferences, typically having to do with limited government, liberty, and other big ideas. Well then, let's consider those alleged policy preferences on their own terms. According to a typical 2019 poll, only 22 percent of Republicans approve of "Obamacare." But majorities of Republicans as high as 80 percent approve of each of the specific provisions of the "Affordable Care Act."[33] Eight in ten Trump supporters favor building a wall along the entire Mexican border in order to stop the massive influx of undocumented immigrants, even though, in fact, there has been a massive decrease in undocumented immigrants, no such wall will ever be built, and no credible expert on any side of the immigration issue thinks it would be useful.[34] The excuse for Trump, we have been told, is that "at least" he gave voice to those who had been forgotten or left behind in the modern economy; the reality is that he stuck them with a bill in the form of tax cuts for the wealthy.

The response to the coronavirus pandemic offered perhaps the most lethal testimony on the state of reason in Trumpland. Universal American stupidity was undoubtedly a comorbidity factor for Covid-19—this is a country where people actually debated whether the virus could be traced back to women having sex with demons or if it was all due to the use of ground-up alien DNA in medicines[35]—but being a Trump voter added to that risk in statistically significant measure. At least three academic studies confirmed that, as one paper put it, "rampant partisanship in the United States may be the largest obstacle to the social distancing most experts see as critical to limiting the spread of the COVID-19 pandemic."[36] You have to read the fine print to figure out that "rampant partisanship" is just a nice way of not saying Trump supporters.[37] Stanford economists used statistical models to infer that Trump's political rallies alone—many of which were held indoors, with little social distancing—resulted in thirty thousand coronavirus infections and seven hundred deaths.[38] And yet—even as he was killing them—Trump won high marks from his supporters for his handling of the pandemic.

Are all Trump supporters nuts? Of course not! Peter Thiel probably doesn't believe any of this nonsense. He just wants his parabiosis stuff and maybe the hundreds of millions of dollars' worth of contracts that his creepy tech company Palantir received from the Trump administration in exchange for, among other things, helping ICE target immigrants for deportation.[39] Even allowing that some of those who supported Trump had "rational" or instrumental reasons for doing so, however, no reasonable person could support Trump and the politics of reason at the same time. Trumpism necessarily ascended to power on the back of unreason, and there is no good excuse for not knowing this.

Are there progressives who suffer from lethal levels of unreason? Of course there are! Food-related paranoias and election conspiracy theories, for example, have historically leaned to the left (though the last one in particular shifted dramatically to the right at Trump's whim in 2020). But there is nothing in the politics of the Democratic Party or the American left in general that depends on the irrationality of its followers in anything like the same way that Trumpism does. Only one party today has the need, the ability, and the absence of integrity to anoint a "birther" as its leader.

This is the fundamental—and obvious—reality about the people "we are supposedly trying to help." The evidence does not necessarily show that individuals on one side of the political divide are more idiotic than the other in some absolute sense. It does show that one side has done a far better job of mobilizing the awesome and universal power of stupid to serve its specific political agendas. As the ancients understood, human idiocy has to be incubated, trained, and pointed in the direction of an enemy in order to be politically useful. Not the absolute level of stupidity, but its mobilization for political purposes, is the core fact in the story of unreason in our times. Where exactly did this politically toxic form of imbecility come from?

THERE CAN BE NO DOUBT that a disposition toward Trumpism arises among the base in some way from the experience of inequality that defines much of life in twenty-first century America. Given the rage that flows like water through so much of Trumpist discourse, it would be reasonable to characterize Trumpism as an expression of resentment against that condition of inequality. Given the heroic levels of distrust, it would be reasonable to characterize Trumpism as a manifestation of the loss in social capital and breakdown in mutual trust that accompanies rising inequality. Given the blatant ignorance that undergirds Trumpism, it also seems reasonable to characterize the movement as a consequence of the education deficits to which inequality gives rise. Given the mindless destruction and self-harm associated with Trumpism, it must be reasonable to interpret the movement as an expression of the nihilism that inequality reliably engenders.

But the fact that Trumpism may reasonably be characterized as a consequence of inequality does not make it a reasonable response to inequality. For one thing, not everyone who experiences inequality becomes a Trumpist. Nonwhite members of the working class, for example, appear to be mostly (though not entirely) immune to the appeal. For another thing, reducing inequalities was rarely among the reasons offered by Trumpists themselves for their support. More importantly, resentment, distrust, ignorance, and nihilism are excuses, not reasons. They are not a policy program. They are typically the prelude to something that reasonable people later come to regret. In fact, Trump's political program had the predictable and intended effect of amplifying the inequality from which it emerged. That's just what tax cuts for the rich and packing the judiciary with conservative ideologues do. (True, there was some upward movement in wages at the bottom in the later stages of the economic boom-from-the-bottom that started in 2009; but even these modest and essentially cyclical gains fell mostly outside of Trump country.)

Perhaps the most obvious reason why the Trumpist population cannot be considered reasonable on its own terms is that the terms on which it reasoned were so evidently not its own. Trumpism did not rise from the bottom up. It was mostly imposed from the top down.

The experience of inequality may have created the disposition toward Trumpism among the base, but shaping that raw material into an instrument of political power took decades of planning and investment. Above all, it took a lot of screen time.

Over the past two decades, much of that screen time (though far from all) was spent on a single "news" channel. Outside observers have compared Fox News to "state TV," and its own current and former staffers describe it as a "destructive propaganda machine," but for our purposes it might simply be called an engine of unreason.[40] (To be sure, Fox is only one part of a right-wing information system that relies heavily on the local television programming of Sinclair Broadcasting, a vast network of syndicated radio talk shows, an archipelago of sympathetic, Christian nationalist churches, and an infamous collection of social media operations.)

Say what you will about the right-wing engine of unreason, it is without question remarkably effective. In 2019, even as surveys showed that a majority of Americans favored not just impeaching but removing President Trump from office, 78 percent of Fox viewers said not just that he was innocent but that he was the greatest president in history.[41] Fox-watching Republicans approved of Trump's job performance more strongly than any other Republican subgroups, including even (the overlapping groups of) white evangelical Republicans and non-college-educated Republicans.[42]

It wasn't that the true believers flocked to Fox; on the contrary, the evidence makes clear that Fox created true believers. Through meticulous analysis of submarkets where Fox went on and off the air for a variety of unconnected reasons, one study estimates that Fox News added 3.59 percent to Republican vote totals in 2004 and 6.34 percent in 2008.[43] Without the Fox effect, John Kerry defeats George W. Bush; Barack Obama buries John McCain under a historic landslide; and, in all likelihood, Trump remains a reality TV cheeseball.

A key to the success of this kind of propaganda operation is not just letting bad information in but keeping good information out. That's why "fake news!" was the single most important catchphrase of Trumpism. And it worked. Seventy-five percent of Republicans approve of their propaganda service at Fox News, but only 24 percent approve of the next favorite, ABC News, and only 20 percent of Republicans extend their trust to "journalists as a group." By contrast 60 percent of Democrats trust journalists as a group.[44]

This kind of disinformation system, more than an assault on particular ideas, is an assault on reason itself. It is an attempt to undermine the capacity of a society to deliberate and act in accordance with fact and logic. In occasional fits of candor, the authors of America's right-wing misinformation machine concede that promoting reason is not high on their list of priorities . "It may be possible for 'irrationally held' views to in fact support good policies," wrote Tyler Cowen, an intellectual godfather of billionaire political activist Charles Koch's crusade against democracy, as Nancy MacLean points out.[45] In fact, the (rather small) minority of Trumpists who display signs of instrumental rationality are descended from a line of political thought that goes back at least to the conservative icon Edmund Burke, that great admirer of Marie Antoinette, who, believing the mass of men altogether incapable of reason, maintained that their inclinations "should be frequently thwarted, their will controlled, their passions brought into subjection," and that this task that could only be accomplished by subjecting them to "a power outside themselves."[46]

The politics of unreason, in short was the product of conscious cultivation. But this fact in turn raises some fundamental questions that must be addressed in any attempt to understand the origin and destiny of the politics of unreason. If one party succeeds in deceiving large numbers of people, and the other party no longer commands the support of these same people, then who will represent their interests? And what happens in a political system where a large number of people are not represented at all?

AT SOME POINT in pretty much every conversation like this one, the polite thing to do is to say with a sigh that we are hopelessly "polarized." For every Fox News, there is an MSNBC, for every Sean Hannity there is a Rachel Maddow, or so the wise writers of the op-ed pages will lament.

We live in "alternative realities" and "echo chambers" separated by an "epistemic divide." We are "tribal," "hyperpartisan," and quite lacking in "civility." In all of these clucking expressions of concern, which form the fundamental platform of Amy Chua's politics of consensus, "we" are rising above the squabbling poles. "We" are being remarkably civil, nonpartisan, and unpolarized.

As a matter of fact, "we" are mostly bananas. More exactly, we are ignoring the facts in order to adopt a specious pose of objectivity. American political discourse is not "polarized," or at least not in any meaningful sense. The thing about poles is that, though they point in opposite directions, they are supposed to look the same in some fundamental way. Whether you think North alone is true or South is the only path, the ends of a magnet are in other respects indistinguishable. The magnet itself does not possess any directionality. But the same is demonstrably not true of American political discourse today.

We could trot through a considerable amount of evidence to explain why it is so indecent to put Sean Hannity in the same sentence as an actual journalist, but fortunately we don't have to. Researchers at the Berkman Klein Center at Harvard conducted a three-year study of 4 million articles across hundreds of media sources, and to no one's surprise, they found a clear division between left and right. Much more interesting is that they also documented a deep asymmetry.[47] There are clearly two sides, but those two sides are not at all the same in shape and other internal properties. "The right is more insular; it is more extreme; it's more partisan," concludes the center's director of research, Robert Faris.[48] "That's not a subjective opinion; that's an empirical observation." BuzzFeed conducted a similar, briefer study and came up with the same result. While both sides make stuff up and pass it along, the right does it more frequently, more blatantly, and with much greater internal consistency. A conference of social scientists at Harvard's Kennedy School in 2017 states the plainly observable fact: "Misinformation is currently predominantly a pathology of the right."[49]

One way to visualize the situation would be to imagine a certain map of the infosphere. Suppose you plot the position of every media source in a multidimensional space where each axis corresponds to the degree of coverage offered on a particular issue (such as, for example: "Hunter Biden's Laptop" or "President Trump's call to Georgia's Secretary of State"). Then draw lines connecting these points in space every time one source cites or borrows a story from the other. Now add a touch of red paint to those interconnections that involve a demonstrable falsehood. Otherwise leave them white.

What would such a mapping of the infosphere look like? In a non-polarized world, you would expect to see a cloud of randomly interconnected dots in the shape of a sphere centered on the midpoint of every axis, with flecks of red scattered evenly throughout. In a perfectly polarized world, you might expect to see two equal but opposite spheres, one on the left and the other on the right, perhaps connected with a few threads of distrust. In America today, however, neither of those shapes obtain.

The infosphere is not a sphere, and it isn't even a pair of spheres joined with a few strings. It has a profoundly unbalanced geometry. Far off to the right, there is a small, compact, densely interconnected, and distinctly reddish nugget, where everybody knows about Hunter Biden's personal issues, no one hears about Trump's possibly felonious conversation with Georgia officials, and the same talking points pass from one source to the next all day long. Just to the left of center, there is a substantially larger, much more widely dispersed, and rather whiter cloud, where the coverage varies independently along the various dimensions and the interconnections are scattered and diverse.

This asymmetrical topography of discourse is so distinctive, and shows up in so many aspects of American political life, that it deserves a name. To me, it looks something like the kind of shuttlecock used in badminton. On the right, you have a hard red rubber ball, densely interconnected and impervious to outside influence. On the left, much closer to the center of the whole and yet not representative of the whole, you have a clutch of feathers, loosely interconnected, mostly white, and soft to the touch. The most important thing to know about a shuttlecock is that it has directionality. When you toss it up in the air, no matter how it flips and spins, it always orients itself in the same direction as it travels through space. The other thing to know is that it always crashes headfirst into the ground.

The unusual geometry of the American infosphere, it is critical to note, is not at all neutral with respect to the hypotheses that might explain the origins of the politics of unreason. For example, the asymmetry largely rules out the popular hypothesis that technological change is the principal factor driving the emergence of the politics of unreason.[50] Twitter and Facebook have undoubtedly made things worse, and they should be fixed, but their emergence alone cannot account for the asymmetry of discourse, because the left and the right have access to the same technologies. More generally, the unbalanced geometry of the infosphere rules out any explanation that relies primarily on some universal attribute of the human condition or human experience that affects all people equally, such as the allegedly "tribal" instincts of humans or their defective psychological faculties. The humans on the left, after all, should be just as tribal, or nutty, as those on the right.

The asymmetry of the shuttlecock, I contend, is the ideological signature of inequality. At an abstract level, the explanation is not hard to see. Money is naturally much more united in its purposes than the absence of money. More exactly—to adjust a thesis put forward by the economist Mancur Olson—human society is always divided to some degree into different interest groups, but extreme inequality necessarily brings forth one interest group that possesses both a high degree of unity and a distinctive and disproportionately effective means to pursue its interests.[51]

The unity at the hard end of the shuttlecock, it's important to emphasize, derives not just from the unity of interest that large concentrations of money create, but from the nature of the means through which the rich must necessarily advance their power. Inequality cannot advance its interests among naturally equal beings by appealing to reason. It succeeds only by appealing to unreason. And the wonderful thing about a lie is that it is usually much less complicated and harder to forget than the truth. The unity on the right is in fact prima facie evidence of its duplicity. The incoherence in the center-left, conversely, is in part evidence of its remaining commitment to the pursuit of truth in a world where all claims to knowledge are properly subject to revision. It is also due in part to the fact that lies are sticky things, and when you're living next to a red-hot ball of them, it isn't easy to remain coherent or truthful.

The role of deceit in shaping the shuttlecock, however, necessarily comes with a heavy price tag. Advancing one's financial interests by actively rendering fellow citizens unreasonable is, in the long term, about as sensible as raising tiger cubs in the spare bedroom. As a general rule, it is a way of using wealth today to destroy the foundation of wealth tomorrow, for the origin of all wealth lies in the cooperation that only a reasonable society can produce. This is why, at the end of the game, the shuttlecock always hits the ground headfirst.

The distinctive geometry of unreason shows up in more than just the media ecosystem, and some consideration of its presence in other fields may help to illustrate its deep connection with inequality. A case in point is the field that is falsely labeled philanthropy. The public devotes much attention to center-left philanthropists such as Bill Gates, Tom Steyer, George Soros, and Warren Buffett, and this gives the impression that the superwealthy represent a balanced diversity of political views. They don't. While an open-minded few scatter their goodwill across the eclectic range of endeavors that happen to capture their imagination, the silent majority of billionaires puts its money into a much harder, much more extreme, much more unified collection of politico-ideological projects.[52]

Considered in the aggregate rather than as individuals, the superwealthy in America are net donors on a massive scale to causes such as: the Republican Party; Donald Trump; deficit hawkishness aimed squarely at devouring entitlement programs; advocacy for tax cuts that ignore said deficit hawkishness; elimination of the estate tax, and say that again many times, because the rich really do rally around the noble goal of passing it all down to their chosen heirs; deregulation, especially where it involves trashing the environment and/or consolidating monopolies; obliterating unions, workers' rights in general, and the minimum wage; religion, especially where it promotes anti-liberal attitudes and right-wing economics; anti-gun safety, wherever it can be counted on to bring out votes for right-wing economic policies; education, mostly of the kind that involves private profits and instruction in the economically correct ideology; American history, to the extent that it can be used to legitimize that ideology; and media, notably of the ethno-nationalist variety. It turns out that the rich really are like you and me: they think they deserve more money than they have.

The asymmetrical ideas and spending habits of the rich, combined with a political system that favors minority rule, have in turn shaped the partisan behavior of lawmakers in accordance with the very same geometry of the shuttlecock. Analyses of voting records in Congress and state legislatures show that party-line voting is up dramatically since 1980, and multiple ideological scoring systems indicate that, unlike forty years ago, the most moderate Republican leader is now well to the right of the most conservative Democrat. The data also reveal, on closer inspection, that the two sides are not at all symmetrical in their characteristics. Summarizing the results of multiple studies over many years, political scientist Nolan McCarty notes that "partisan polarization is strongly asymmetric in the postwar era; the median of the Republican Party has moved further to the right than the median of the Democratic Party has moved to the left."[53] More than that, the data show a tighter grouping around core issues on the right than the left. When lawmakers' positions are mapped into a multidimensional space, where each axis corresponds to a particular issue, the Republicans are bunched together like a solid rubber ball, while the Democrats remain more dispersed, like a bundle of feathers. Further study reveals that this shuttlecock pattern is directly associated with inequality. "Income inequality has a statistically significant, positive, and quantitatively large effect on political polarization" across states, says McCarty.[54] In brief, what we (mistakenly) call political polarization is mostly the noise that inequality makes as it gains control of a political system and generates a politics of unreason.

The same, asymmetric geometry has filtered down from politics to religion (which has in any case become increasingly indistinguishable from politics). On the right, longtime theological adversaries from evangelical Protestant, charismatic, and conservative Catholics sects, who spent much of the preceding several centuries condemning one another to hell, have united around a political theology defined by hard-rubber positions on policing gender hierarchies in American society, depriving LGBT people of civil rights, defending the tax status of politically active religious organizations, and securing the long-term profits of capital, with a particular sympathy for fossil fuel companies.[55] The mainstream and the religious left, meanwhile, represent a cloud of liberal religionists, humanists, and atheists who hover around the center of the political spectrum but spend much of their time politely disagreeing with one another.

The last time the American religious world looked like this, curiously, was in the period preceding the Civil War, when all of the most powerful and established denominations in North and South were united around a small, hard religion that emphasized the literal truth of the Bible and divine approval for the institution of slavery, while at the same time a loose, querulous, and ultimately ineffective gaggle of heterodox sects collected on the center and left of religious belief in opposition to both biblical literalism and slavery.[56]

In the American slave republic just as in the present, the connection between this imbalance in religion and inequality is plainly visible in the aggregate data. In research extending across thirty countries over fifty years, sociologist Frederick Solt finds that "rising levels of inequality are soon followed by rising levels of religiosity."[57] More than that, rising inequality is associated with changes in the nature as well as the level of religiosity. In general, inequality promotes the extreme varieties of religion, that is, religion that involves belief in the supernatural, that distinguishes strongly between the in-group and the out-group, that favors hierarchical structures of authority, and that imposes stiff requirements on its practitioners. Inequality also tends to divide the religious sphere between a hardened, dogmatic core and a loose, fragmented collection of liberal dissenters. These changes in the quantity and nature of religion, Solt argues, result from the increasing power of wealthy people to influence the beliefs of other people, either through direct investment in religion or through the example they set and the social power they wield.

The unbalanced geometry of the shuttlecock is also distinctly visible in the ideas that dominate the legal community and the judiciary. It isn't news that the Supreme Court, for example, is divided between left and right.[58] Much more interesting is the fact that the right is much farther to the right and much more united in its agendas than the left relative to the center of debate either in the legal community or among the general public. The real enigma of decisions such as *Citizens United*, which famously twisted the First Amendment into an excuse for granting dark money the power to purchase the American political system, is not that there are some legal minds capable of imagining that a constitutional right unambiguously intended to ensure that the truth cannot be excluded from public deliberation could be used to justify a system where the ownership of corporate entities privileges the wealthy to drown out the truth in floods of anonymously funded propaganda, but that five such legal minds landed on the Supreme Court. How did they get there?

The short answer, of course, is the Federalist Society. The society is in essence an affirmative action program for conservative legal ideologues. The criteria for winning its affection have everything to do with fidelity to doctrine and little to do with talent in the pursuit of truth and justice. It accounts for a mere 5 percent of attorneys in the United States and (one may suppose) a comparable minority of law school faculty, and yet Justices Kavanaugh, Gorsuch, Alito, Thomas, and Roberts (possibly), along with a remarkable 90 percent of Trump's appellate court appointees, are current or former members. In the legal community today, hundreds (indeed thousands) of other legal minds representing a feathery diversity of legal opinion will agonize for days over the wording of a letter intended to explain why a particular individual is unfit to serve, and yet that individual will still end up serving on the Supreme Court, provided he or she is a hardcore member of the Federalist Society.

The Federalist Society, moreover, is nothing if not a creature of escalating inequality. The $27 million annual budget for the society, the bulk of which comes from superwealthy donors, is just the group's lunch money. The $154 million expended to secure a last-minute seat on the Supreme Court for Federalist representative Amy Coney Barrett is a better measure of the level of resources involved in the effort to game the American legal mind. The payoff for the Federalist Society's superwealthy backers is not different in principle from the payoff that southern slaveholders received in exchange for their investment in the Supreme Court that delivered the Dred Scott decision of 1857. Their property rights are vigorously secured—at least until the game ends, when it all crashes into the ground.

Which brings up the other thing that the geometry of discourse in unequal times shares with an actual shuttlecock: the way the game ends. Human beings raised under the historically anomalous condition of relative equality take for granted that the extremes on the left will correct the extremes on the right, and that the outcome of a seemingly evenhanded debate will always lie in the sensible middle. In times of inequality, this assumption is false and dangerous. As money presses in, rational deliberation yields to a simulacrum of rationality, and those who pretend to stand for the pursuit of truth are usually the ones leading the charge into mutual destruction. If we return to that small world of the 9.9 percent where the Yale Law School looks almost like the hub of the universe, you will see what I mean.

So, WHAT IS AN ASPIRING MEMBER of the intellectual vanguard of the 9.9 percent to do? The charter of that vanguard in a democratic society is to operate the machinery of reason. Its members are there to draft the legal briefs, write up the policy proposals, manage the technology, and in general oversee all of the many operations that allow the rest of society to cooperate in a reasonable and productive way. But they've also got careers and projects in self-realization to pursue. It would be surprising if they managed to remain reasonable in a decidedly unreasonable system—especially considering that they themselves are the ones operating the system. In New Haven, at least, they clearly do not.

Let's say you clawed your way in to Yale Law School, but once you get there, you get this bad feeling that you don't belong. Maybe it's because you are Black and, like Clarence Thomas, you succumb to a frenzy of self-pity and somehow convince yourself that you will never overcome the stigma of having been accepted only through affirmative action. "All the Law School cares about is its own image among know-it-all elites,"[59] you might conclude, as Thomas did. Or maybe it's because you identify with some white religion, and you feel you are the real victim here. Or maybe it's something else altogether, something weird, personal, or random. The truth is, there doesn't have to be a reason. As inequality rises, the competition for recognition grows ever more intense. Everybody feels judged, most are found wanting, and only the paranoid survive. The decisive question is whether you happen to focus your resentments and anxieties on the very idea of Yale Law School, which is to say, on the smug, ostentatiously liberal, virtue-signaling professors who claim to speak for the institution. That's when you join the angry young people of the Federalist Society.

It's not an easy proposition. That's why the number who take it up are so few, and the anger they harbor so great. You need to have a great deal of passion, or world-historical levels of callow ambition, to push yourself past the paradoxes. You have to be willing to bash those dreaded elites that come out of places like Yale even though you yourself are coming out of Yale. You have to pretend that you are merely a seeker of truth joining a debating society, even though your debating society and every idea it promotes is bought and paid for by extreme wealth. And then you have to sign up for work on building the hard, rubbery end of the politics of unreason. It has often been suggested that anti-intellectualism arises like a fungus from the neglected members of the uneducated classes. In fact, the only kind of anti-intellectualism that really matters comes from other members of the intellectual class. It is the archetypal form of the treason of the intellectuals.

But let's say that, like most of the people who navigate the treacherous admissions process, you are a more well-adjusted type. You didn't come to Yale to nurse a grievance. You're more like a tiger mother— gung-ho on the system and focused mainly on succeeding within its terms. This is where the predicament of the 9.9 percent is particularly poignant. You get that your mission is to stand up for reason, and that your guiding principle is objectivity. But you soon grasp that the stock-in-trade of the day-to-day intellectual is really only the appearance of objectivity. The currency of intellectual success is not truth itself but the authority to speak for it that comes with a distinguished position within a hierarchy of learning. The human condition being what it is, some trade-off is inevitable. The question is how much of the truth you sacrifice in exchange for the privilege of pretending to speak for it from those care-free positions of intellectual authority known as professorships at Yale Law School.

As inequality seeps into institutions of higher learning through every pore of a society flush with excess cash and imposes its grim stratification schemes even on intellectual labor, the calculus of the trade-off between objectivity and the appearance of objectivity changes. The reward for conflating the two increases with the rising value of prestige and its ever-greater dependence on the benevolence of extreme wealth.

Even more problematically, rising inequality itself expands the gap between objectivity and the appearance of objectivity. Human beings intuitively judge the appearance of objectivity with respect to an implicit standard of equality. They take for granted that everyone has an "equally valid" perspective, and that everyone's perspective is their own. This is a fine thought, and where the equality of basic conditions makes possible a genuine equality of mutual regard, it is a useful thought as well. In the distorted world of rising inequality, however, it is a bad thought. It means sacrificing reason for the sake of appearing to be reasonable.

What should an intellectual to do under these conditions? Socrates was pretty clear on that point. In unequal times, he understood, to be for the consensus is to be against truth, and to advance the genuine interest of the people is necessarily to disagree with them. Thus, the truth, if it is to survive, must be defended against the conventional opinions. Which is not always easy to do, as Socrates himself might have pointed out, just before drinking that lethal dose of hemlock. Which doesn't really make it any easier.

People on the outside of the game have no idea how many sacrifices you have to make to secure a position on the Yale Law School faculty. They really don't know what it takes to snag one of those Supreme Court clerkships for one's daughter. That's why people on the outside don't matter. So, the game turns inward. This is the life of the mind in the twilight of the meritocracy: cliquish, careerist, and militantly committed to the mere appearance of objectivity. Relativism is just another form of the treason of the intellectuals. It is a gentler way of serving power than joining the Federalist Society.

When this treason of the intellectuals is mapped back into American political discourse, the consequences are easy to see. The nihilistic ideologues of the right have made it possible for the Republican Party to become the party that deceives other people in order to promote inequality. And self-delusion in the upper economic reaches of the left risks turning the Democratic Party into a home for an affluent, educated elite that seeks to correct every form of injustice except the inequality that is the actual basis of its privilege. The role of the 9.9 percent, in brief, is to distribute the blindfolds through which inequality perpetuates itself in a politics of unreason.

THE OUTLINES OF A SOLUTION aren't complicated. If inequality is the remote cause of political unreason, then restoring a politics of reason must ultimately depend on establishing the equality of mutual regard that is the necessary foundation for rational action among humans. Even so, reason does not require that we wait until equality obtains before we act. The proximate causes of the politics of unreason are visible, too, and they may be addressed more directly. The first step in restoring a politics of reason is to address the disinformation problem that now plagues the infosphere.

The root of the crisis in media today is that the "public square" has been privatized and pillaged. The communications infrastructure on which any democracy depends has been turned over to private corporations that have learned how to sell off the public interest for private gain. Even worse, it has been turned over to private monopolies and oligopolies whose only enduring interest is to sustain the inequalities from which they arise. Public media, meanwhile, has atrophied to the point of near irrelevance.

Any solution to the present disinformation problem must therefore begin with the understanding that this "public square" properly belongs to the public. It is a piece of what Henry George and Thomas Paine would have called "the earth." This does not mean that every actor in the infosphere should work for some central government agency. It does mean that every actor should be working within a system that is held accountable to the public good. One way to establish such a system would be to create a viable public option that can serve as a real check on disinformation. Another important step would be to rigorously separate the communications infrastructure that supplies the platform of discussion from the purveyors of information who depend upon it. A further critical step would be to break up the oligopolies that have infested the media world at all levels.[60]

If we are to change the infosphere for the better, however, we will also need better ideas about what kind of thing it is. This is where the ideas that guide the 9.9 percent matter. Restoring the politics of reason rests on reviving the understanding that the pursuit of truth is a public good. It means acknowledging that journalism, for example, is a public service and that education is a public good. These ideas were once built in to the machinery that produced America's professional classes. Sustaining them in the face of escalating inequality must be at the core of any effort to save democracy in America. It will be the principal task of the enlightened successors to the 9.9 percent. To be clear, such a project in enlightenment can succeed only if equality prevails on the ground and in the economy; and yet it is a necessary piece of any plan that will allow us to establish such an equality.

How We Might Get a Clue

On a fall morning in 1785, Thomas Jefferson set off for a hike in the mountains around Fontainebleau, a gated community forty miles south of Paris that served as a playground for the French king and his enablers among the 9.9 percent of the time (who represented about 2.9 percent of the population, the times being what they were). As he walked past vast tracts of prime suburban real estate reserved for the use of aristocratic hunting parties, the American diplomat fell into conversation with a minimum wage peasant woman. She told him of the brutal circumstances of her life as a worker in the gig economy. Every morning she would load up her hand-operated GPS and set off in search of a paying job in the fields, she explained, but many nights she would return home with no bread and no money. Often, she skipped meals, and some evenings she put her two children to bed hungry. Plagues and junk food were regular visitors. When their paths parted, Jefferson handed the woman 24 sous—pocket change for him, three days' wages for her—and she burst into tears.[1]

That evening, Jefferson composed a letter to James Madison, his powerful political ally in the Virginia legislature. The "unequal division of property" in Europe, he writes, produces "numberless instances of wretchedness" and brings "misery to the bulk of mankind." The situation in France is unsustainable, he suggests—which, in view of the revolution that took place four years later, it surely was. Lawmakers in America, he argues, should spare no effort in devising policies to prevent such dangerous and unjust economic inequalities from taking root. In sharp contrast with the ideologues of the oligarchy today, he takes as a given that extreme inequality is a natural result not of the creation of wealth but of its destruction. He proposes to remedy the situation with a tax on "property in geometrical progression"—that is, a progressive wealth tax, or what on certain propaganda networks today would be instantly identified as "socialism." He also advocates reforms to inheritance law to prevent the accumulation of large estates—that is, a "death tax," as some would say today.

Jefferson was far from the only founder of the American republic to advocate such putatively socialistic proposals. Benjamin Franklin and John Adams, among others, supported forms of progressive taxation, as did Adam Smith, the founding father of modern economics, from whom America's leaders drew many of their insights on economic questions. Perhaps the most striking proposals came from Thomas Paine. In his 1797 pamphlet on *Agrarian Justice*, Paine outlines a plan for charging a "ground-rent" of 10 percent of the value of an estate upon a landowner's death and distributing the proceeds in the form of a lump sum or "inheritance" for every citizen upon reaching the age of twenty-one as well as an annual pension for every person over fifty. The plan is in essence the eighteenth-century version of social security, universal basic income, and an estate tax rolled into one.[2]

These early moves toward the future are particularly noteworthy in light of the fact that, for most of recorded time, economic inequality was so much a feature of life that asking about its origins would have made as much sense as asking why mountains are high or water is wet. Yet, for many of America's founders, it was visible as a problem—a human problem, with a human solution. Why did this happen? How did Jefferson, who was himself the enslaver of 218 human beings, manage to see the world from the perspective of a peasant woman—rather than from, say, the perspective of the aristocrats with whom he was there to mingle?

Much of the commentary today on America's founders focuses on the inequalities that they themselves represented and practiced, notably with respect to native peoples, enslaved peoples, the un-propertied classes, and women. But the rush to police their imperfections risks obscuring the extraordinary place of the American experience in the history of equality. In the eyes of Jefferson, Paine, and many of America's founders, the extreme inequality carved into the European landscape stood out as a visible and extremely dangerous problem precisely on account of the extraordinary experience of (relative) equality among white people in America. In the eyes of high-born European visitors, such as Hector St. John de Crèvecoeur and Alexis de Tocqueville, conversely, the social and economic equality that reigned in American life was its most distinctive feature, and they wrote of it as a development of world-historical consequence.

The economic data from the period, limited as it is, indicate that their perceptions were accurate. At least for the white European settlers involved in the project, the opening of the North American continent resulted in a degree of leveling with few parallels in western history. Even the largest estates of the emerging American elite were meager by the standards of the British empire. George Washington's Mount Vernon would have counted as a guest cottage at the Duke of Marlborough's Blenheim Palace.

Although it would be pleasant to suppose that this extraordinary leveling was due to some suite of superior ideas, a far more likely suspect in the plot is the simple accident of terrestrial geography. The weakness of the old hierarchies across the ocean, in contrast with what Paine called "the natural mightiness of America,"[3] thwarted for a time the elites who might otherwise have figured out how to capture the wealth of the new continent for themselves and reduce the people once again to servitude. The temporary result was a land where wages for free labor were unusually high, where the common people enjoyed relatively abundant opportunities to achieve economic self-determination, and where the gap between rich and poor, though not inconsiderable, rested at a tiny fraction of what it was in Europe. Only for a moment—and only for some—geography was destiny.

In the most consequential part of his letter from Fontainebleau, Jefferson puts his finger on the general principle that guides his thinking on the origins of and the solutions to the problem of extreme economic inequality. "Wherever there is in any country uncultivated lands and unemployed poor, it is clear that the laws of property have been so far extended as to violate natural right," he writes. Jefferson's distinction between "the laws of property" and "natural right"—and his recognition that the two can be in conflict—is remarkable, and worth attention now. It is a direct appeal to the political philosophy encoded in the Declaration of Independence. It makes clear that, contrary to the relentless messaging from the defenders of unearned wealth today, collectively addressing the problem of inequality through the instruments of government and law is not only consistent with the original vision of the American republic but required by it.

Today, unfortunately, "liberalism" is often falsely identified with what Jefferson calls "the laws of property." Especially under the deceitful name of "neoliberalism," it has been mistaken for a regime that enforces a particular set of legal rights, most of them having to do with the ownership rights of individuals and corporate entities. In its original form, however, as I have explained elsewhere,[4] liberalism is grounded on what Jefferson calls "natural right." "The laws of property," though a necessary feature of any liberal society, must answer to natural right. To identify liberalism with a set of legal rights, as many superficial commentators today do, is to confuse the instruments of liberalism with its principles.

Although the language of natural right has long gone out of fashion (and has in recent years been misappropriated by conservative ideologues who systematically pervert its meaning), the relevant aspects of the idea are easy to state. "Natural right" just means freedom. But it comes with the understanding that there is no freedom without reason. Among naturally equal beings that depend upon one another for their survival and self-realization, it adds, reason is not empty. Reason requires that we seek to cooperate with one another in pursuit of common goods on the basis of equal mutual regard. It further tells us that there are some goods—Jefferson and Paine both gathered them under the label of "the earth"—that human beings can only possess in common. Natural right in this sense calls for a system of laws of property through which individuals may collaborate on the basis of equal mutual regard. But it also stipulates that no system of laws may ever be permanently identified with the grounding principle of liberalism, because laws are not reasons. When a system of law becomes unreasonable, it is the law that must change. This is the simple yet pregnant idea of liberalism that Jefferson issued from Fontainebleau and wrote into the Declaration of Independence: freedom arises from equal justice; there is no justice without law; and no law is just that fails the test of reason.

Where did this radical idea of original liberalism come from, and why did it take root in America? Religious and nationalist mythmakers at this point typically invoke some idea of "heritage," by which they mostly mean to say that it involved some inherited dogma that makes their culture superior and imbues it with a right to dominate all others. Jefferson himself pointed to a better answer when he observed, late in life, that the Declaration of Independence aimed not for "originality of principle or sentiment" but rather amounted to "an expression of the American mind."[5] That mind was made up in America. And the distinguishing feature of American life, as we already know, was the relative (if still highly imperfect) equality in social and economic circumstances that it had achieved even before the Revolution, thanks principally to geography. An emerging American elite signed on to the self-evident truth that all men are created equal because—to a limited degree, sufficient mainly to produce the glimmer of consciousness—people were already equal.

As a general rule, equality happens on the ground before it happens in the mind. It follows from this fact that the story that progressives prefer to tell today, that justice advances inexorably forward one identity group at a time from a blinkered past to a woke present, is unfortunately too simple to be true. If material equality is the condition of justice, then material inequality will produce injustice, and it will manufacture whatever new identity groups it needs for the purpose, as discussed in preceding chapters. To the extent that this general rule holds, the prospects for creating a more just world would seem to lie trapped in a chicken-and-egg predicament. We can only count on people to pursue equality when the world is already, to some degree, equal. This is why, as historian Walter Scheidel points out, plagues, famines, wars, and the collapse of states are, tragically, the most reliable way to lay the foundations of justice.[6]

If we consider the origins of American liberalism more closely, however, a more hopeful picture emerges. It is embedded in both the context of Jefferson's work and the text, and in the nature of the republic they sought to establish. Liberal democracy is misunderstood if it is represented, as it often is today, merely as a device for tabulating the opinions of a population. Liberal democracy does not in fact take its start from the assumption that human beings are largely self-sufficient rational actors in need of some minor assistance in maximizing their pre-existing preferences. On the contrary, its most basic assumptions are that humans left to their own devices are generally quite unreasonable.

The point of the separation of powers, the checks and balances, the inherently public character of deliberation and legislation, the election of representatives, the guaranteed rights, especially of expression, and all of the other mechanisms of a functioning liberal democracy is to ensure as much as possible that the understanding on which public action takes place is accountable to reason. Properly conceived, liberal democracy is a truth machine. Its most fundamental premise is that every step in the direction of reason is also a step in the direction of justice. It takes for granted that, in the same way that injustices like racism and sexism are not just legacies from the past but outcomes of a series of injustices that multiply themselves out in the present, so, too, are justice and equality reproduced in the present, step by step, wherever and in whatever degree power is held accountable to reason. This truth machine cannot withstand any degree of inequality—we're pushing the limit now—but, within certain confines, it can reverse the normal tide of human history, because reason always dissolves inequality. Indeed, Jefferson himself proposed some reasonable ways to dissolve inequality in his time, and we have similar options available today in the land of the 9.9 percent.

MAYBE THE MOST REMARKABLE ASPECT of the tax proposal that Jefferson promulgates in the letter from Fontainebleau is how little of substance in it needs to be updated. The arguments for a progressive wealth tax are just as good now as they were when Jefferson walked the hills of the Ancien Régime. And you don't have to go back to the eighteenth century to make the case: the United States taxed the wealthy at much higher rates in the post–World War II period than it does today, and had much higher growth rates to show for it. The existing distribution of the tax burden in America is inexcusable. The question is why we put up with it.

The most obvious explanation for the persistence of our inequitable tax system, already discussed previously, is that greedy rich people have purchased the political system and bought the tax code they desire. Another, equally obvious explanation is that the same people, through their control of the ideological apparatus of the modern American political system, have successfully indoctrinated large numbers of college Republicans and other useful people in the belief that subsidizing the rich is the only way to provide toys for everyone and avoid turning into Venezuela. Another explanation is that the rich have successfully manipulated uneducated white people into thinking that not taxing the rich is the best way to stop wasting money on undeserving people of other racial identities, and yet another explanation adds that the not-so-rich have struck a deal to give the rich what they want in exchange for whatever psychic or cultural benefits flow from imposing their religious convictions on the rest of society. There is a lot of truth to all of these suggestions. Yet there is an additional explanation, complementary to all of these worthy hypotheses, and it deserves more attention than it gets because it points to an easier and less appreciated set of solutions—and because it involves the 9.9 percent directly. It starts with the fact that Americans are deluded about the actual nature of their tax code.

The American system of taxation is notoriously complex, expensive, and opaque. Most of the time, the barbarism of the system is represented as either an accident of history or the inevitable by-product of bureaucracy, and its impact is thought to be spread out indifferently across the population. In fact, the obscurity in the code exists to perpetuate the illusions that have flourished in American culture with the rise of the 9.9 percent, and it ultimately works to redistribute wealth from the 90 percent to the top. Some of this redistributive impact follows from the direct costs of complexity—only the rich can afford the lawyers and accountants needed to game the system—but more of it derives from the lack of transparency and the resulting misperceptions that it encourages.

Consider, for example, the question whether the American system of taxation is progressive. It is an article of faith among Americans in general and the 9.9 percent in particular that the existing system of taxation takes proportionally more money from "us"—meaning hardworking, mostly white, "successful" Americans—and gives proportionally more to "them"—meaning the less fortunate, the less able, and the less white. Mitt Romney gave voice to this assumption when he famously suggested that 47 percent of Americans pay no taxes and therefore have "no skin in the game."

But this article of faith is quite false. The federal income tax system is indeed progressive, as Romney suggests, but it represents only about one third of the total tax burden on Americans, as Romney conveniently ignores. Federal payroll taxes, which represent roughly a quarter of all taxes, are steeply regressive; every penny earned above a cap conveniently situated around the bottom of the 9.9 percent income level is payroll-tax-free. State taxes take the next largest bite, but many states continue to rely on sales taxes on the kinds of things that poor people buy in greater proportion to their income than rich people. And then there are local taxes, most of them property taxes, that spare the very rich (whose wealth is concentrated in financial assets, not houses), and return much of the revenue collected back to their middle-class base in the form of local schools and services. When you put the whole house of cards together, as Emmanuel Saez and Gabriel Zucman show, it turns out that the working class pays about 25 percent of its income on tax, the middle class pays 28 percent, and the richest four hundred Americans pay 23 percent.[7] In other words, the United States spends a fortune on accountants and lawyers to manage a byzantine code that delivers an essentially flat tax for most of the population with a massive dollop of regressive taxation at the top end. But sure, it *feels* like the system is taxing only hardworking (white) Americans, and letting *other people* get a free ride—and that's really all that the oligarchs need you to feel.

It gets worse. The tax code is more than a device for collecting money. It's a way of handing out public money, too, only without having to go to the trouble of writing a check on the public treasury. Most of the love falls on the 9.9 percent, and it happens by means that are often so delicately invisible that it is easily mistaken for a sign of divine affection. The problem starts with a cognitive shortcoming in humans that makes it difficult to grasp that an income tax deduction is just a public expenditure by another name—with the added twist that it often permits private individuals to decide exactly how public resources will be allocated.

The invisible welfare system of tax expenditures now accounts for more federal spending than Medicare. According to the Congressional Budget Office, the federal government spends three times as much subsidizing tax-free employer-sponsored health care ($250 billion) as it does on subsidies to those who can't afford insurance in the non-tax-free private market ($84 billion). It spends three times as much on subsidies to wealthy homeowners as it does on affordable housing. It spends three times as much absolving wealthy heirs of capital gains taxes on estates as it does on the school lunch programs that feed 30 million low-income children every school day. It lavishes as much money on churches and religious organizations simply for being religious as it does on the entire federal Department of Education. It hands out about as much money to the few tens of thousands of students attending universities with the largest tax-advantaged endowments as it does to the 7 million low-income students that receive Pell Grants.[8]

The granddaddy of all tax subsidies is the preferential treatment of capital income over labor income. Somehow—actually, we know how, and it involved quite a few distinguished professors of economics—the rich managed to convince the public that income earned while sitting on the sofa and watching your stock portfolio grow is far more commendable than income earned while working. The subsidy that flows to those who make sofa money ($190 billion) would be more than enough to solve the problems of higher and lower education.

Step back to the level of principle and it becomes clear that the situation with the American tax system differs little from the fundamental condition that Jefferson observed in the hills of Fontainebleau. Under the cloak of an impenetrably complex tax code, the laws of property have been extended in such a way as to violate natural right. The tax code in its present form, in other words, is not a product of liberalism but of its absence. It reflects a failure to supply the transparency that a liberal democracy requires in all of its public policy in order to hold power accountable to reason. You can't solve a problem if you don't see it.

Merely recognizing the injustice, to be sure, won't bring equality back. That's why we will need Jefferson's progressive wealth tax. And it should not be modest. There just isn't any good reason to keep billionaires around. But it also follows from the insights that Jefferson lays down that the path to justice generally does not pass through violent upheavals of the sort that took place in France in 1789 and that are mistakenly called "revolutions." The only real revolutions happen through acts of reason, and in the end, precisely because they answer to reason, they look more like what we call "reform."

On this slow path to sensible reform, the 9.9 percent have a special role to play. No less than in Jefferson's time, a key to the possibility of meaningful change is having a 9.9 percent capable of seeing their gated communities from the perspective of those on the outside. It means trying a little harder to see the world through the eyes of those who by natural right are the actual source of all wealth in human society.

IN RETROSPECT, IT IS ASTONISHING that Teddy Roosevelt chose to take his stand in Osawatomie, Kansas.[9] Only fifty-four years had passed since the bloody summer of 1856, when "Border Ruffians" burned the settlement down and killed five antislavery "Free-Staters," including one of John Brown's sons. This was where John Brown, a wanted man and a terrorist in the eyes of many of his contemporaries, turned to another of his sons and vowed, "There will be no more peace in this land until slavery is done for." Yet here it was that, on August 31, 1910, at the dedication of the John Brown Memorial Park, fresh from an African safari and standing before an audience of thirty thousand, Roosevelt delivered what one listener described as the greatest speech by the greatest person in the greatest country in the history of the world.

In the speech, the erstwhile president lays out the defiantly progressive program that he hoped would carry him back to the leadership of the Republican Party and then back to the White House. The program calls for, among other things: a vigorous anti-trust policy to rein in the monopolies that were strangling the economy and corrupting the political system; labor reforms intended to strengthen the hand of workers in negotiating fair compensation; the establishment of a national health agency and a system of social security; conservation of the environment for future generations; and tax reforms, including a federal income tax and an inheritance tax. Much of government hitherto has merely attempted to defend the rights of the propertied, Roosevelt argues, echoing Jefferson's message from Fontainebleau; it must now be "interested primarily in human welfare rather than property."

Progress, Roosevelt further explains, depends on bringing all unearned power and money to justice. "This conflict between the men who possess more than they have earned and the men who have earned more than they possess is the central condition of progress," he declares. "At every stage, and under all circumstances, the essence of the struggle is to equalize opportunity, destroy unearned privilege, and give to the life and citizenship of every individual the highest possible value both to himself and the commonwealth."

Roosevelt was instantly and predictably denounced as a "communist agitator," an "anarchist," and a "socialist"—and his bid for a return to the presidency failed. And yet all of the reforms he listed were implemented at least in part over the coming years, and all remain central to any progressive program. The problem with the American economy today, just as in Roosevelt's, is not that we have a "free market" but that we pretend to have it. Americans, with the ostentatious help of the 9.9 percent, have confused the paraphernalia of free exchange with the substance. They infer that wherever there is a large corporation, a brand, and an MBA, there is free market and prosperity. Or they falsely conclude that the free market itself is to blame for all the consequences of a captured market.

The reality is that the fictitious creatures of corporate law have destroyed many of our markets, diminished actual wealth, and converted what are supposed to be exercises in free exchange into acts of ransom—and the 9.9 percent have provided ideological cover for this destruction of wealth even as they oversee the operation of the machines that reproduce it. Any credible program to address the unjust inequalities of the present must begin with the effort to liberate productive human collaboration from the dead hand of the corporate apparatus. But that also means liberating the mind from the meritocratic framework through which Americans systematically represent actual corporate activity.

Though the details of any progressive program today will differ, the substance is the same as that which Roosevelt proposed. Progress requires pursuing an anti-trust policy that is not just a pro-trust policy in disguise. It means obliterating the specious consumer price rationales for licensing the destruction of markets and instead breaking up the oligopolies and quasi-monopolies that now rule in financial services, telecommunications, social media, online retail, internet search, airlines, pharmaceuticals, and many other industries.[10] It also means vaporizing once and for all the noxious dogma that corporations have obligations only to their shareholders. A good place to start on that project would be to modify corporate governance to require that all corporations, not just those that are publicly listed, provide transparency sufficient to justify the licenses that they acquire from the public, and to further require that they include representation on their governing boards not just of those lucky enough to work for them but all other constituencies and the general public. The idea of a "private" corporation is and always has been a contradiction in terms. The corporate form can be very useful, to be sure; but corporations should be tools for humans, not the other way around.

Any credible program to advance justice today would also seek to reempower workers, as Roosevelt's program promised to do. A first step would be to return to workers the rights that employers, through their paid agents in government, have taken from them. There is no excuse for a legal code that allows corporations to require employees to sign away their right to compete and their right to pursue disputes through the courts rather than through privatized systems of arbitration. It is also time to consider alternatives to collective bargaining that might permit workers to organize across firms and sectors.

It is true, of course, that labor organizations can and do interfere with free exchange and democratic processes in the same way that corporations do, and that public sector unions in particular can become a legitimate source of concern. But the bad behavior in some contexts does not change the tremendous, aggregate imbalance of power that tilts against labor in the modern American economy. The best way to "redistribute" the wealth is, as ever, to ensure that people have the power to negotiate their rightful claims to the wealth that they actually produce.

At Osawatomie, Roosevelt decried the influence of special interest money in politics. The situation hasn't changed much. Today, we need a system of public funding of political campaigns—much of which can be supplied at no direct cost by simply allocating use of public airwaves and platforms. Perhaps even more important than campaign finance today, however, are the electoral reforms required to restore American democracy. The electoral college is an economic inequality issue, not just a political inequality issue. So is voter suppression. So are gerrymandering, the Supreme Court selection process, the filibuster, and the U.S. Senate itself. Everything that permits minority rule opens the door that much wider for plutocracy and corruption. As Abraham Lincoln (supposedly) said, you can fool some of the people all of the time—and, unfortunately, in America right now, that's all you need to do to establish a permanent rule by the rich.

There is something else that remains relevant about Roosevelt's performance at Osawatomie, however, and it goes beyond the continuities in the policy programs. It has to do with the problem represented by the 9.9 percent. Although the speech swiftly gained Roosevelt a reputation as a socialist or worse, it is worth remembering that he was in fact a child of privilege, the scion of a wealthy New York business family. It's worth adding that his speechwriter Gifford Pinchot—the national conservation leader whose radical turns of phrase are embroidered throughout Roosevelt's speech—was equally well-born. Yet that did not stop those two men and many of their supporters from taking the perspective of the common people and making it the center of their vision.

Roosevelt had the usual allotment of shortcomings and prejudices of his time (as represented in his taste for African safaris, for example), and yet he managed to make the commitment to the good of all people an explicit part of his speech at Osawatomie. The meaning of the struggle for economic justice, Roosevelt says, is to increase the worth of all individuals in their own eyes and those of society. Thus he finds the cornerstone of progress in the recognition of the dignity of humankind. This dignity, as Roosevelt well understood, was not merely a matter of making fine declarations of principle. Dignity is ultimately available only to those who have the requisite power over the material conditions of their own lives.

HARRY TRUMAN GOT THE POINT. He figured it out in the army. He was thirty-three years old when he volunteered for service in the First World War and still had rather little to show for his time on the planet: one solitary year in college, a stint as a railroad clerk, long hours on a small farm, a string of business ideas that went nowhere, and the cold slap of rejection from Bess in his first proposal of marriage. But out in the killing fields of Europe, he discovered something about himself. In the "Battle of Who Run," when the men in his battalion began to turn and flee a German onslaught, the shy, shortsighted man from Missouri unleashed a furious torrent of salty invectives and revealed a talent for leadership that he did not know he possessed.[11]

Apart from teaching him something about himself, the army taught Truman a great deal about his fellow Americans. He got to know a thousand or so men in his command, and back home after the war, the same men and their families would supply the votes that launched his political career. As an officer in the reserve, and later as a member of the Senate Armed Services Committee, he came across thousands more soldiers from across the country. Among the many things he learned about this population of American men, one in particular would prove unexpectedly significant. They were shockingly unhealthy.

When the nation called up 5 million men for service during the war, Truman noted in 1945, it found that fully 30 percent of American men aged eighteen to thirty-seven suffered from health conditions that made them physically unfit to serve. Of those who did enlist, a million and a half were later discharged on account of pre-existing health conditions unconnected with their service. Life in America was hard on many people, and it showed in their bodies. This awareness of the unhealthy condition of much of the American population stayed with Truman when he ascended into the presidency upon the death of Franklin Roosevelt, and it supplied the motivation behind his boldest failure, the proposed National Health Act of 1945.[12]

The problem, according to Truman's analysis, was not that America lacked the medical technology or the aggregate wealth to care for its population. The problem was that the poor and even the middle classes did not have access to decent health care and had no insurance to fall back upon when catastrophe struck. The wealthy had their doctors and their hospitals, and the rest had to make do with prayers. The solution, according to Truman, was a compulsory, universal health insurance that would cover every American. It was a conclusion that the leadership of pretty much every other industrialized country arrived at more or less the same time.

The American Medical Association, however, had other ideas. The group hotly denounced the National Health bill as "socialized medicine." A national insurance program was "the first step in a plan for general socialization not only of the medical profession, but all professions, business and labor," AMA leaders thundered. It represented "the kind of regimentation that led to totalitarianism in Germany." The AMA's allies in Congress agreed. Senator Robert Taft, a Republican of Ohio, denounced Truman's bill as "the most socialistic thing" he'd ever seen. In the 1946 midterm elections, the Republicans roared back into control of Congress, and that reversal, combined with Truman's chronic unpopularity in his first term, effectively killed off the plan for national health insurance.[13]

Twenty years later, Lyndon Johnson successfully revived the over-sixty-five part of the plan, when he managed to push Medicare past the same hysterical accusations of socialism and totalitarianism (some of them coming this time from actor-turned-politician Ronald Reagan).

Forty-five years after Medicare, in the face of the evergreen cant about "socialism," and in the context of massive increases in the relative and absolute cost of health care, President Obama filled in some of the holes in coverage among low-income and other workers with the Affordable Care Act. Although these reforms improved coverage and outcomes in the United States considerably, they left the bulk of the system in the hands of pseudo-private insurance companies, and these have largely succeeded in exploiting their public subsidies and licenses to hold the health of the public for ransom—and then perpetuating themselves by reinvesting their winnings in manipulating the political system to their advantage.

With the benefit of seventy-five years of hindsight, it is now fair to say that the failure to embrace a national health care program along the lines Truman proposed in 1945 has cost the United States more years of lost life and more dollars in medical expenses and lost economic output than all of the wars fought during that period combined. Disease and death directly attributable to massive health care policy failure was and remains a far more real danger to American lives than any military enemy.[14]

Health care, however, was not the only scene of needless destruction in struggle for domination in postwar American society. Truman's health bill was just one part of the economic bill of rights that FDR had put forward in his State of the Union address of January 1944. Though sometimes pitched as a "second" bill of rights, the new bill is an extension of rights that Jefferson and Madison would have recognized as belonging to the first, and it subsequently influenced the United Nations' declaration of universal human rights. Apart from access to health care, the economic bill of rights also included, among other things, the right "to a decent home" and the right "to a good education." At the beginning of the postwar period, the United States invested substantial sums in a welfare system that helped secure those rights for the white middle classes. With the triumph of inequality, however, these rights were converted into privileges for the few, while the rest were encouraged to take on reckless levels of debt to acquire them.

The erosion of the economic bill of rights was the work of many actors and many factors working together. Undoubtedly, major economic players—the health-care-industrial complex, the car and fossil fuel companies, the education privatizers, and so on—played a starring role. But the ideas and the people who ultimately formed the 9.9 percent had their fingerprints all over the scene of the crime, too. The AMA—which, together with its sister organizations among the medical professions, now represents the single largest block of paid-up members of the 9.9 percent—supplied the archetype for the reaction with their sabotage of the national health insurance plan. The ultimate beneficiaries were the health care corporations and the executives who captured them, but the medical professionals came in a close second (though their time may be running out). The capture of the education sector, too, could not have happened without self-congratulatory efforts of the 9.9 percent, who insisted on educational credentials as indisputable proof of merit even as they ignored overwhelming evidence of massive disparities in access to education. The conversion of housing from a right into a method for separating winners from losers likewise could not have happened without the rise of the 9.9 percent. There is no housing "affordability" crisis; there is only a housing availability crisis, and it exists mostly because the 9.9 percent have captured the regulation of local space and because the system actively punishes renters and others who fail to inherit a home or get help on the down payment.

Now is the time to set aside the preconceptions of the 9.9 percent and make room for public options not just in health care insurance and education (where forms of a public option have existed for some time) but also in child care, internet access, telecommunications, banking, and tax accounting. Jefferson, Paine, Henry George, and Teddy Roosevelt understood that "the earth" belongs to all; it's time to recognize that cyberspace is part of the earth, too. The Federal Reserve Bank is our common property, too, for that matter and it ought to be able to open accounts for individuals, and not just for banks as a means of funneling public subsidies to the behemoths of the financial services industry.

In the homilies intended to make the world safe for oligarchy, efforts to secure a basic equality of material conditions through access to a good education, decent housing, and affordable health care are often represented as attempts to expand government power at the expense of economic growth. The moral of the story typically turns on a trade-off between equality on the one hand and freedom and prosperity on the other. Every step we take toward equality, the fable tells us, costs us a little piece of freedom and a lot of money, until at last we end up like Cuba or Venezuela, or some such impoverished totalitarian socialist regime with a cigar-chomping dictator. In fact, it works the other way around. The rise of a self-involved, self-seeking, and fundamentally corrupt upper class in places like Cuba and Venezuela, uncomfortably akin to our own 9.9 percent, is precisely what produced the reactionary regimes that ultimately impoverished those countries. The equality of the basic material conditions is and has long been understood as a natural right because it is both the basis of the creation of wealth in a society and the foundation of individual freedom.

AMERICAN HISTORY CONSIDERED IN ITS BROADEST SWEEP makes abundantly clear that collective action through a democratically elected government has been and must remain an indispensable tool in advancing the cause of equal justice. The idea that the market or civil society, left to their own devices, will organize a fair tax code, break up monopolies, ensure universal access to health and education is and always has been fatuous. It is usually the mantra of those who rely on the hidden powers of government to sustain their own privilege.

Among the 9.9 percent, this self-serving abdication from politics often takes the form of virtuous consumerism. We don't need to think about a carbon tax because we can solve the problem of climate change by carefully choosing what we will have for dinner, or so the thinking goes. We can compensate for collecting on the race dividend by carefully policing our own thoughts about race. But the widespread belief that every political issue comes down to the personal choices and actions we make as individuals is one of the delusions of inequality. It is a way of disempowering the public by replacing active citizens with passive consumers.

Even so, the sweep of American history also shows that the formal apparatus of lawmaking and control that we associate with government in a modern society is far from the only source of meaningful change. The distinction that matters here is not between private and public actions, but between two kinds of public action. Government in the formal sense is far from the only tool available for advancing justice—because government in this narrow sense is not the only way we govern ourselves. The schools, businesses, churches, community groups, cooperatives, unions, extended families, and other institutions that make up what we customarily call the "private" sphere, or civil society, are an extension of the common project of human self-governance, not an exception to it.

Civil society is a historical and political achievement; it does not spring up like a bed of flowers from a meadow when government goes away. Directly or indirectly, it always rests on the delegated powers of a sovereign people, and its institutions act rightly when they answer to the common good. Whenever we hold power accountable, in any social institution, and every time we demand that it explain itself according to universal principles, even in small circumstances, we are to some degree legislating on behalf of humanity. The teacher who devotes himself to the education of students from all circumstances in life; the business that honors its duty to serve all customers equally and treat all of its employees with equal dignity; and the activist group that works to promote understanding across racial and social dividing lines—all of these and many other actors in a healthy civil society are committing public acts of justice, not private acts of charity. This is why many of the great reform movements in American history got their start when people decided that they didn't have to sit at the back of the bus or on some other lunch counter, even if those movements necessarily culminated in more formal public actions and laws.

The destruction of this element of justice in civil society, conversely, is and always has been one of the principal means through which inequality advances. This is the story of the 9.9 percent. Rising inequality has undermined families, disassembled communities, perverted the institutions of education, and, in general, strip-mined civil society for short-term financial gain. Left unchecked, this process will whittle down the list of winners, replacing society with a shrinking clique at the top shrieking about socialism and a disaffected rabble below shrieking about imaginary alien enemies, leaving behind yet another one of those decadent aristocracies that fill up the backlist of human history and the backwaters of the global economy. This is also the scene of action for much of the 9.9 percent now. The task now is not merely to advocate for political reform but to reconstitute civil society—not in opposition to politics, but as part of a political project that ties the norms of everyday life to the requirements of justice.

All of this is easy enough to see if one takes the trouble to look. The justification for stating the obvious in this book is that inequality itself stands in the way of seeing it. Inequality in America has given rise to the culture of the 9.9 percent, and this culture has willfully blinded itself to its own role in reproducing inequality and undermining the conditions of its own existence. This culture stands for some decent ideals, but it is fast leaving those original principles behind. There is something good about wanting to be the best parent ever, about striving for the best education, about believing in merit, trusting in the outcome of free exchanges, building strong neighborhoods, and doing all the other things that the 9.9 percent aspire to do. It just stops making sense when you mistake a privilege for a right. The problem is not that the paid-up members of the 9.9 percent are an exceptionally self-interested or immoral group. The problem is their failure to grasp that it is very difficult to act justly in an unjust society.

Change necessarily involves some sacrifice for those who see themselves as winners under the current system. To the extent that equality and justice are the actual foundation of freedom and prosperity, as I have maintained in this book, however, these moderate losses for the few translate into a gain for all in the aggregate. It's worth adding what every 9.9 percenter senses at some level, that our present winnings are not quite the thing we imagine them to be. Inequality places all who strive within it in status competitions that we cannot realistically hope to win while remaining true to ourselves. So we turn ourselves into what we are not and adopt fictional identities that better serve our chances for survival. We take for granted that the protection of these imaginary alter egos, fabricated out of all the prejudices and preconceptions of an unreasonable society, is the path to happiness. We thus transpose the disorder in the world into a kind of disorder in our minds, strive for things that, in the end, are the opposite of what we wanted, and confuse self-subordination with freedom. All of which leads us away from the awareness of how much our happiness depends on understanding our actual relations with other people and our place in nature. In the end, we have nothing to lose but our illusions.

Acknowledgments

This book began life as an essay, "The Birth of a New American Aristocracy," published in the June 2018 issue of the *Atlantic*. I am grateful to Don Peck, my editor there, and the staff at that magazine for their invaluable assistance in shaping the project. I would also like to thank the many readers of that essay—too many to acknowledge individually here—who wrote in with often very perceptive and useful insights.

In the course of writing this book, it was my good fortune to be able to test-run some of its ideas and sections before several critical audiences. I am particularly indebted for the conversation and feedback at events organized by Bob Milnikel and David Rowe at Kenyon College; Daniel Nuckols at Austin College; Tony Fleo and Michael Sorrell at Paul Quinn College; Todd Jick and Bruce Usher, both of the Columbia Business School, in Youngstown, Ohio; Giampaolo Greco at the Icahn School of Medicine at Mount Sinai; Greg Epstein of the Human Hub together with Nick Hanauer at MIT; and Lisa Baker of the Milton Academy at the Humanities Workshop of Boston.

A work such as this one, which pretends only to synthesize the facts uncovered by others, necessarily owes a debt of gratitude to the many researchers and writers in the fields of economics, sociology, political theory, public policy, and other subjects on whose labors it depends. In the footnotes, I have listed as many sources as practicable and made mention of some with whom I have consulted personally. I encourage interested readers to pursue the material further, and I offer my general thanks here.

This book has also benefited from anecdotes and insights supplied by many fellow members of the cultural universe it hopes to describe, a number of whom appear in anonymous guises in the text itself. Since they have wisely preferred not to be named, I would like to express my gratitude for their collaboration here.

This book is no exception to the rule that every book is the work of many hands. It has been my privilege to be represented by Andrew Stuart, my literary agent for the past two decades. I am grateful as well to my editor, Bob Bender, and his team at Simon & Schuster. I owe thanks also to Ben Lahey for his work as a research assistant.

Finally, my thanks go to those who cannot be thanked enough: Katherine, Sophia, and Aaron, not just for putting up with the author but for their many substantive contributions to the work itself, many of which were affectionately delivered across the kitchen table or on the drive to school.

Notes

Chapter 1 Who We Are

1 For more on Robert Wright Stewart, see Paul H. Giddens, *The Standard Oil Company (Indiana): Oil Pioneer of the Middle West* (New York: Appleton-Century-Crofts, 1955); Laton McCartney, *The Teapot Dome Scandal: How Big Oil Bought the Harding White House and Tried to Steal the Country* (Random House, 2008); and Daniel Yergin, *The Prize: The Epic Quest for Oil, Money, and Power* (New York: Simon & Schuster, 1990).

2 The study of economic inequality has now reached that point in the development of a discipline where no individual can claim to be the master of the entire domain. In these notes I will identify those sources that have guided this project and that might be useful for readers interested in further exploration.

For reasons made clear in subsequent chapters, I have preferred to center the discussion on wealth distribution as opposed to income distribution. The wealth distribution is substantially more skewed than the income distribution, but it is a better measure of the differentials in social, cultural, and political power. There are a number of methodological issues that arise in attempting to measure wealth and income distributions. Some sources make use of survey data, for example, while others rely more on income tax reporting data. For the purposes of this project and for most readers, however, these differences can be set aside, since all credible sources agree on the fundamental conclusions. For a survey of the methodological issues, see Gabriel Zucman, "Global Wealth Inequality," NBER Working Paper No. 25462, January 2019.

The most useful data on both wealth and income come from the various databases and publications put forward by Thomas Piketty, Emmanuel Saez, and Gabriel Zucman. See in particular "Distributional National Accounts:

Methods and Estimates for the United States," *The Quarterly Journal of Economics* 133, no. 2 (May 2018), and associated Data Appendix and online databases, which may be found at gabriel-zucman.eu/usdina and at the World Inequality Database (wid.world).

Also consulted were the data (with different methodologies) from the Urban Institute (urban.org), which were used to calculate the amounts and ratios of wealth between the 0.1 percent, the 9.9 percent, and the 90 percent. Additional data may be found at the Economic Policy Institute (epi.org) and at the OECD Institute for Policy Studies.

Additional essential resources for further study of economic inequality are Thomas Piketty, *Capital in the Twenty-First Century* (Cambridge, MA: Harvard University Press, 2013); Thomas Piketty, *Capital and Ideology* (Cambridge, MA: Harvard University Press, 2019); Joseph Stiglitz, *People, Power, and Profits: Progressive Capitalism for an Age of Discontent* (New York: Norton, 2019); and Joseph Stiglitz, "The American Economy Is Rigged," *Scientific American*, November 1, 2018.

For a case that the problem, or a big part of it, comes from the top 20 percent, see Richard Reeves, *Dream Hoarders: How the American Upper Middle Class Is Leaving Everyone Else in the Dust, Why That Is a Problem, and What to Do About It* (Washington, DC: Brookings Institution Press, 2017).

3 Katie Warren, "Comparing Forbes' Lists of America's Richest People from 1982 and 2019," *Business Insider*, November 6, 2019; Katie Warren, "The Richest American 37 Years Ago Wouldn't Even Make It onto the Forbes Billionaires List Today," *Business Insider*, October 3, 2019.

4 These numbers are my calculations based on data from the Urban Institute. Other sources cited in notes above yield slightly different numbers.

5 Chuck Collins et al., *Dreams Deferred: How Enriching the 1 Percent Widens the Racial Wealth Divide*, Institute for Policy Studies, 2019; Chuck Collins et al., "Report: The Road to Zero Wealth," Institute for Policy Studies, September 11, 2017. Note that there are a number of other sources providing slightly different estimates for the racial wealth gap. Though the numbers vary somewhat, the results are directionally identical.

6 Carlota Balestra, "Inequalities in Household Wealth Across OECD Countries," OECD Working Paper No. 88, June 20, 2018.

7 Matthias Doepke and Fabrizio Zilibotti, *Love, Money, and Parenting: How Economics Explains the Way We Raise Our Kids* (Princeton, NJ: Princeton University Press, 2019), p. 67.

8 David Leonhardt, "The Fleecing of Millennials," *New York Times*, January 27, 2019; Emma Kalish, "Millennials Are the Least Wealthy, but Most Optimistic, Generation," Urban Institute, April 2016; Christopher Kurz et al., "Are Millennials Different?," FEDS, 2018-080.

9 Matthew Desmond, "How Homeownership Became the Engine of American Economic Inequality," *New York Times Magazine*, May 9, 2017.

10 Volker Grossman et al., "The Macroeconomics of Housing and the Dynamics of Wealth Inequality," First WID.world Conference, December 14, 2017.

11 Laura Feiveson and John Sabelhaus, "How Does Intergenerational Wealth Transmission Affect Wealth Concentration?," *FEDS Notes*, June 1, 2018.

12 Jung Hyun Choi et al., *Intergenerational Homeownership: The Impact of Parental Homeownership and Wealth on Young Adults' Tenure Choices*, Research Report, Urban Institute, October 2018; Desmond, "How Homeownership Became the Engine of American Economic Inequality," *New York Times*, May 9, 2017.

13 Drew Delsilver, "For Most U.S. Workers, Real Wages Have Barely Budged in Decades," Pew Research Center, August 7, 2018.

14 "Americans and CEO Pay: 2016 Public Perception Survey on CEO Compensation," Stanford Graduate School of Business, Rock Center for Corporate Governance, February 2016. The locus classicus for surveys on Americans' absurd misperceptions about the distribution of wealth is Michael Norton and Dan Ariely, "Building a Better America, One Wealth Quintile at a Time," *Perspectives on Psychological Science* 6, no. 1 (January 2011): 9–12.

15 Lawrence Mishel and Julia Wolfe, "CEO Compensation Has Grown 940 Percent Since 1978," Economic Policy Institute, August 14, 2019. See also Equilar Institute, which sets the median for the top two hundred CEOs at $18.6 million in 2018.

16 Nathan Vardi, "The Highest-Earning Hedge Fund Managers and Traders," Forbes, March 20, 2019; Nathan Vardi, "The Top 25 Highest-Earning Hedge-Fund Managers," Forbes, April 17, 2018.

Chapter 2 Why We Have Such Amazing Children

1 Peppy Noor, "Must Ski, Cook and Know Excel," *Guardian*, January 24, 2020; Ruth Graham, "An Interview with the Woman Who Wrote the Viral 1,000 Word Job Listing for a 'Household Manager/Cook/Nanny,'" *Slate*, January 25, 2020. The ad itself was consulted but is no longer available online.

2 "High Quality Early Learning Settings Depend on a High-Quality Workforce," U.S. Department of Health and Human Services/Department of Education, June 2016; Linda Burnham and Nik Theodore, "Home Economics: The Invisible and Unregulated World of Domestic Work," National Domestic Workers Alliance, 2012; Sonali Kohli, "America Undervalues Childcare So Much, Nearly Half of Its Nannies Are on Welfare," *Quartz*, April 16, 2015. The Bureau of Labor Statistics says 2019 median pay for child care workers was $24,230 per year and $11.65 per hour.

3 Judy (Syfers) Brady, "I Want a Wife," *New York*, December 1971.

4 The ad was placed on monster.com and in print; a screenshot is in my possession.

5 Nanny salaries in Boston, Massachusetts, area, Glassdoor.

6 Wendy Rose Gould, "Here Are Five Nannies Who Make over $100,000 a Year," SWAAY, January 30, 2017.

7 Anna Bahney, "What It Takes to Be a $200,000-a-Year-Nanny," CNN Business, June 13, 2019.

8 Ads taken from British American Household Staffing on July 29, 2020: Hamptons, Boston, Connecticut, Los Angeles, Pacific Palisades.

9 The app is called Life360.

10 *Stuff: A Cluttered Life: Middle Class Abundance*, UCTV series, UCLA Center on Everyday Lives of Families, December 23, 2013; Jack Feuer, "The Clutter Culture," UCLA *Magazine*, July 1, 2012.

11 Annette Lareau, *Unequal Childhoods: Class, Race, and Family Life* (Berkeley, CA: University of California Press, 2011).

12 Alvin Rosenfeld and Nicole Wise, *The Overscheduled Child: Avoiding the Hyper-Parenting Trap* (New York: St. Martin's Griffin, 2001); Richard Reeves, "How to Save Marriage in America," *Atlantic*, February 13, 2014; Esther Wojcicki, *How to Raise Successful People* (New York: Penguin, 2019); "Parenting Methods Are Exacerbating Social Divisions," Special Report, *Economist*, January 3, 2019;

13 Patrick Ishizuka, "Social Class, Gender, and Contemporary Parenting Standards in the United States," *Social Forces* 98, no. 1 (September 2019): 31–58.

14 Pamela Druckerman, "A Cure for Hyper-Parenting," *New York Times*, October 12, 2014. On the other hand, parents from many countries think American parents have gone nuts: Lela Moore, "From Tokyo to Paris, Parents Tell Americans to Chill," *New York Times*, August 2, 2018.

15 Matthias Doepke and Fabrizio Zilibotti, *Love, Money, and Parenting: How Economics Explains the Way We Raise Our Kids* (Princeton, NJ: Princeton University Press, 2019), 128; Robert Putnam, *Our Kids* (New York: Simon & Schuster, 2015), 127. For an early overview: Garey Ramey and Valerie A. Ramey, "The Rug Rat Race," NBER Working Paper No. 15284, August 2009.

16 Sabino Kornrich, "Inequalities on Spending on Young Children: 1972 to 2010," SAGE Journals, June 8, 2016, combined with Claire Cain Miller, "The Relentlessness of Modern Parenting," *New York Times*, December 25, 2018.

17 Jason Smith, "Paying to Play: How Much Do Club Sports Cost?," *USA Today*, August 1, 2017; Ben Radding, "The Three Most Expensive Sports for Kids," *Fatherly*, October 28, 2017; Nadine Jolie Courtney, "These 19

Institutions Are the Best Summer Camps in the Country," *Town & Country*, July 28, 2017.

18 Joe Nocera, "Hamptons Houses Are Now Luxury Coronavirus Bunkers," Bloomberg, March 30, 2020.

19 Jennifer Senior, "All Joy and No Fun," *New York Times*, July 2, 2010; Center on Everyday Lives of Families, UCLA.

20 Benedict Carey, "Families' Every Fuss, Archived and Analyzed," *New York Times*, May 22, 2010.

21 For more on the uneven division of household labor by gender, see Tsui-Tai, "Housework Task Hierarchies in 32 Countries," *European Sociological Review* 29, no. 3 (August 2013): 780–91; Jessica Grose, "Cleaning: The Final Feminist Frontier," *New Republic*, March 19, 2013; Soraya Chernaly, "At Work as at Home, Men Reap the Benefits of Women's 'Invisible Labor,'" *Quartz*, January 22, 2016.

22 Jennifer Glass, Robin W. Simon, and Matthew A. Anderson, "Parenthood and Happiness: Effects of Work-Family Reconciliation Policies in 22 OECD Countries," *American Journal of Sociology* 122, no. 3 (November 2016).

23 Shantel Meek and Conor P. Williams, "How to Build a Better Childcare System," *New York Times*, May 29, 2020; Anneken Tappe, "The Economy Can't Recover Until Parents Have Childcare Again," CNN Business, May 2, 2020.

24 U.S. Department of Health and Human Services/Department of Education, "High-Quality Early Learning Settings Depend on a High-Quality Workforce," June 2016.

25 Caitlyn Collins, *Making Motherhood Work: How Women Manage Careers and Caregiving* (Princeton, NJ: Princeton University Press, 2019).

26 Daniel Schneider et al., "Income Inequality and Class Divides in Parental Investments," *American Sociological Review*, May 21, 2018.

27 Holly H. Schiffrin et al., "Helping or Hovering? The Effects of Helicopter Parenting on College Students' Well-Being," *Journal of Child and Family Studies*, February 9, 2013.

28 Madeline Levine, *The Price of Privilege* (New York: HarperCollins, 2006).

29 Suniya S. Luthar et al., "'I Can Therefore I Must': Fragility in the Upper-Middle Classes," *Developmental Psychopathology*, November 2013.

30 Paula Fornby and Kelly Musick, "Mothers' Time, the Parenting Package, and Links to Healthy Child Development," *Journal of Marriage and Family* 80 no. 1: March 2018, 166–81.

31 Jan Macvarish, "Babies' Brains and Parenting Policy: The Insensitive Mother," in E. Lee, ed., *Parenting Culture Studies* (New York: Palgrave MacMillan, 2014), pp.165–83.

32 Matthias Doepke and Fabrizio Zilibotti, "The Parent Trap," *Washington Post*, February 22, 2019; Doepke and Zilibotti, *Love, Money, and Parenting*.

33 On mobility data, several sources have been combined. IGE data were provided to me in a spreadsheet by Miles Corak. See Miles Corak, "Income
Inequality, Equality of Opportunity, and Intergenerational Mobility," *Journal
of Economic Perspectives* 27, no. 3 (Summer 2013): 79–102; and Miles Corak
et al., "A Comparison of Upward and Downward Intergenerational Mobility
in Canada, Sweden, and the United States," *Labour Economics* 30 (October
2014): 185–200. On absolute mobility data, see Opportunity Insights, which
collects mobility data, as well as Opportunity Atlas, which follows on a series
of seminal papers from Raj Chetty and several collaborators, including "Is the
United States Still a Land of Opportunity? Recent Trends in Intergenerational
Mobility," NBER Working Paper No. 19844, January 2014; and "Where Is
the Land of Opportunity?," NBER Working Paper No. 19843, June 2014. On
occupational status mobility, see, Michael Hout, "Americans' Occupational
Status Reflects the Status of Both of Their Parents," *PNAS*, July 18. 2018. For
international IGE, see Ambar Narayan et al., "Fair Progress? Economic
Mobility Across Generations Around the World," World Bank, 2018.

34 See Corak et al., "A Comparison of Upward and Downward Intergenerational Mobility in Canada, Sweden, and the United States."

35 The decline in mobility can also be measured in terms of job status mobility,
that is, the chances that individuals will move from the status-tier of their
parents. See Hout, "Americans' Occupational Status Reflects the Status of
Both of Their Parents." The decline in mobility can also be measured in
absolute terms, that is, the probability that individuals will earn more than
their parents (at the same age, and adjusted for inflation). Chetty (2014),
for example, shows that whereas 92 percent of Americans born in 1940
satisfied this definition of upward mobility, only 50 percent of those born
in 1980 did better than their parents.

36 Alan B. Krueger, "The Rise and Consequences of Inequality in the United
States," Remarks as prepared for delivery, chairman, Council of Economic
Advisers, January 12, 2012.

37 Margaret Thatcher, "Interview for Women's Own, September 23, 1987,
Margaret Thatcher Foundation.

38 David French, "The Right Should Reject Tucker Carlson's Victimhood
Populism," *National Review*, January 4, 2019.

39 On this admittedly big topic, one could do worse than start with Friedrich
Engels, *The Origin of the Family, Private Property and the State*, 1884, trans.
Ernest Untermann (Chicago: Charles Kerr & Co., 1902). See also Sarah
Blaffer Hrdy, *Mothers and Others: The Evolutionary Origins of Mutual
Understanding*, (Cambridge, MA: Harvard University Press, 2011).

40 Dayna M. Kurtz, "We Have a Child-Care Crisis in This Country. We Had
the Solution 78 Years Ago," *Washington Post*, July 23, 2018.

Chapter 3 Why We Get Along So Well with the Other Sexes

1 Susan A. Patton, Class of 1977, "Advice for the Young Women of Princeton," *Daily Princetonian*, March 29, 2013.

2 See The Princeton Momster, *Marry Smart, OR DIE* (Amazon, 2014).

3 Susan Patton, *Marry Smart* (New York: Gallery Books, 2014), and *Marry by Choice, Not by Chance* (New York: Gallery Books, 2014).

4 Grace Wyler, "Princeton Alumna to Female Princeton Students: Find a Husband Before Graduation," *Business Insider*, March 29, 2013.

5 From *New York Times*, June 7, 2019, June 18, 2006, October 14, 2011. See David Brooks, *Bobos in Paradise* (New York: Simon & Schuster, 2001), for more on *New York Times* weddings.

6 Braden Leap, "A New Type of (White) Provider: Shifting Masculinities in Mainstream Country Music from the 1980s to the 2010s," *Rural Sociology*, April 26, 2019; Tom Jacobs, "Country Hits Increasingly Objectify Women and Glorify Whiteness," *Pacific Standard*, May 7, 2019.

7 Mark A. Flynn et al., "Objectification in Popular Music Lyrics: An Examination of Gender and Genre Difference," *Sex Roles: A Journal of Research* 75, nos. 3–4 (July 2016): 164–76.

8 Nicholas A. Valentino et al., "Mobilizing Sexism: The Interaction of Emotion and Gender Attitudes in the 2016 US Presidential Election," *Public Opinion Quarterly* 82, S1 (April 2018): 799–821.

9 Stephanie Russell-Kraft, "The Rise of Male Supremacist Groups," *New Republic*, April 4, 2018; "Male Supremacy," Southern Poverty Law Center, splccenter.org, accessed January 22, 2021.

10 For data on the growing gender gap in party voting, see "Trends in Party Affiliation Among Demographic Groups," Pew Research Center, March 20, 2018.

11 "An Examination of the 2016 Electorate, Based on Validated Voters," Pew Research Center, August 9, 2018.

12 There is an extensive and not always edifying debate about "red" families and "blue" families. For a legal systems perspective, see Naomi Cahn and June Carbone, *Red Families v. Blue Families* (New York: Oxford University Press, 2011). For the sociology, see Jennifer Glass, "Red States, Blue States, and Divorce: Understanding the Impact of Conservative Protestantism on Regional Variation in Divorce Rates," *American Journal of Sociology* 118, no. 4 (January 2014): 1002–46; and "Red States, Blue States, and Divorce," Council on Contemporary Families, January 16, 2014. For a critique of the suggestion that Republicans fail to practice what they preach on family values, see W. Bradford Wilcox and Vijay Menon, "No, Republicans Aren't Hypocrites on Family Values," *POLITICO Magazine*, November 28, 2017.

Unfortunately, Wilcox and Menon, like many participants in the debate, misses the point by personalizing politics. The issue is not that Republicans are hypocrites in their personal behavior; it is that their "pro-family" politics is a response to the perception of family instability among other people in the world they inhabit—an instability brought about not by their personal behavior but (here is where the hypocrisy lies) by the same policies and culture they promote.

13 Stephen J. Rose, "Still a Man's Labor Market," Institute for Women's Policy Research, November 26, 2018; Nicholas Kristof and Sheryl WuDunn, "Americans Are Right to Think the Economy Is Rigged," LitHub, January 20, 2020; "Economic Inequality Across Gender Diversity," inequality.org, accessed January 22, 2021.

14 Kevin Miller et al., *Deeper in Debt: Women and Student Loans*, American Association of University Women, 2017.

15 Catherine Collinson et al., *The New Social Contract: Achieving Retirement Equality for Women*, Aegon Retirement Readiness Survey, 2019.

16 Elizabeth Warren and Amelia Warren Tyagi, *The Two-Income Trap: Why Middle-Class Parents Are Going Broke* (New York: Basic Books, 2004).

17 Stacy A. Anderson et al., "Women Staging a Labor Force Comeback," Brookings, March 26, 2019.

18 On assortative mating, see Yonzen Nishant, "Assortative Mating and Labor Income Inequality: Evidence from Fifty Years of Coupling in the US," Stone Center Working Paper Series no. 15, June 2020; Robert D. Mare, "Educational Homogamy in Two Gilded Ages: Evidence from Intergenerational Social Mobility Data," The Annals, AAPSS, 663, January 2016; Jeremy Greenwood et al., "Marry Your Like: Assortative Mating and Income Inequality," NBER Working Paper No. 19829, January 2014; Mauricio Bucca et al., "Changing Patterns of Educational Assortative Mating and Income Inequality: The Case of Chile," NBER Conferences, September 29, 2016; and Robert Putnam, *Our Kids* (New York: Simon & Schuster, 2015).

19 "How's Life: Measuring Well-being," OECD, 2017.

20 W. Bradford Wilcox et al., "The Marriage Divide: How and Why Working Class Families Are More Fragile Today," Institute for Family Studies, September 25, 2017; Claire Cain Miller, "How Did Marriage Become a Mark of Privilege?," *New York Times*, September 25, 2017; Sharon Sassler and Amanda Jayne Miller, Cohabitation Nation: Gender, Class, and the Remaking of Relationships (Berkeley, CA: University of California Press, 2017); Andrew J. Cherlin, *Labor's Love Lost* (New York: Russell Sage Foundation, 2014).

21 Diane Whitmore Schauzenbach et al., "Who Is Out of the Labor Force?," The Hamilton Project, August 17, 2017.

22 Richard V. Reeves and Katherine Guyot, "Black Women Are Earning More College Degrees, but That Alone Won't Close Race Gaps," Brookings, December 4, 2017.

23 Hillary Hoffower, "Wealthy New Yorkers Are Dropping $375 an Hour on Prep Courses to Get Their Kids into $50,000 'Baby Ivy' Kindergartens," *Business Insider*, May 29, 2019; Suzanne Woolley and Katya Kazakina, "At $50,000 a Year, the Road to Yale Starts at Age 5," Bloomberg, March 27, 2019.

24 Gretchen Livingston, "Stay-at-Home Moms and Dads Account for About One-in-Five Parents," Pew Research Center, September 24, 2019.

25 Diane Whitmore Schauzenbach et al., "Who Is Out of the Labor Force?," The Hamilton Project, August 17, 2017.

26 Joni Hersch, "Opting Out Among Women with Elite Education," *Vanderbilt Law and Economics Research Paper No. 13-05*, May 15, 2013.

27 For a similar analysis of class at elite private schools, see Shamus Rahman Khan, *Privilege: The Making of an Adolescent Elite* (Princeton, NJ: Princeton University Press, 2011).

28 Isabel Sawhill, "Purposeful Parenthood," *Brookings*, February 26, 2015.

29 Raj Chetty et al., "Where Is the Land of Opportunity?," NBER Working Paper 19843, June 2014.

30 David Autor et al., "When Work Disappears: Manufacturing Decline and the Falling Marriage Market Value of Young Men," NBER Working Paper 23173, December 2018.

31 Christian Groes-Green, "Hegemonic and Subordinated Masculinities: Class, Violence and Sexual Performance Among Young Mozambican Men," *Nordic Journal of African Studies* 18, no. 4 (2009): 286–304.

32 Khandis R. Blake et al., "Income Inequality Not Gender Inequality Positively Covaries with Female Sexualization on Social Media," *PNAS* 115, no. 35 (August 28, 2018): 8722–27.

33 Charles Fourier, The Social Destiny of Man, or Theory of the Four Movements, trans. Albert Brisbane (USA: R. M. Dewitt, 1857), p. 119.

34 Exodus 20:17.

35 M. Dyble, "Sex Equality Can Explain the Unique Social Structure of Hunter-Gatherer Bands," *Science*, May 15, 2015.

Chapter 4 **Why We Are So Highly Educated**

1 Matthew Goldstein et al., "College Admission Scandal's Other Big Names Are Titans of Finance and Law," *New York Times*, March 13, 2019.

2 Mark Vandevelde, "How US College Bribery Scandal Shattered Bill McGlashan's Image," *Financial Times*, April 4, 2019; Alicia McElhaney,

"Bill McGlashan Fights Back in College Bribery Case," *Institutional Investor*, December 18, 2019.

3 therisefund.com, accessed July 29, 2019.

4 "The Rise Fund Investing $130 Million in K-8 Math Education Technology Company DreamBox Learning," *Businesswire*, July 31, 2018.

5 Leslie P. Norton, "TPG Cracks the Code for Impact Investing," *Barron's*, September 21, 2018.

6 William D. Cohan, "How Bono's Investment Partner Got Busted in the College-Admissions Scandal," *Vanity Fair*, May 2, 2019.

7 Vanity Fair New Establishment Summit, 2017.

8 Jessica Werner-Zeck, "'10 Americans' Hits Home for Mill Valley Mom," *San Francisco Chronicle*, SFGATE, March 16, 2009.

9 Levi Sumagaysay, "College Admissions Scandal: Investor Bill McGlashan Has Many Ties in Bay Area, Hollywood, and Beyond," *Mercury News*, March 13, 2019; Gary Klein, "Marin Residents Charged in College Bribery Scandal," *Marin Independent Journal*, March 12, 2019; tuition from Marin Academy.

10 Quotes and descriptions taken from the FBI affidavit in support of the criminal complaint, available at "College Admissions Bribery Scheme Affidavit," *Washington Post*, March 12, 2019. See also Holly Yan, "The CEO Behind the College Admissions Cheating Scam Wanted to Help the Wealthy. But That's Not All," CNN, March 12, 2019.

11 McGlashan would later deny the allegation. Matthias Gafni, "College Admissions Scandal: Mill Valley Dad Denies 'Side Door' Got Son into USC," *San Francisco Chronicle*, March 30, 2019; John Woolfolk, "Mill Valley Investor for U2's Bono Insists College Admissions Charges Are Wrong," *Mercury News*, January 31, 2020. As of this writing, this case and others continue to slither through the legal system: Lori Loughlin was released in December 2020, after serving a two-month sentence, just as her husband, who also pled guilty, was set to begin his five-month sentence.

12 Aaron Fels, "College Scam Mastermind Photoshopped Students' Faces onto Athletes: Prosecutors," *New York Post*, March 12, 2019.

13 Kelly McLaughlin, "A Private Equity Firm Executive Had His Son Pose as a Football Player," *Insider*, March 13, 2019.

14 Daniel Golden, *The Price of Admission* (New York: Broadway Books, 2007); Daniel Golden, "The Story Behind Jared Kushner's Curious Acceptance into Harvard," *ProPublica*, November 18, 2016.

15 Gregory Korte, "The Rise of Rick Singer: How the Mastermind of College Admissions Scandal Built an Empire on Lies, Exploited a Broken System," *USA Today*, June 24, 2019.

16 Ray Sanchez et al., "Lori Loughlin and Mossimo Giannulli Plead Guilty in College Admissions Scam," CNN, May 22, 2020.

17It's safe to guess that they didn't know that ASU has been ranked "#1 in Innovation" in a *U.S. News & World Report* survey five years in a row, or that under President Michael M. Crow's dynamic leadership it has become a major research university, or that its alumni include members of Congress, a senator, a MacArthur "Genius Grant" recipient, and sharp-witted celebrities like Jimmy Kimmel. For more on the vision behind ASU, as well as interesting insights on higher education in America, see Michael M. Crow and William B. Dabars, *The Fifth Wave: The Evolution of American Higher Education* (Johns Hopkins University Press, 2020); and Michael M. Crow and William B. Dabars, *Designing the New American University* (Baltimore, MD: Johns Hopkins University Press, 2015).

18Benjamin Rush, American Museum, January 1787. See Albert Castel, "The Founding Fathers and the Vision of a National University," History of Education Quarterly 4, no. 4 (December 1964): 280–302.

19Thomas Jefferson to George Wythe, August 13, 1786, in Julian P. Boyd, ed., *The Papers of Thomas Jefferson* (Princeton, NJ: Princeton University Press, 1958–), vol. 10, pp. 243-5.

20John Adams to John Jebb, September 10, 1785, in Gregg L. Lint et.al., eds., *The Adams Papers*, (Cambridge, MA: Harvard University Press, 2014), vol. 17, p.422.

21George Washington, "First Annual Message," January 8, 1790, National Archives.

22Thomas Jefferson, "Bill for the More General Diffusion of Knowledge," in Julian P. Boyd, ed., *The Papers of Thomas Jefferson* (Princeton, NJ: Princeton University Press, 1958–), vol. 2, pp. 526—35.

23For more on the expropriation of native land, see Michael V. Martin and Janie Simms Hipp, "A Time for Substance: Confronting Funding Inequities at Land Grant Institutions," *Tribal College: Journal of American Indian Higher Education* 29, no. 3 (Spring 2018).

24David J. Staley, "Democratizing American Higher Education: The Legacy of the Morrill Land Grant Act," *Origins* 6, no. 4 (January 2013).

25Jeffrey T. Demning, "ProPelled: The Effects of Grants on Graduation, Earnings, and Welfare," *American Journal of Applied Economics* 11, no. 3 (July 2019): 193–234.

26Mariana Mazzucato, *The Entrepreneurial State* (New York: Anthem Press, 2011); Mariana Mazzucato, *The Value of Everything* (New York: Public Affairs, 2018).

27Claudia Goldin and Lawrence F. Katz, "The Shaping of Higher Education: The Formative Years in the United States, 1890 to 1940," *Journal of Economic Perspectives* 13, no. 1 (Winter 1999): 37–62.

28Data from nces.org, National Center for Education Statistics.

29 "Higher Education for American Democracy: A Report of the President's Commission on Higher Education," text available on Internet Archive; Claire Gilbert and Donald Heller, *The Truman Commission and Its Impact on Federal Higher Education Policy from 1947 to 2010*, Center for the Study of Higher Education, Working Paper No. 9, November 2010.

30 Here's a list of eighteen camps that go for $11,000 and up not including transportation and extras: Meredith Galante, "Send Your Kid to One of These 18 Absurdly Expensive Summer Camps," *Business Insider*, June 8, 2012.

31 See Maine Camp Experience, mainecampeexperience.com.

32 Scott Jaschik, "$1.5 Million to Get into an Ivy," *Inside Higher Ed*, February 12, 2018.

33 Hillary Hoffower, "Wealthy New Yorkers Are Dropping $375 an Hour on Prep Courses to Get Their Kids into $50,000 'Baby Ivy' Kindergartens," *Business Insider*, March 28, 2019.

34 Beth Teitell, "What's the Craziest Thing About a $16,000 College Application Boot Camp: That It Has a Wait List, or Its Secret Location?," *Boston Globe*, August 14, 2018.

35 Adam Harris, "Parents Gone Wild: High Drama Inside D.C.'s Most Elite Private School," *Atlantic*, June 5, 2019.

36 Rick Perlstein, *Nixonland: The Rise of a President and the Fracturing of America* (New York: Scribner, 2010), p. 83.

37 American Academy of Arts and Sciences, *Public Research Universities: Changes in State Funding* (Washington, DC: The Lincoln Project, 2015).

38 "Trends in College Pricing 2019," The College Board, 2019.

39 Ronald Brownstein, "American Higher Education Hits a Dangerous Milestone," *Atlantic*, May 3, 2018.

40 Ben Miller, "The Student Debt Problem Is Worse than We Imagined," *New York Times*, August 25, 2018; Riley Griffin, "The Student Loan Crisis Is About to Get Worse," *Bloomberg*, October 17, 2018.

41 Robert D. Atkinson and Caleb Foote, "US Funding for University Research Continues to Slide," Information Technology and Innovation Foundation, October 21, 2019.

42 Crystal Han et al., Recruiting the Out-of-State University: Off Campus Recruiting by Public Research Universities, The Joyce Foundation, March 2019.

43 Stephanie Hall, "How Much Education Are Students Getting for Their Tuition Dollar?," The Century Foundation, February 28, 2019.

44 Derek Newton, "20,000 More Reasons to Never Go to a For-Profit School," *Forbes*, December 9, 2018.

45 Luis Armosa et al., "How Does For-Profit College Attendance Affect Student Loans, Defaults, and Labor Market Outcomes?," NBER Working Paper No.

25042, September 2018; Kevin Lang and Russell Weinstein, "Evaluating Student Outcomes at For-Profit Colleges," NBER Working Paper No. 18201.

46 Brownstein, "American Higher Education Hits a Dangerous Milestone."

47 See also Jonathan Metzl, *Dying of Whiteness* (New York: Basic Books, 2019); Suzanne Mettler, *Degrees of Inequality: How the Politics of Higher Education Sabotaged the American Dream* (New York: Basic Books, 2014), and Suzanne Mettler, *The Government-Citizen Disconnect* (New York: Russell Sage Foundation, 2018).

48 Judith Scott-Clayton, "Black-White Disparity in Student Loan Debt More than Triples After Graduation," Brookings, October 20, 2016.

49 EveryCRSReport.com, May 4, 2018.

50 Heather Joslyn, "Giving to Colleges Up 6 Percent in 2017," *The Chronicle of Philanthropy*, February 6, 2018. The earnings number is based on my own calculation from posted returns and net asset values.

51 Rick Seltzer, "Endowment Returns Slow, Survey Offers Peak at Spending," *Inside Higher Ed*, January 31, 2019.

52 The $130 million estimate assumes a marginal tax rate of 33 percent for Paulson.

53 This is my own very rough estimate, and assumes that contributions and investment income would otherwise be subject to an average tax rate of 33 percent.

54 Richard K. Vedder, "Princeton Reaps Tax Breaks as State Colleges Beg," *Bloomberg Opinion*, March 18, 2012.

55 Valerie Strauss, "How Gov. Walker Tried to Quietly Change the Mission of the University of Wisconsin," *Washington Post*, February 5, 2015.

56 Jesse Opoien, "Scott Walker: Scrapping 'Wisconsin Idea' Was a 'Drafting Error,'" *The Cap Times*, February 4, 2015.

57 CNN exit polls.

58 Michael W. Sances, "How Unusual Was 2016? Flipping Counties, Flipping Voters, and the Education-Party Correlation," *Perspectives on Politics* 17, no. 3 (September 2019): 666–78.

59 Kim Parker, "The Growing Partisan Divide in Views of Higher Education," Pew Research Center, August 19, 2019.

60 *Education at a Glance*, OECD, 2018; Preston Cooper, "The Crazy Amount America Spends on Higher Education, in One Chart," *Forbes*, September 12, 2018.

61 Ryan McMaken, "The US Is Already Spending More on Higher Education than Many Countries with 'Free' College," Foundation for Economic Education, April 29, 2019.

62 "Education Expenditures by Country," *The Condition of Education*, The National Center for Education Statistics, May 2020.

63 Amanda Ripley, "Why Is College in America So Expensive?," *Atlantic*, September 11, 2018.

64 "Survey of Adult Skills," Program for the Assessment of Adult Competencies, OECD, 2011-.

65 Kevin Carey, "Americans Think We Have the World's Best Colleges," *New York Times*, June 18, 2014.; see also Michael M. Crow and William B. Dabars, *Fifth Wave: The Evolution of American Higher Education* (Baltimore, MD: Johns Hopkins, 2020).

66 "Young Adult Educational and Employment Outcomes by Family Socioeconomic Status," *The Condition of Education*, The National Center for Education Statistics, May 2019.

67 Raj Chetty et al., "Mobility Report Cards: The Role of Colleges in Intergenerational Mobility," NBER Working Paper No. 23618, July 2017.

68 Ibid.

69 Raj Chetty et al., "Income Segregation and Intergenerational Mobility Across Colleges in the United States," *Quarterly Journal of Economics*, 135 no. 3 (February 2020): 1567–1633.

70 "College Scorecard," U.S. Department of Education, collegescorecard.ed.gov.

71 Richard Zweigenhaft, "The Role of Elite Education for White Men, White Women, and People of Color in the U.S. Corporate Elite," in G. William Domhoff, ed., *Studying the Power Elite: Fifty Years of Who Rules America* (New York: Routledge, 2017).

72 Joni Hersche, "Catching Up Is Hard to Do: Undergraduate Prestige Elite Graduate Programs and the Earnings Premium," *Vanderbilt Public Law Research Paper No. 16–17*, SSRN, July 20, 2019.

73 Derek Witteven and Paul Attwell, "The Earnings Payoff from Attending a Selective College," *Social Science Research* 66 (August 2017): 154–69.

74 Jane Buckingham and Marcus Buckingham, "Note to Gen Y Workers: Performance on the Job Actually Matters," *Time*, September 28, 2012.

Chapter 5 **Why Our Neighborhoods Are the Best**

1 Biographical details in this chapter taken from Edward T. O'Donnell, *Henry George and the Crisis of Inequality* (New York: Columbia University Press, 2015).

2 Ibid., p. 23

3 Henry George, *Progress and Poverty* (New York: Appleton, 1879), p. 6.

4 Zillow Research, Zillow.com, April 9, 2018.

5 ATTOM Data Solutions, "Median-Priced Homes Remain Unaffordable for Average Wage-Earners in 74 Percent of US Housing Markets," attomdata .com, September 24, 2019.

6 Volker Grossman et al., "The Macroeconomics of Housing and the Dynamics of Wealth Inequality," *First WID.world Conference*, December 14, 2017.

7 Moritz Kuhn et al., "Income and Wealth Inequality in America, 1949–2016," Opportunity and Inclusive Growth Institute, Federal Reserve Bank of Minneapolis, Working Paper No. 9, June 2018.

8 Matthew Desmond, "How homeownership Became the Engine of American Economic Inequality," *New York Times Magazine*, May 9, 2017.

9 Joint Center for Housing Studies of Harvard University, Harvard College, 2019.

10 Christopher Kurz et al., "Are Millennials Different?," FEDS, Federal Reserve Bank, 2018-080.

11 Jung Hyun Choi et al., *Explaining the Black-White Homeownership Gap*, Urban Institute, October 2019.

12 Greg Martin and Steven Webster, "The Real Culprit Behind Geographic Polarization," *Atlantic*, November 26, 2018.

13 Bruce Kennedy, "America's 11 Poorest Cities," CBSNews, February 18, 2015.

14 Home value data from Zillow.

15 Emma Martin, "In San Francisco, Households Earning $117,000 Qualify as 'Low Income,'" CNBC, June 18, 2018.

16 Richard Fry and Paul Taylor, "The Rise of Residential Segregation by Income," Pew Research Center, August 1, 2012.

17 Sean F. Reardon and Kendra Bischoff, "No Neighborhood Is an Island," *The Dream Revisited*, NYU Furman Center, November 2014.

18 Robert B. Reich, "Secession of the Successful," *New York Times Magazine*, January 20, 1991.

19 On Lizzie Magie, Henry George, and Monopoly, details here taken from Mary Pilon, *The Monopolists: Obsession, Fury, and the Scandal Behind the World's Favorite Board Game* (New York: Bloomsbury, 2015).

20 George, *Progress and Poverty*, 370.

21 "The Time May Be Right for Land-Value Taxes," *Economist*, August 9, 2018.

22 "Historical Census of Housing Tables," U.S. Census Bureau; Na Zhao, "Homeownership Rate Bounces Back, National Association of Homebuilders, October 29, 2019.

23 F. John Devaney, *Tracking the American Dream: 50 Years of Housing History from the Census 1940 to 1990*, U.S. Department of Commerce, May 1994.

24 The analysis of this development begins with Kenneth Jackson, *Crabgrass Frontier: The Suburbanization of the United States* (New York: Oxford University Press, 1985).

25 Matthew Chambers et al., "The New Deal, the GI Bill, and the Post-War Housing Boom," Federal Reserve Bank of St. Louis, February 14, 2012; and more recent: "The Postwar Conquest of the Home Ownership Dream," Towson University Working Paper Series, No. 2016-07, April 2016.

26 David Albony and Mike Zabek, "Housing Inequality," NBER Working Paper No. 21916, January 2016.

27 Richard Florida, "Is Housing Inequality the Main Driver of Economic Inequality?," Bloomberg City Lab, April 13, 2018.

28 Will Fischer and Barbara Sard, "Chart Book: Federal Housing Spending Is Poorly Matched to Need," Center on Budget and Policy Priorities, March 8, 2017.

29 Robert Collinson, "Low-Income Housing Policy," NBER Working Paper No. 21071.

30 Raj Chetty et al., "The Long-Term Effects of Exposure to Better Neighborhoods: New Evidence from the Moving to Opportunity Experiment," Harvard University Working Paper No. 2015; "The Opportunity Atlas: Mapping Childhood Roots of Social Mobility," Center for Econoimc Studies, U.S. Census Bureau, September 2018.

31 Joint Committee on Taxation, Congress of the United States, "Estimated Revenue Effects of the Revenue Provisions Contained in H.R. 6800," May 15, 2020.

32 Christopher Pulliam and Richard Reeves, "The SALT Deduction Is a Handout to the Rich," Brookings, September 4, 2020.

33 Richard Reeves and Christopher Pulliam, "The Tax Cut for the Rich That Democrats Love," New York Times, September 7, 2020.

34 "Imputed Rental of Owner-Occupied Housing," Economic Research, Federal Reserve Bank of St. Louis, August 29, 2019.

35 Francesco Figari et al., "Removing Homeownership Bias in Taxation: The Distributional Effects of Including Imputed Rent in Taxable Income," Fiscal Studies 38, no. 4 (2017): 525–57.

36 "Housing and the Economy: Policies for Renovation," Economic Policy Reforms, 2011, OECD.

37 Bruce Bartlett, "Taxing Homeowners as if They Were Landlords," New York Times, September 3, 2013.

38 William A. Fischel, The Homeowner Hypothesis: How Home Values Influence Local Government, Taxation, School Finance, and Land-Use Policies (Cambridge, MA: Harvard University Press, 2005).

39 Michael Hankinson, "When Do Renters Behave like Homeowners? High-Rent, Price Anxiety and NIMBYism," Harvard University Working Paper, February 2017.

40 Michael Hobbes, "Progressive Boomers Are Making It Impossible for Cities to Fix the Housing Crisis," Huffington Post, July 8, 2019.

41 Posted on The C is for Crank, May 3, 2018, http://publicola.com/2018/05/03/tonight-in-ballard-two-hours-hate/.

42 Benjamin Oreskes, "To Block Homeless Shelter, San Francisco Residents Are Suing on Environmental Grounds," *Los Angeles Times*, July 10, 2019.

43 Richard V. Reeves, "How Land-Use Regulations Are Zoning Out Low-Income Families," Brookings, August 16, 2016.

44 Michael C. Lens and Paavo Monkkonen, "Do Strict Land-Use Regulations Make Metropolitan Areas More Segregated by Income?," *Journal of the American Planning Association* 82, no. 1 (December 28, 2015).

45 On the need for construction of new housing units, see "The State of the Nation's Housing 2019," Joint Center for Housing of Harvard University, 2019.

46 See Chetty et al., "The Effects of Exposure to Better Neighborhoods on Children."

47 Joseph P. Williams, "In an Unequal America, Getting to Work Can Be Hell," *The Nation*, January 29, 2019.

48 "Dismissed: America's Most Divisive Borders," EdBuild, August 2019.

49 Adam Cohen, *Supreme Inequality: The Supreme Court's Fifty-Year Battle for a More Unjust America* (New York: Penguin, 2020), p. 91.

50 Richard Murrane and Sean Reardon, "US Private Schools Increasingly Serve Affluent Families," Voxeu/CEPR, August 31, 2017.

51 Zola Canady, "What Yale Could Have Paid," *The New Journal* 42, no. 35 (April 2020).

52 Robert Manduca and Robert J. Sampson, "Punishing and Toxic Neighborhood Environments Independently Predict the Intergenerational Social Mobility of Black and White Children," *PNAS* 116, no. 16 (April 18, 2018): 7772–77; Lincoln Quillian, "Neighborhood and the Intergenerational Transmission of Poverty," *Focus* 33, no. 2 (Spring/Summer 2017): 22–28.

53 Chetty et al., "The Long-Term Effects of Exposure to Better Neighborhoods."

54 Annette Lareau, "Parental Challenges to Organization Authority in an Elite School District: The Role of Social, Cultural, and Symbolic Capital," *Teachers College Record* 120, no. 1 (2018): 1–46.

55 Derek Thompson, "Why Manhattan's Skyscrapers Are Empty," *Atlantic*, January 16, 2020.

56 Ryan Avent, "Moving Toward Stagnation," *Economist*, September 27, 2011.

57 Enrico Moretti, *The New Geography of Jobs* (Boston, MA: Mariner Books, 2013).

58 Henry George, *Progress and Poverty*, (in an edition from London: Kegan Paul, 1883), 471.

59 O'Donnell, *Henry George and the Crisis of Inequality*, p. 160ff.

60 Details from Pilon, *The Monopolists*.

Chapter 6 **Why We Believe in Merit**

1 Walt Bogdanich and Michael Forsythe, "How McKinsey Has Helped Raise the Stature of Authoritarian Government," *New York Times*, December 15, 2018.

2 Calvert W. Jones, "All the King's Consultants," *Foreign Affairs*, May/June 2019; Jackie Cameron, "McKinsey Works for Authoritarian, Corrupt Governments Everywhere!," *BizNews*, December 19, 2018; Sheelah Kolhatkar, "McKinsey's Work for Saudi Arabia Highlights Its History of Unsavory Entanglements," *New Yorker*, November 1, 2018.

3 On McKinsey's work for drugmakers, see court documents: Commonwealth of Massachusetts v. Purdue Pharma et al., Suffolk Superior Court C.A. No. 1884-cv-01808 (BLS2). On McKinsey and ICE, see Ian MacDougall, "How McKinsey Helped the Trump Administration Detain and Deport Immigrants," *ProPublica*, December 3, 2019. McKinsey posted a response on its website on December 4, 2019, and ProPublica published a response to the response on December 16.

4 There are various sources of data on elite college hiring trends, some cited in my own, *The Management Myth* (New York: W. W. Norton, 2009). See more recently the op-ed by Riya Sood, "Is a Consulting Job Ever Just a Job?," *Harvard Crimson*, December 13, 2019; and Amy Weiss-Meyer, "Case Study: Consulting After College," *Harvard Crimson*, November 6, 2014, who puts the number of Harvard grads taking jobs in consulting immediately upon entering the job market at 14 percent.

5 E. Mazareaunu, "Number of Management Consultants Employed in the U.S. 2012–2019," *Statista*, April 20, 2020.

6 Beecher Tuttle, "Proof That a Lot of Strategy Consultants Leave After Two Years," efinancialcareers.com, February 19, 2019.

7 "Statement on New York Times Article on McKinsey Work in Southeast Asia, China, Eastern Europe and the Middle East," posted on McKinsey website, December 16, 2018.

8 Thomas Jefferson to John Adams, October 28, 1813, in Lester Cappon, ed., *The Adams-Jefferson Letters* (Chapel Hill, NC: University of North Carolina Press, 1988), vol. 2, p. 387.

9 For example, "wages are generally determined by skills and productivity," in David Brooks, "The Bernie Sanders Fallacy," *New York Times*, January 6, 2020.

10 Charles Murray and Richard J. Herrnstein, *The Bell Curve* (New York: Free Press, 1994).

11 Jean-Jacques Rousseau, *A Discourse upon the Origin and the Foundation of the Inequality Among Mankind* (London: Dodsley, 1761), p. 7.

12 In PBS documentary, *Amazon Empire: The Rise and Reign of Jeff Bezos*, *Frontline*, PBS, February 18, 2020.

13 Michael Young, *The Rise of the Meritocracy* (London: Thames & Hudson, 1958)

14 Michael Young, "Down with Meritocracy," *Guardian*, June 28, 2001.

15 Daniel Markovits, *The Meritocracy Trap* (New York: Penguin, 2019).

16 Data here from Derek Thompson, "Are We Truly Overworked?," *Atlantic*, June 2013.

17 Elizabeth Day, "Moritz Erhardt: The tragic death of a city intern," *Guardian*, October 5, 2013.

18 John Pencavel, *The Productivity of Working Hours*, IZA (Institute for the Study of Labor), April 2014.

19 CDC, "Work Schedules: Shift Work and Long Hours," National Institute for Occupational Safety and Health (NIOSH), https://www.cdc.gov/niosh /topics/workschedules/default.html.

20 Bob Sullivan, "Want a Raise? Try Taking a Vacation," CNBC, August 27, 2014; Bob Sullivan, "Is Going on Vacation Becoming Too Much Work?," CNBC, August 14, 2014.

21 Erin Griffith, "Why Are Young People Pretending to Love Work?," *New York Times*, January 26, 2019; Derek Thompson, "Workism Is Making Americans Miserable," *Atlantic*, February 24, 2019.

22 Jean-Paul Sartre, *Being and Nothingness*, trans. Hazel Barnes (New York: Washington Square Press, 1956), p. 101ff.

23 The Amazon workplace culture has been the subject of considerable discussion and controversy. A starting point is: Jodi Kantor and David Streitfeld, "Inside Amazon: Wrestling Big Ideas in a Bruising Workplace," *New York Times*, August 15, 2015. The piece elicited a vigorous riposte from Amazon's communications office, and many further responses to the response.

24 Matthew Stewart, *The Management Myth* (New York: W. W. Norton, 2009).

25 Ibid., p. 244.

26 Cited in Kantor and Streitfeld, "Inside Amazon: Wrestling Big Ideas in a Bruising Workplace."

27 Peter Graeber, *Bullshit Jobs: A Theory* (New York: Simon & Schuster, 2018).

28 Stewart, The Management Myth.

29 John Maynard Keynes, "Economic Possibilities for our Grandchildren," *Essays in Persuasion*. (New York: W. W. Norton, 1963).

30 For more on these issues, see Robert Frank, *Success and Luck: Good Fortune and the Myth of Meritocracy* (Princeton, NJ: Princeton University Press, 2016); A. Pluchino et al., *Talent vs. Luck: The Role of Randomness in Success and Failure*, ResearchGate, February 2018; and Stephen J. McNamee and Robert K. Miller, *The Meritocracy Myth* (Lanham, MD: Rowman & Littlefield, 2009).

31 Jonathan Rothwell, *A Republic of Equals: A Manifesto for a Just Society* (Princeton, NJ: Princeton University Press, 2019).

32 Jay Zagonsky, "You Don't Have to Be Smart to Be Rich," *Science Daily*, Ohio State University, April 27, 2007

33 Dacher Keltner, *The Power Paradox: How We Gain and Lose Influence* (New York: Penguin, 2017); Dacher Keltner et al., "Higher Social Class Predicts Increased Unethical Behavior," *PNAS* 109, no. 11 (March 13, 2012): 4086–91; Emilio J. Castilla and Stephen Benard, "The Paradox of Meritocracy in Organizations," *Administrative Science Quarterly*, December 1, 2010; Aldo Rustichini, "Merit and Justice: An Experimental Analysis of Attitude to Inequality," *PLOS One*, December 9, 2014; Chunliang Feng et al., "The Flexible Fairness: Equality, Earned Entitlement, and Self-Interest," *PLOS One*, September 9, 2013.

34 Frederick Solt et al., "Economic Inequality and Belief in Meritocracy in the United States," *Research & Politics*, October 19, 2016.

35 Daiane Borges Machado et al., "Impact of Inequality and Other Social Determinants on Suicide Rate in Brazil," *PLOS One*, April 30, 2015; Daniel Kim, "The Association Between US State and Local Spending, Income Inequality, and Individual All-Cause and Cause-Specific Mortality," *Science Direct*, 2015.

Chapter 7 Why We Make So Much Money

1 Caroline Binham, "Goldman Sachs's Griffiths Says Inequality Helps All," *Bloomberg*, October 21, 2009.

2 Reuters, November 8, 2009.

3 Deirdre McCloskey, "The Formula for a Richer World? Equality, Liberty, Justice," *New York Times*, September 2, 2016.

4 Note that the common interpretation of Adam Smith as a proponent of inequality is quite false. Like Jefferson and Paine, Smith saw the operation of the market as a force for equality, and attributed inequality generally to rents, captured markets, and domination. See Deborah Boucoyannis, "The Equalizing Hand: Why Adam Smith Thought the Market Should Produce Wealth Without Steep Inequality," *Perspectives on Politics*, December 10, 2013, Cambridge University Press.

5 On the general trend toward market concentration and capture in the U.S., see Tim Wu, *The Curse of Bigness* (New York: Columbia Global Reports, 2018); Brink Lindsey and Steven M. Teles, *The Captured Economy: How the Powerful Enrich Themselves, Slow Down Growth, and Increase Inequality* (New York: Oxford University Press, 2017); Thomas Philippon, *The Great Reversal: How America Gave Up on Free Markets* (Cambridge, MA: Harvard University Press, 2019); Jonathan Tepper, *The Myth of Capitalism:*

Monopolies and the Death of Competition (Hoboken, NJ: Wiley, 2019); and Gustavo Grullon, Yelena Larkin, and Ron Michaely, "Are US Industries Becoming More Concentrated?," *Swiss Finance Institute Research Paper Series*, No 19-41, August 2019.

6 Tim Wu, "Be Very Afraid of Economic 'Bigness,' Be Very Afraid," *New York Times*, November 10, 2018.

7 Germán Gutiérrez and Thomas Philippon, "How EU Markets Became More Competitive than US Markets: A Study of Institutional Drift," NBER Working Paper No. 24700, June 2019.

8 See Philippon, *The Great Reversal*; and Tepper, *The Myth of Capitalism*.

9 Mara Faccio and Luigi Zingales, "Political Determinants of Competition in the Mobile Telecommunication Industry," NBER Working Paper No. 23041, January 2017.

10 Irene Papanicolas et al., "Healthcare Spending in the United States and Other High Income Countries," *JAMA* 319, no. 10 (March 13, 2018): 1024–39.

11 Emily Stewart, "America's Monopoly Problem, Explained by Your Internet Bill," *Vox*, February 18, 2020.

12 "No Relief: Denial of Bathroom Breaks in the Poultry Industry," *Oxfam Report*, Oxfam, May 2016.

13 "Bank Market Share by Size of Institution," Institute for Local Self-Reliance, May 14, 2019.

14 "To the shareholders of Berkshire Hathaway Inc," Annual Report, 1995.

15 Bureau of Economic Analysis, U.S. Department of Commerce, July 26, 2020.

16 Robert H. Bork, *The Antitrust Paradox: A Policy at War with Itself* (New York: Basic Books, 1978); Barak Y. Orbach, "The Antitrust Consumer Welfare Paradox," *Journal of Competition Law and Economics* 7, no. 1 (March 2011): 133–64.

17 Daisuke Wakabayashi, "Big Tech Funds a Think Tank Pushing for Fewer Rules. For Big Tech," *New York Times*, July 26, 2020.

18 Lina Khan and Sandeep Vaheesan, "Market Power and Inequality," 11 *Harvard Law & Policy Review* 235(2017), February 22, 2017; Lina M. Khan, "Amazon's Antitrust Paradox," *Yale Law Journal* 126, no. 3 (January 2017): 864–907.

19 Elizabeth Anderson, Private Government: How Employers Rule Our Lives (and Why We Don't Talk about It) (Princeton, NJ: Princeton University Press, 2017).

20 Kris Janisch, "Do Employees Have Any Privacy at Work?," *GovDocs*, November 14, 2019 ("The short answer is no."); Lisa Guerin, "Email Monitoring: Can Your Employer Read Your Messages?," Nolo.

21 See Joel Bakan, *The Corporation: The Pathological Pursuit of Profit and Power* (New York: Free Press, 2005).

22 See Anderson, *Private Government*, who aptly compares the absence of awareness of that half of the economy that involves the relations of domination within firms to hemiagnosia, or the condition in which people are unable to sense half of their bodies. See also James Kwak, *Economism: Bad Economics and the Rise of Inequality* (New York: Pantheon, 2017), for a takedown of the reductionist ideology of "Economics 101." Within the economics profession, there have been many efforts to absorb lessons from the aporias of market theory, by extending the discipline to cover market imperfections due to institutional arrangements and irrational behavior. See Richard Thaler, *Misbehaving: The Making of Behavioral Economics* (New York: W. W. Norton, 2016). However, these refined thoughts among the economics professoriat have not, on the whole, undone the damage of decades of ideology masquerading as coursework, nor do they entirely escape the limitations of economistic thinking.

23 Armen A. Alchian and Harold Demsetz, "Production, Information Costs, and Economic Organization," *American Economic Review* 62, no. 5 (1972): 777–95. See also Anderson, *Private Government*.

24 Compare Katharina Pistor, *The Code of Capital: How the Law Creates Wealth and Inequality* (Princeton, NJ: Princeton University Press, 2019).

25 Elizabeth Tandy Shermer, "The Right to Work Really Means the Right to Work for Less," *Washington Post*, April 24, 2018; *Sunbelt Capitalism: Phoenix and the Transformation of American Politics* (Philadelphia: University of Pennsylvania Press, 2015).

26 Heidi Shierholz, "The Number of Workers Represented by a Union Held Steady in 2019, While Union Membership Fell," Economic Policy Institute, January 22, 2020.

27 David Cooper, "Raising the Federal Minimum Wage to $15 by 2024 Would Lift Pay for Nearly 40 Million Workers," Economic Policy Institute, February 9, 2019.

28 "The Productivity-Pay Gap," Economic Policy Institute, July 2019.

29 Josh Bivens and Heidi Shierholz, "What Labor Market Changes Have Generated Inequality and Wage Suppression?," Economic Policy Institute, December 12, 2018.

30 David Armiak and Alex Kotch, "ALEC Leading Right-Wing Campaign to Re-Open Economy Despite COVID-19," Center for Media and Democracy, April 30, 2020.

31 The theory of the firm has a long history and is usually dated to Ronald H. Coase, "The Nature of the Firm," *Economics* 4, no. 16 (November 1937): 386–405.

32 Stewart, *The Management Myth*.

33 David L. McKnight and Paul J. Hinton, *International Comparisons of Litigation Costs*, U.S. Chamber Institute for Legal Reform, June 2013.

34 Lyman Stone, "The Boomers Ruined Everything," *Atlantic*, June 24, 2019.

35 See data provided by The New Faculty Majority, newfacultymajority.info; Herb Childress, *The Adjunct Underclass: How America's Colleges Betrayed Their Faculty, Their Students, and Their Mission* (Chicago: University of Chicago Press, 2019); Benjamin Ginsburg, *The Fall of the Faculty: The Rise of the All-Administrative University and Why It Matters* (New York: Oxford University Press, 2011).

36 Dan Baumann et al., "Executive Compensation at Public and Private Colleges," *Chronicle of Higher Education*, July 17, 2020.

37 Zephyr Teachout, *Break 'Em Up: Recovering Our Freedom from Big Ag, Big Tech, and Big Money*, (New York: Macmillan, 2020); Tim Wu, *The Curse of Bigness: Anti-Trust in the New Gilded Age*, (New York: Columbia Global Reports, 2018).

Chapter 8 Why We Are So Fit

1 Asher Klein and Shira Stoll. "Many Cringe at How Peloton's New Ad Treats Its Female Lead 'Grace from Boston,'" NBCBoston, December 3, 2019.

2 Ben Midgley, "The Six Reasons the Fitness Industry Is Booming," *Forbes*, September 26, 2018; "Personal Trainers in the US-Market Research Report," IbisWorld, April 2020.

3 Life expectancy by city neighborhood taken from Dan Kopf and Daniel Wolfe, "Map: What story does your neighborhood's life expectancy tell?," *Quartz*, December 10, 2018.

4 "The Royal Tombs of Ur Reveal Mesopotamia's Ancient Splendor," *National Geographic*, May 22, 2019.

5 Mark Nathan Cohen and George J. Armelagos, *Paleopathology at the Origins of Agriculture* (Gainesville, FL: University Press of Florida, 1984), pp. 52–68.

6 For surveys of the extensive data on height, see Carles Boix, *Political Order and Inequality: Their Foundations and Their Consequences for Human Welfare* (Cambridge, MA: Cambridge University Press, 2015), pp. 174–84; Walter Scheidel, *The Great Leveler: Violence and the History of Inequality from the Stone Age to the Twenty-first Century* (Princeton, NJ: Princeton University Press, 2017); Michael Hermanussen, "Stature of Early Europeans," *Hormones* 2, no. 3 (2003): 175–78; John Komlos, "On English Pygmies and Giants: The Physical Stature of English Youth in the Late 18th and Early 19th Centuries," *Research in Economic History* 25, December 18, 2007.

7 *The Epic of Gilgamesh*, trans. Maureen Gallery Kovacs, (Redwood City, CA: Stanford University, 1989); see also *The Epic of Gilgamesh*, trans. Andrew George (New York: Penguin, 1999).

8 Homer, *Iliad*, Book XVIII, trans. Alexander Pope.

9 Ibid., Book II.

10 Estimate from Eric Lander in Karen Weintraub, "In the Heart of Biotech, Leaders Explain the Boston Area's 'BioBoom,'" WBUR, June 4, 2018.

11 Satta Sarmah-Hightower, "How Massachusetts Built a Booming Biotech Ecosystem," wework, September 24, 2018.

12 My calculation based on: "Data Brief: Health Professions Data Series-Physicians 2014," Massachusetts Department of Health, April 2016.

13 From Laurie Garrett, in Frank Bruni, "She Predicted the Coronavirus. What Does She Foresee Next?," New York Times, May 2, 2020.

14 Steven Woolf, "Life Expectancy and Mortality Rates in the United States, 1959–2017, JAMA 322, no. 20 (2019): 1996–2016; Lenny Bernstein, "US Life Expectancy Declines Again," Washington Post, November 29, 2018.

15 Catherine Rampell, "The Top 1 Percent: Executives, Doctors, and Bankers," New York Times, October 17, 2011.

16 Dean Baker, "The Problem of Doctors' Salaries," The Agenda, October 25, 2017.

17 Jerry Y. Du et al., "The Growing Executive-Physician Wage Gap," Clinical Orthopaedics and Related Research 426, no. 10 (October 2018): 1910–19.

18 Bob Herman, "Healthcare CEO Pay Tops $1 Billion in 2018 So Far," Axios, April 8, 2019.

19 Most recently in Anne Case and Angus Deaton, Deaths of Despair and the Future of Capitalism (Princeton, NJ: Princeton University Press, 2020). The paper that started it all is: "Rising Morbidity and Mortality in Midlife Among White Non-Hispanic Americans in the 21st Century," PNAS 112, no. 49 (December 8, 2015): 15078–83.

20 "Long-Term Trends in Deaths of Despair," United States Congress Joint Economic Committee, September 5, 2019.

21 Dante Chinni, American Communities Project, July 23, 2020.

22 Data from the CDC and from HHS.gov.

23 Jean M. Twenge, "Time Period and Cohort Differences in Depressive Symptoms in the US, 1982–2013," Social Indicators Research, June 5, 2014.

24 Jacob S. Hacker and Paul Pierson, American Amnesia: How the War on Government Led Us to Forget What Made America Prosper (New York: Simon & Schuster, 2016).

25 See Jane Jacobs, Economy of Cities (New York: Vintage, 1970), p. 119, arguing that poverty does not have causes, only prosperity does. The underlying assumption is that scarcity is the default condition of humankind.

26 Steven Pinker, "Why Income Inequality Is Not the Injustice We Perceive It to Be," Big Think, February 13, 2018; Steven Pinker, Enlightenment Now: The Case for Reason, Science, Humanism, and Progress (New York: Viking, 2018). It is very odd that a declared champion of the Enlightenment should so easily dismiss equality, one of the cardinal principles of the Enlightenment,

but there you have it. The ideologues at the think tanks of the oligarchy certainly appreciated the gesture: Marian Tupy, "Income Inequality Is No Measure of Human Progress," in CapX, CATO Institute, May 2, 2018, and Foundation for Economic Education, May 3, 2018.

27 Harry Frankfurt, *On Inequality* (Princeton, NJ: Princeton University Press, 2015). Frankfurt's book is drawn mostly from an essay published three decades earlier. Frankfurt argues that an agenda of imposing economic equality, or making sure that everyone has the same amount of stuff, is a bad way to organize a political movement. This is the kind of tendentious argument that only an analytic philosopher could love. One does not have to argue for extreme economic egalitarianism (I certainly do not) in order to show that unjust distributions of wealth are bad.

28 Joseph Watts et al., "Ritual Human Sacrifice Promoted and Sustained the Evolution of Stratified Societies," *Nature* 532 (April 4, 2016): 228–31.

29 Peter Turchin, Ultrasociety: How 10,000 Years of War Made Humans the Greatest Cooperators on Earth (Chaplin, CT: Beresta Books, 2016), p. 148ff.

30 See ibid., p. 148. Inscription available at mcadams.posc.mu.edu.

31 For a more in-depth argument along these lines, see James C. Scott, *Against the Grain: A Deep History of the Earliest States* (New Haven, CT: Yale University Press, 2017).

32 In the optimistic narratives favored today, the multi-millennial humanitarian crisis known as ancient civilization, if it receives attention at all, is typically brushed aside as an incidental expense of the agricultural revolution. The excuse is that humans collectively opted for a sensible trade-off, giving up the nutritional and antibiotic benefits of life in the wild for a stable food source and the delights of urban living. But it is far from obvious that any such collective decision was ever made, except by default, or even whether, from the perspective of most individuals, it really was such a great deal. (It took the services of a "harlot" to bring Enkidu in from the wild.) More to the point, varieties of agriculture preceded civilization by a thousand years or more, and the studies now indicate that the additional food sources, not surprisingly, tended at first to improve human well-being. See Eva Rosenstock et al., "Human Stature in the Near East and Europe ca. 10,000–1000 B.C.," *Archaeological and Anthropological Sciences* 11 (July 29, 2019): 5657–90.

33 Santiago Lago et al., "Socioeconomic Status, Health Inequalities, and Non-Communicable Diseases: A Systematic Overview," *Zeitschrift fur Gesundheitswissenschaften* 26, no. 1 (2018): 1–14.

34 Carol Graham, "Stress, Worry, and Social Support: Inequality in America's Cities," Brookings, November 5, 2015; Carol Graham, *Happiness for All? Unequal Lives and Hopes in Pursuit of the American Dream* (Princeton, NJ: Princeton University Press, 2017).

35 Jacob S. Hacker, "The Great Risk Shift That Helped Deliver Donald Trump,"
     TPM Series, October 24, 2018. See also book by same title and author.
36 Andrew Van Dam, "Is It Great to Be a Worker in the U.S.? Not Compared
     with the Rest of the Developed World," *Washington Post*, July 4, 2018.
37 "Poll: Nearly 1 in 4 Americans Taking Prescription Drugs Say It's Difficult
     to Afford Their Medicines . . . ," *KFF*, March 1, 2019.
38 Antonio Olivo, "He Lost His Insurance and Turned to a Cheaper Form of
     Insulin," *Washington Post*, August 3, 2019.
39 Heather Long, "Every American Basically Pays an $8,000 'Poll Tax' Under
     U.S. Health System, Top Economists Say," *Washington Post*, January 7, 2020.
40 David U. Himmelstein et al., "A Comparison of Hospital Administrative
     Costs in 8 Nations: US Costs Exceed All Others by Far," *HealthAffairs* 33, no. 9
     (September 2014); Katherine Wilson, "Health Care Costs Accounted for 17.7
     Percent of GDP in 2018," California Health Care Foundation, June 2, 2020.
41 Max Abelson, "Rich and Powerful Jump to the Front of the Line for Tests,"
     Bloomberg, March 20, 2020.
42 Angus Maddison, *Contours of the World Economy 1–2030 AD* (London:
     Oxford University Press, 2007).
43 There is a surprisingly finicky debate about the labor-time involved in the
     construction of the pyramids. The 400,000 man-years appears in Turchin,
     Ultrasociety, p. 9, and Mark Lehner, "Who Built the Pyramids?," *Nova*,
     February 4, 1997. Others offer lower estimates. Nobody really knows, except
     that it clearly took a large number of laborers to build.
44 Megan Gannon, "China's First Emperor Ordered Official Search for Immor-
     tality Elixir," *LiveScience*, December 27, 2017.
45 Jonathan D. Ostry et al., *Redistribution, Inequality, and Growth*, IMF Dis-
     cussion Note, February 2014; Ostry et al., "Redistribution, Inequality, and
     Growth: New Evidence," *Journal of Economic Growth* 23, no. 3 (September
     2018): 259–305.
46 Jeff Bercovici, "Peter Thiel Is Very, Very Interested in Young People's Blood,"
     Inc., August 1, 2016.
47 Douglas Rushkoff, "Survival of the Richest," medium.com, September 5, 2018.
48 Jonathan Shaw, "Who Built the Pyramids?" *Harvard Magazine*, August
     2003; Owen Jarus, "Giza Secret Revealed: How 10,000 Pyramid Builders
     Got Fed," *LiveScience*, April 23, 2013.

Chapter 9 **Why Other People Are So Racist**

1 Accessed July 27, 2020: https://www.youtube.com/watch?v=yMleEXTx41w.
 2 See Chapters 1 and 4 above. See also Ana Patricia Muñoz et al., "The
     Color of Wealth in Boston," Federal Reserve Bank of Boston; and Kilolo

Kijakari et al., "The Color of Wealth in the Nation's Capital," Urban Institute, November 1, 2016.

3 Valerie Wilson, "Racial and Ethnic Income Gaps Persist Amid Uneven Growth," Economic Policy Institute, September 11, 2019.

4 Patrick Bayer and Kerwin Kofi Charles. "Divergent Paths: A New Perspective on Earnings Differences Between Black and White Men Since 1940," *The Quarterly Journal of Economics* 133, no. 3 (August 2018): 1459–1501; Becky Pettit, *Invisible Men: Mass Incarceration and the Myth of Black Progress* (New York: Russell Sage Foundation, June 2012); Michelle Alexander, *The New Jim Crow: Mass Incarceration in the Age of Colorblindness* (New York: The New Press, 2010); John Gramlich, "The Gap Between the Number of Blacks and Whites in Prison Is Shrinking," Pew Research Center, April 30, 2019; Chuck Collins et al., "Report: The Road to Zero Wealth," Institute for Policy Studies, September 2017.

5 Frederick Douglass, *The Life and Writings of Frederick Douglass*, Philip S. Foner, ed. (New York: International Publishers, 1955), vol. 4, p. 169.

6 Matthew S. Gottlieb, "James W. Hunnicutt (1814–1880)," *Encyclopedia Virginia*, August 27, 2015; Richard G. Lowe, *Republicans and Reconstruction in Virginia, 1857–70* (Charlottesville, VA: University Press of Virginia, 1991).

7 Details from W. E. B. Du Bois, *Black Reconstruction in America* (New York: Oxford University Press, 2007); Eric Foner, *Reconstruction: America's Unfinished Revolution, 1863–78*, updated edition (New York: HarperCollins, 2007).

8 Frederick Douglass, "Speech on the Occasion of the Twenty-Sixth Anniversary of Emancipation," April 16, 1888, *The Life and Writings of Frederick Douglass*, Philip S. Foner, ed. (New York: International Publishers, 1955), vol. 5, p.379.

9 Theodore Parker, *Discourses of Slavery*, 2 volumes., in Francis Power Cobbe, ed., *The Collected Works of Theodore Parker*, Vols. 5-6 (London: Trubner & Co., 1864); Frederick Law Olmsted, *A Journey in the Seaboard Slave States, with Remarks on The Economy* (New York: Mason Brothers, 1861); Hinton Rowan Helper, *Compendium on the Impending Crisis of the South* (New York: A. B. Burdick, 1860).

10 Hinton Rowan Helper, *The Impending Crisis in the South* (New York: A. B. Burdick, 1857), p. 373.

11 Douglass, The Life and Writings of Frederick Douglass, vol. 4, p. 289.

12 Ibid., vol. 4, p. 519.

13 Jefferson Davis, *The Essential Writings*, William J. Cooper, ed. (Random House, 2004), p. 160

14 See Robert Putnam, *The Upswing* (New York: Simon & Schuster, 2020).

15 Andre M. Perry et al., "The Devaluation of Assets in Black Neighborhoods: The Case of Residential Property," Brookings, November 27, 2018; Oscar

Perry Abello, "Why Black Neighborhoods Are Valued Less than Other Neighborhoods," nextcity.org, November 29, 2018; Jung Hyun Choi et al., "Housing and Housing Finance," The Urban Institute, February 28, 2019.

16 Frederick Douglass, *My Bondage and My Freedom* (New York: Miller, Orton, 1857), pp. 42, 77, 131.

17 Frederick Douglass, *Life and Times of Frederick Douglass* (Hartford, CT: Park Publishing, 1882), p. 445.

18 Sociologist Douglas S. Massey observes that "racial segregation constitutes the 'structural linchpin' of racial stratification in the United States." Douglas S. Massey, "Residential Segregation Is the Linchpin of Racial Stratification," *City Community* 15, no. 1 (March 29, 2016): 4–7.

19 Richard Rothstein, *The Color of Law: A Forgotten History of How Our Government Segregated America* (New York: Liveright, 2017).

20 Megan E. Irons, "Researchers Expected Outrageously High Discrimination Against Black Renters. What They Found Was Worse than Imagined," *Boston Globe*, July 1, 2020.

21 Jorge De La Roca, "Race and Neighborhoods in the 21st Century: What Does Segregation Mean Today?," *Regional Science and Urban Economics*, September 24, 2013; Edward Glaeser and Jacob Vigdor, "The End of the Segregated Century: Racial Segregation in America's Neighborhoods, 1890–1910," *Civic Report* 6 (January 2002).

22 Erica Frankenberg et al., *Harming Our Common Future: America's Segregated Schools 65 Years After Brown*, The Civil Rights Project, May 10, 2019; Emma Garcia, "Schools Are Still Segregated, and Black Children Are Paying a Price," Economic Policy Institute, February 12, 2020.

23 Richard Rothstein, "For Public Schools, Segregation Then, Segregation Since," Economic Policy Institute, August 27, 2013.

24 Tony Pals and Collin Boylin, "School Segregation Worsens for Latino Children Compared with a Generation Ago," American Educational Research Association, July 30, 2019.

25 Cited in Alvin Chang, "White America Is Quietly Self-Segregating," *Vox*, July 31, 2018.

26 Chase Billingham and Shelley Kimeberg, "Identifying the Urban: Resident Perceptions of Community Character and Local Institutions in Eight Metropolitan Areas," Wiley Online Library, September 27, 2018.

27 Chase Billingham and Matthew O. Hunt, "School Racial Composition and Parental Choice: New Evidence on the Preferences of White Parents in the United States," *Sociology of Education*, March 2, 2016.

28 Ann Owens, "Unequal Opportunity: School and Neighborhood Segregation in the USA," *Race and Social Problems* 12 (January 20, 2020): 29–41.

29 David Card, Alexandre Mas, and Jess Rothstein, "Tipping and the Dynamics of Segregation," *The Quarterly Journal of Economics*, Harvard, February 2008.

30 Sloane Heffernan, "'Keep This Area Upscale' Warns Letter to Interracial Wake Forest Family," WRAL.com, July 6, 2020.

31 Donna St. George, "Study Shows Wide Varieties in Discipline Methods Among Very Similar Schools," *Washington Post*, July 19, 2011.

32 Micki Lisa Cole, "Understanding the School to Prison Pipeline," *ThoughtCo.*, May 30, 2019.

33 Tessa Charlesworth and Mahzarin Banaji, "Patterns of Implicit and Explicit Attitudes: Long-Term Changes from 2007–2016," *Psychological Science* 30, no. 2 (January 2019): 174–92.

34 Daniel J. Hopkins and Samantha Washington, "The Rise of Trump, the Fall of Prejudice? Tracking White Americans' Racial Attitudes 2008–2018 via a Panel Survey," SSRN, October 1, 2019.

35 John Sides, Michael Tesler, and Lynn Vavreck, *Identity Crisis: The 2016 Presidential Campaign and the Battle for the Meaning of America* (Princeton, NJ: Princeton University Press, 2018).

36 Michael Tesler, "Views About Race Mattered More in Electing Trump than in Electing Obama," *Washington Post*, November 22, 2016.

37 Philip Klinkner, "The Easiest Way to Guess if Someone Supports Trump? Ask if Obama Is a Muslim," *Vox*, June 2, 2016.

38 Griffin Sim Edwards and Stephen Rushin, "The Effect of President Trump's Election on Hate Crimes," SSRN, January 14, 2018; Ayal Feinberg et al., "The Trump Effect: How 2016 Campaign Rallies Explain Spikes in Hate," *Washington Post*, March 22, 2019.

39 John Sides, Michael Tesler, and Lynn Vavreck, *Identity Crisis: The 2016 Presidential Campaign and the Battle for the Meaning of America* (Princeton, NJ: Princeton University Press, 2018).

40 Jon Green and Sean McElwee, "The Differential Effects of Economic Conditions and Racial Attitudes in the Election of Donald Trump," *Perspectives on Politics* 17, no. 2 (June 2019): 358–79.

41 Carlos Algara and Isaac Hale, "The Distorting Effects of Racial Animus on Proximity Voting in the 2016 Elections," *ScienceDirect*, February 2019.

42 Samuel Sommers and Michael Norton, "White People Think Racism Is Getting Worse, Against White People," *Washington Post*, July 21, 2016; Don Gonyea, "Majority of White Americans Say They Believe Whites Face Discrimination," NPR, October 24, 2017.

43 Sides, Tesler, and Vavreck, *Identity Crisis*; Tesler, "Views About Race Mattered More in Electing Trump than in Electing Obama.".

44 For a strong recent statement of the case for the top-down creation of racism, see Jacob S. Hacker and Paul Pierson, *Let Them Eat Tweets: How the Right Rules in an Age of Extreme Inequality* (New York: Liveright, 2020).

45 Thomas Edsall, *Chain Reaction: The Impact of Race, Rights, and Taxes on American Politics* (New York: W. W. Norton, 1972); "The Deepening 'Racialization' of American Politics," *New York Times*, February 27, 2019.

46 Adam M. Enders and Jamil Scott, "White Racial Resentment Has Been Gaining Political Power for Decades," *Washington Post*, January 15, 2018.

47 Mark Muro et al., "Biden Counties Equal 70 Percent of America's Economy," Brookings, November 10, 2020.

48 Mark Muro and Jacob Whiton, "America Has Two Economies—And They Are Diverging Fast," Brookings, November 19, 2019; Marc Muro and Sifan Liu, "Another Clinton-Trump Divide: High-Output America vs Low-Output America," Brookings, November 29, 2016.

49 Jennifer Malat, Sarah Gallo, and David Williams, "The Effects of Whiteness on the Health of Whites in the USA," *Social Science and Medicine* 199 (July 2017).

50 Suzanne Mettler, *The Government-Citizen Disconnect* (New York: Russell Sage Foundation, 2017); Heather Hahn et al., "Why Does Cash Welfare Depend on Where You Live?," The Urban Institute, June 5, 2017.

51 Jonathan Metzl, *Dying of Whiteness: How the Politics of Racial Resentment Is Killing America's Heartland* (New York: Basic Books, 2019).

52 Eitan Hersh, *Politics Is for Power* (New York: Simon & Schuster, 2020); "College-Educated Voters Are Ruining American Politics," *Atlantic*, January 20, 2020.

Chapter 10 Why Everyone Is So Unreasonable

1 Lucy Rock, "After Being the Tiger Mom, Amy Chua Turns to Political Tribalism," *Guardian*, March 1, 2018.

2 Amy Chua, "Kavanaugh Is a Mentor to Women," *Wall Street Journal*, July 12, 2018.

3 Jeremy Stahl, "Daughter of Fierce Kavanaugh Defender Amy Chua to Clerk for . . . Brett Kavanaugh," *Slate*, June 10, 2019.

4 Alexandria Hutzler, "Amy Chua Denied Grooming Female Students to Clerk for Brett Kavanaugh," *Newsweek*, June 6, 2019.

5 Sarah Jones, "So Much for Worshipping Meritocracy," *The Cut*, June 12, 2019.

6 Mihir Zaveri, "Yale Law Professor Is Suspended After Sexual Harassment Inquiry," *New York Times*, August 26, 2020.

7 Hannah Arendt, *The Origins of Totalitarianism* (New York: Schocken, 1951).

8 Amy Chua, *Political Tribes: Group Instinct and the Fate of Nations* (New York: Penguin, 2018), p. 3.

9 Ibid., p. 203ff.

10 Ibid., p. 153ff.

11 Much of this kind of thinking, which has many historical antecedents, is now concentrated in "moral foundations theory." See Jesse Graham. Jonathan Haidt, Sena Koleva, Matt Motyl, Ravi Iyer, Sean P. Wojcik, and Peter H. Ditto, "Moral Foundations Theory: The Pragmatic Validity of Moral Pluralism," in Patricia Devine and Ashby Plant, eds., *Advances in Experimental Social Psychology* 47 (Cambridge, MA: Academic Press, 2013); John R. Hibbing, Kevin B. Smith, and John R. Alford, *Predisposed: Liberals, Conservatives, and the Biology of Political Differences* (New York: Routledge, 2013).

12 "Feelings-First Voters Have Found a Voice in Donald Trump," *Economist*, September 15, 2016.

13 Francis Fukuyama, *Identity: The Demand for Recognition and the Politics of Resentment*, (New York: Farrar, Straus and Giroux, 2018).

14 The claim that Coulter said this has been fact-checked by snopes.com and been rated as "true." Bethania Palma, "Did Ann Coulter say this about the Oklahoma City bomber?," snopes,com, February 2, 2019.

15 Katherine Stewart, "The roots of Josh Hawley's rage," *New York Times*, January 11, 2021.

16 Chua, *Political Tribes*, pp. 100–15.

17 Kathleen McAuliffe, "Liberals and Conservatives React in Wildly Different Ways to Repulsive Pictures," *Atlantic*, March 2019; Hibbing, Smith, and Alford, *Predisposed*.

18 David Lazer et al., "Combating Fake News: An Agenda for Research and Action," Conference Report, February 17–18, 2017, Harvard Kennedy School, Shorenstein Center.

19 Aristotle, *Politics*, IV, 11.

20 Polybius, *The Histories*, VI, ii, 5.

21 This is the case I make in Matthew Stewart, *Nature's God: The Heretical Origins of the American Republic* (New York: W. W. Norton, 2014).

22 Walter Scheidel and Steven Friesen, "The Size of the Economy and the Distribution of Income in the Roman Empire," *The Journal of Roman Studies* 99 (November 2009): 61–91; Walter Scheidel, *The Great Leveler: Violence and the History of Inequality from the Stone Age to the Twenty-First Century* (Princeton, NJ: Princeton University Press, 2017).

23 Zachary Wolff, "How Voters Shifted During Four Years of Trump," CNN, November 7, 2020.

24 Mark Muro et al., "Biden Counties Equal 70 Percent of America's Economy," Brookings, November 10, 2020; Denise Lu, "How Did Trump Do in Counties That Backed Him in 2016," *New York Times*, November 12, 2020.

25 Michal Kranz, "These Maps Show That Counties Where Opioid Death and Prescription Rates Are Highest Are Also Places Where Trump Won Big in 2016," *Business Insider*, November 3, 2017.

26 Daniel Cox of the American Enterprise Institute.

27 Thomas Piketty, "Brahmin Left v. Merchant Right," World Inequality Database, 2018.

28 "GOP Unifies Around Trump, Clinton Still Has Modest Lead," Public Policy Polling, May 10, 2016.

29 Poll by *The Economist*/YouGov, November 8–10, 2020.

30 Devi Lockwood, "What a Trump Rally Looks Like from the Inside," *New York Times*, February 10, 2020.

31 Yale Program on Climate Change Communication, *Politics and Global Warming*, March 2018.

32 Frank Newport and Andrew Dugan, "College Educated Republicans Most Skeptical of Global Warming," Gallup, March 26, 2015.

33 Ashley Kirzinger et al., "6 Charts About Public Opinion on the Affordable Care Act," KFF, November 27, 2019.

34 John Gramlich, "Trump Voters Want to Build the Wall," Pew Research Center, November 29, 2016; "Trump's Border Wall Plan Is Unrealistic and Useless, Experts Say," *The Tribune Express*, August 26, 2016.

35 Gary Detman, "Throw God's Wonderful Breathing System Out the Door, Mask Debate Turns Fiery," cbs12news, June 24, 2020.

36 Joshua Clinton et al., "Partisan Pandemic: How Partisanship and Public Health Concerns Affect Individuals' Social Distancing During COVID-19," SSRN, June 29, 2020; Christos Makridis and Jonathan T. Rothwell, "The Real Cost of Political Polarization: Evidence from the COVID-19 Pandemic," SSRN, June 29, 2020; Anton Golwitzer et al., "Partisan Differences in Physical Distancing Are Linked to Health Outcomes During the COVID-19 Pandemic," *Nature Human Behavior* 4 (2020): 1186–97.

37 Clinton et al., "Partisan Pandemic." See also "The Relation Between Media Consumption and Misinformation at the Outset of the SARS-CoV-2 Pandemic in the US," *The Harvard Kennedy School Misinformation Review*, April 2020, vol. 1, Special Issue.

38 B. Douglas Berheim et al., "The Effects of Large Group Meetings on the Spread of COVID-19: The Case of Trump Rallies," Stanford Department of Economics, October 30, 2020,

39 Douglas MacMillan, "The War Inside Palantir," *Washington Post*, August 22, 2019; April Glaser, "Palantir's Pandemic Contracts Stir Concern," NBC News, July 22, 2020.

40 Matt Gertz, "Destructive Propaganda Machine: How Current and Former Staffers Have Ripped into Fox News," *Media Matters*, July 10, 2019.

41 Maxwell Tani, "Poll: 78 Percent of Fox News Viewers Say Trump Is Best President Ever," *Daily Beast*, March 21, 2019.

42 "Fractured Nation: Widening Partisan Polarization and Key Issues in 2020 Presidential Elections," *PRRI*, October 20, 2019.

43 Gregory J. Martin and Ali Yurukoglu, "Bias in Cable News: Persuasion and Polarization," *NBER* Working Paper No. 20798, June 2016.

44 The Media Insight Project, "How Much Republicans and Democrats Trust or Understand the News Media," American Press Institute, June 11, 2018.

45 Nancy MacLean, "Since We Are Greatly Outnumbered," in *The Disinformation Age: Politics, Technology, and Disruptive Communication in the United States*, W. Lance Bennett and Steven Livingston, eds. (Cambridge, MA: Cambridge University Press, 2020), p. 121.

46 This is James Wilson's roughly accurate transcription of a passage from Edmund Burke, *Reflections on the Revolution in France* (J. Dodsley, 1790), pp. 88–89; James Wilson, *Pennsylvania Packet*, October 10, 1787.

47 Yochai Benkler, Bob Faris, and Hal Roberts, *Network Propaganda: Manipulation, Disinformation, and Radicalization in American Politics* (Cambridge, MA: Berkman Klein Center, 2018). See also Bennett and Livingston, eds., *The Disinformation Age*.

48 Carolyn E. Schmitt, "Network Propaganda," *Harvard Gazette*, October 25, 2018.

49 Lazer et al., "Combating Fake News."

50 See Yochai Benkler, "A Political Economy of the Origins of Asymmetric Propaganda in American Media," in Bennett and Livingston, eds., *The Disinformation Age*.

51 Mancur Olson, *The Logic of Collective Action* (Cambridge, MA: Harvard University Press, 1965) and *The Rise and Decline of Nations* (New Haven, CT: Yale University Press, 1982).

52 Benjamin L. Page, Jason Seawright, and Matthew J. Lacombe, *Billionaires and Stealth Politics* (Chicago: University of Chicago Press, 2018)

53 John Voorheis, Nolan McCarty, and Boris Shor, "Unequal Incomes, Ideology, and Gridlock: How Rising Inequality Increases Polarization," SSRN, August 21, 2015; Nolan McCarty, "What We Know and Don't Know About Our Polarized Politics," *Washington Post*, January 8, 2014.

54 Ibid.

55 See the Manhattan Declaration and the Cornwall Alliance for expressions of this kind of theological unity on the basis of politics.

56 Frederick Douglass, *The Life and Writings of Frederick Douglass*, Philip S. Foner, ed. (New York: International Publishers, 1955), vol. 3, p. 499.

57 Frederick Solt, "Reversing the Arrow? Economic Inequality's Effect on Religiosity," in *Religion and Inequality in America: Research and Theory on*

Religion's Role in Stratification, L. Keister and D. Sherkat, eds. (Cambridge, MA: Cambridge University Press, 2015).

58 Adam Cohen, *Supreme Inequality: The Supreme Court's Fifty-Year Battle for a More Unjust America* (New York: Penguin, 2020).

59 Clarence Thomas, *My Grandfather's Son*, (New York: HarperCollins, 2007); Jeffrey Toobin, "Unforgiven," *New Yorker*, November 5, 2007.

60 For further, interesting proposals on how to correct for the market failure that is the modern media system, see Victor Pickard, *Democracy Without Journalism? Confronting the Misinformation Society* (New York: Oxford University Press, 2020).

Chapter 11 How We Might Get a Clue

1 Thomas Jefferson to James Madison, October 28, 1785, in Julian P. Boyd, ed., *The Papers of Thomas Jefferson* (Princeton, NJ: Princeton University Press, 1958), vol. 8, p. 681.

2 Thomas Paine, *Agrarian Justice* (Paris: W. Adelard, 1797).

3 Thomas Paine to George Staunton, Spring 1789, in Moncure Conway, ed., *The Writings of Thomas Paine* (New York: Putnam, 1896), vol. 4, p. 443

4 Matthew Stewart, *Nature's God: The Heretical Origins of the American Republic* (New York: W. W. Norton, 2014).

5 Thomas Jefferson to Henry Lee, May 8, 1825, *Papers of Thomas Jefferson*, Retirement Series (early access through Library of Congress, loc.gov).

6 Walter Scheidel, *The Great Leveler: Violence and the History of Inequality from the Stone Age to the Twenty-First Century* (Princeton, NJ: Princeton University Press, 2017).

7 Emmanuel Saez and Gabriel Zucman, *The Triumph of Injustice: How the Rich Dodge Taxes and How to Make Them Pay* (New York: W. W. Norton, 2019).

8 Congressional Budget Office, "The Distribution of Major Tax Expenditures in the Individual Income Tax System," May 2013.

9 Speech available at "The New Nationalism," Theodore Roosevelt Association. For detail on the setting, see Robert S. La Forte, "Theodore Roosevelt's Osawatomie Speech," *Kansas History: A Journal of the Central Plains* 32, no. 2 (Summer 1966): 187–200.

10 Zephyr Teachout, *Break 'Em Up: Recovering Our Freedom from Big Ag, Big Tech, and Big Money* (New York: All Points Books, 2020).

11 For biographical detail, see David McCullough, *Truman* (New York: Simon & Schuster, 1992).

12 For details on Harry Truman's national health insurance proposal, see Howard Markel, "Give 'em Health, Harry," *Milbank Quarterly* 93, no. 1 (March 5, 2015): 1–7; Truman's Address to the Congress of the United States,

November 19, 1945, and other supporting documents, National Archives, Harry S. Truman Library.

13 Joseph Connor, "Howls of Socialism Killed Truman Health Insurance," HistoryNet, October 2019.

14 Anne Case and Angus Deaton, *Deaths of Despair and the Future of Capitalism* (Princeton, NJ: Princeton University Press, 2020), make this point well.

Index

Page numbers beginning with 293 refer to notes.